First World War
and Army of Occupation
War Diary
France, Belgium and Germany

36 DIVISION
Headquarters, Branches and Services
Commander Royal Artillery
27 November 1915 - 28 February 1919

WO95/2494/1

The Naval & Military Press Ltd
www.nmarchive.com
Published in association with The National Archives

Published by

The Naval & Military Press Ltd

Unit 10 Ridgewood Industrial Park,

Uckfield, East Sussex,

TN22 5QE England

Tel: +44 (0) 1825 749494

www.naval-military-press.com

www.nmarchive.com

This diary has been reprinted in facsimile from the original. Any imperfections are inevitably reproduced and the quality may fall short of modern type and cartographic standards.

© **Crown Copyright**
Images reproduced by permission of The National Archives, London, England, 2015.

Contents

Document type	Place/Title	Date From	Date To
Heading	WO95/2494/1 Commander Royal Artillery.		
Heading	36th Division C.R.A. Nov 1915-Feb 1919 (Jly 1917-Sep 1917 Missing)		
Heading	C.R.A. 36th Div Vol: 3 121/7809 Nov & Decr 15.		
War Diary		27/11/1915	29/02/1916
Heading	C.R.A. 36 Div Vol 6		
War Diary		01/03/1916	31/05/1916
Heading	36th Divisional Artillery C.R.A. 36th Division. June 1916.		
War Diary		01/06/1916	30/06/1916
War Diary	Bombardment Table for Night 3/4th June, 1916. Appendix 1.	03/06/1916	03/06/1916
Map			
Miscellaneous	Programme of Raid to be carried out on W/X night. Point of Raid R.19.c. 1055. Appendix 2.	23/06/1916	23/06/1916
Miscellaneous	Headquarters, R.A., Xth Corps.	09/06/1916	09/06/1916
Miscellaneous	36th Divisional Artillery. Battery Positions, shewing O.P's & Arcs of Fire. Right Group.	18/06/1916	18/06/1916
Operation(al) Order(s)	36th Divisional Artillery Order No. 1.	17/06/1916	17/06/1916
Miscellaneous	Instructions for Artillery During Gas Discharge and Raid.	24/06/1916	24/06/1916
Miscellaneous	Amendment to 36th Divisional Artillery Order No. 1.	18/06/1916	18/06/1916
Miscellaneous	Table B.	24/06/1916	24/06/1916
Map	The villages (except Pozieres) within the German lines are shown according to latest information available.		
Miscellaneous		15/06/1916	15/06/1916
Miscellaneous	Intensive Bombardment & Table of Lifts. (Hamel Sub-Sector).	20/06/1916	20/06/1916
Miscellaneous	Appendix "E" Intensive Bombardment and Table of Lifts (Thiepval Sub-Sector)	20/06/1916	20/06/1916
Miscellaneous	Amendments to Appendix E.	27/06/1916	27/06/1916
Heading	36th Divisional Artillery. C.R.A. 36th Division. July 1916.		
War Diary		01/07/1916	31/07/1916
Operation(al) Order(s)	36th Divisional Artillery Order No. 2.	13/07/1916	13/07/1916
Miscellaneous	March Table July 14th.	14/07/1916	14/07/1916
Miscellaneous	March Table July 15th.	15/07/1916	15/07/1916
Miscellaneous	March Table July 16th.	16/07/1916	16/07/1916
Miscellaneous	March Table July 17th.	17/07/1916	17/07/1916
Miscellaneous	March Table 18th July.	18/07/1916	18/07/1916
Operation(al) Order(s)	36th Divisional Artillery Order No. 3.	17/07/1916	17/07/1916
Operation(al) Order(s)	36th Divisional Artillery Order No. 4.	19/07/1916	19/07/1916
Operation(al) Order(s)	36th Divisional Artillery Order No. 5.	19/07/1916	19/07/1916
Miscellaneous	March Table 20th July.	20/07/1916	20/07/1916
Miscellaneous	Amendment to 36th Divisional Artillery Order No. 6.	28/07/1916	28/07/1916
Operation(al) Order(s)	36th Divisional Artillery Order No. 6.	27/07/1916	27/07/1916
Operation(al) Order(s)	36th Divisional Artillery Order No. 7.	30/07/1916	30/07/1916
Miscellaneous	36th Divisional Artillery. Table of Reliefs, 30/31 July.	30/07/1916	30/07/1916
Miscellaneous	36th Divisional Artillery. Table of Reliefs, 31st July,/1st August, 1916.	31/07/1916	31/07/1916

War Diary		01/08/1916	31/10/1916
Heading	War. Diary. Simpsons Group. October 1st to 10th 1916.		
War Diary	Kemmel	01/10/1916	10/10/1916
Miscellaneous	Relief of the 3rd Canadian Divisional Artillery. Appendix (1).		
Miscellaneous	Defence Scheme Simpsons Group. Appendix ii.	01/10/1916	01/10/1916
Miscellaneous	Simpson Group Supplement to reference scheme. Appendix (iii).	06/10/1916	06/10/1916
Miscellaneous	Relief of simpson group by 16th Div. Artillery. Appendix (iv).		
War Diary		01/11/1916	31/05/1917
War Diary	Ref Map France Sheet 28 S.W. 1/20000.		
War Diary	Preliminary Artillery action.		
War Diary		01/06/1917	05/06/1917
War Diary	Y Day	06/06/1917	06/06/1917
War Diary	Z Day.	07/06/1917	30/06/1917
Heading	Jly-Sep 1917 Missing.		
War Diary	Ytres Wood	01/10/1917	10/10/1917
War Diary	Ytres Wood	06/10/1917	15/10/1917
War Diary	Ytres	16/10/1917	20/10/1917
War Diary	Ytres	16/10/1917	31/10/1917
Heading	War Diary of C.R.A. 36th Division November 1917.		
Miscellaneous	1/7 D of W.		
War Diary	Ytres	01/11/1917	19/11/1917
War Diary	Ytres	14/11/1917	26/11/1917
War Diary	Little Wood Ytres	29/11/1917	30/11/1917
War Diary	Ytres	01/12/1917	05/12/1917
War Diary	Sorel Le Grand	05/12/1917	20/12/1917
War Diary	Little Wood R.E. Camp Ytres.	22/12/1917	31/12/1917
War Diary	Treux	01/01/1918	01/01/1918
War Diary	Corbie	02/01/1918	06/01/1918
War Diary	Quesnel	07/01/1918	10/01/1918
War Diary	Roye	11/01/1918	12/01/1918
War Diary	Nesle	13/01/1918	14/01/1918
War Diary	Ollezy	15/01/1918	28/02/1918
Heading	36th Divisional Artillery. C.R.A. 36th Division March 1918. Appendices attached:- Narrative of Operations 21st-31st March. Artillery Orders.		
War Diary	Ollezy	01/03/1918	21/03/1918
Miscellaneous	Colonel Potter, D.S.O., R.F.A.	21/03/1918	21/03/1918
Miscellaneous	Copy of 36th Divisional Artillery Order, issued on 24th March.	24/03/1918	24/03/1918
Operation(al) Order(s)	Copy of 36th Divisional Artillery Order No. 33.	26/03/1918	26/03/1918
Miscellaneous	Mr Cordery		
Miscellaneous	Narrative of the Operations Carried out by the 36th Divisional Artillery for the period March 21st-March 31st Inclusive.	21/03/1918	21/03/1918
Miscellaneous	Left Group.		
Miscellaneous	Trench Mortars.	21/03/1918	21/03/1918
Miscellaneous	Narrative of the Operations Carried out by the 36th Divisional Artillery for the period March 21st-March 31st Inclusive. Appendix 'A'.	21/03/1918	21/03/1918
Miscellaneous	Left Group.		
Miscellaneous	Trench Mortars.	21/03/1918	21/03/1918
Miscellaneous	Colonel Potter, D.S.O., R.F.A.	21/03/1918	21/03/1918

Miscellaneous	Copy of 36th Divisional Artillery Order, issued on 24th March.	24/03/1918	24/03/1918
Operation(al) Order(s)	Copy of 36th Divisional Artillery Order No. 33.	26/03/1918	26/03/1918
Heading	36th Divisional Artillery. C.R.A. 36th Division. April 1918.		
War Diary	Etouy	01/04/1918	03/04/1918
War Diary	Morvillers	03/04/1918	04/04/1918
War Diary	Moyencourt Sous Poix	08/04/1918	08/04/1918
War Diary	Pont du Metz	11/04/1918	14/04/1918
War Diary	Monastery Mont Des Cats.	15/04/1918	24/04/1918
War Diary	Ten Elms Camp	25/04/1918	25/04/1918
War Diary	Border Camp.	25/04/1918	27/04/1918
War Diary	Dragon Camp	28/04/1918	30/04/1918
Operation(al) Order(s)	36th Divisional Artillery Order No. 34.	01/04/1918	01/04/1918
Miscellaneous	March Table.		
Operation(al) Order(s)	36th Divisional Artillery Order No. 35.	03/04/1918	03/04/1918
Miscellaneous	March Table.		
Operation(al) Order(s)	36th Divisional Artillery Order No. 36.	03/04/1916	03/04/1916
Operation(al) Order(s)	36th Divisional Artillery Order No. 37.	07/04/1918	07/04/1918
Miscellaneous	March Table.		
Operation(al) Order(s)	36th Divisional Artillery Entrainment Order No. 1.	10/04/1918	10/04/1918
Miscellaneous	Entraining Table No. (I). Entraining Station St Roch (Station 'A') Detraining Station Hopoutre.		
Miscellaneous	Entraining Table No. (II). Entraining Station St Roch (Station 'B'). Detraining Station. Peselhoek.		
Operation(al) Order(s)	36th Divisional Artillery Order No. 38.	11/04/1918	11/04/1918
Operation(al) Order(s)	36th Divisional Artillery Order No. 39.	13/04/1918	13/04/1918
Miscellaneous	March Table.		
Operation(al) Order(s)	36th Divisional Artillery Order No. 40.	22/04/1918	22/04/1918
Operation(al) Order(s)	36th Divisional Artillery Order No. 41.	23/04/1918	23/04/1918
Operation(al) Order(s)	36th Divisional Artillery Order No. 42.	24/04/1918	24/04/1918
Operation(al) Order(s)	36th Divisional Artillery Order No: 43.	25/04/1918	25/04/1918
Operation(al) Order(s)	36th Divisional Artillery Order No. 44.	25/04/1918	25/04/1918
Operation(al) Order(s)	36th Divisional Artillery Order No. 44.	26/04/1918	26/04/1918
Operation(al) Order(s)	36th Divisional Artillery Order No: 45.	26/04/1918	26/04/1918
Operation(al) Order(s)	36th Divisional Artillery Order No; 46.	27/04/1918	27/04/1918
Miscellaneous	Fu 2986		
War Diary	Dragon Camp A.15.b.3.4.	01/05/1918	01/05/1918
War Diary	Dragon Camp.	02/05/1918	07/06/1918
War Diary	Couthove Chateau	08/06/1918	20/06/1918
War Diary	Couthove Chateau	12/06/1918	30/06/1918
War Diary	Couthove	01/07/1918	08/07/1918
War Diary	Mont Des Cats	09/07/1918	13/07/1918
War Diary	Terdeghem	14/07/1918	31/08/1918
War Diary		01/08/1918	28/08/1918
War Diary	Terdeghem	29/08/1918	31/08/1918
War Diary	Int Des Cats.	01/09/1918	01/09/1918
War Diary	St Jans Cappel	02/09/1918	21/09/1918
War Diary	Esdale	20/09/1918	30/09/1918
War Diary	Sheet 28 K.7.d.3.1.	01/10/1918	04/10/1918
War Diary	Farm at K.7.d.3.1 (Sheet 28)	05/10/1918	07/10/1918
War Diary	Junction Camp C.27.c.8.7.	08/10/1918	08/10/1918
War Diary	Junction Camp	09/10/1918	11/10/1918
War Diary	K.7.c	12/10/1918	14/10/1918
War Diary	Ashmore Farm	15/10/1918	16/10/1918
War Diary	Ashmore Farm L.15.c.9.0	16/10/1918	16/10/1918

War Diary	Farm at F.26.b.35.50. (Sheet 28)	17/10/1918	17/10/1918
War Diary	Lendelede (A.18.d.2.3) Sheet 29.	18/10/1918	20/10/1918
War Diary	Lendelede	20/10/1918	23/10/1918
War Diary	House at I.3.a.55.90.	24/10/1918	28/10/1918
War Diary	Belleghem	28/10/1918	30/11/1918
War Diary	Mouscron	01/12/1918	31/12/1918
War Diary	Mouscron	11/12/1918	11/12/1918
War Diary	Mouscron	01/01/1919	31/01/1919
War Diary	Mouscron	30/01/1919	28/02/1919

WO 95/2494/1
Commanders Royal Artillery

36TH DIVISION

C. R. A.
Nov ~~OCT~~ 1915-FEB 1919
(JLY 1917-SEP 1917 MISSING)

Cav. 26th Str.
Vol. 3

131/7809

Nov & Dec. 15

Army Form C. 2118.

Headquarters 36th Divisional Artillery

WAR DIARY
or
INTELLIGENCE SUMMARY.
(Erase heading not required.)

Hour, Date, Place	Summary of Events and Information	Remarks and references to Appendices
27th Novr/15	H.Q. R.A. Ulster Division landed at HAVRE about 11 am and entrained for PONT REMY near ABBEVILLE in the IIIrd Army area about 6.30 pm the same night.	
28th Novr.	Arrived at PONT REMY about 5 am and went into billets at FRANCIÈRES. Brigades were billetted as under 153rd Bde. LONG. and LONGVET 154th Bde. COCQUEREL. 172nd Bde. BOUCHON and LONG. 173rd Bde. YAVOHELLE and MOUFLERS. Div. Am. Col. VILLERS-SUR-AILLY.	
29th Novr	Brigades moving in all day. 153rd and 172nd &173rd completely in. Lieut Lockyer A.D.C. put in arrest and sent to 153rd Bde R.F.A.	

Instructions regarding War Diaries and Intelligence Summaries are contained in F.S. Regs., Part II. and the Staff Manual respectively. Title pages will be prepared in manuscript.

Army Form C. 2118.

WAR DIARY
or
INTELLIGENCE SUMMARY.
(Erase heading not required.)

Instructions regarding War Diaries and Intelligence Summaries are contained in F.S. Regs., Part II. and the Staff Manual respectively. Title pages will be prepared in manuscript.

Hour, Date, Place	Summary of Events and Information	Remarks and references to Appendices
30th Nov.	D.A.C. wired in billets. 154th Bde. not arrived yet. Orders issued regarding moves of batteries to different billets owing to very bad accommodation at VAU CHELLES.	

Army Form C. 2118.

WAR DIARY
or
INTELLIGENCE SUMMARY.
(Erase heading not required.)

Instructions regarding War Diaries and Intelligence Summaries are contained in F.S. Regs., Part II. and the Staff Manual respectively. Title pages will be prepared in manuscript.

Hour, Date, Place	Summary of Events and Information	Remarks and references to Appendices
1st December /15	154th Bde not yet arrived. Arranged the places for winter Horse Standings. Summary of Evidence on Lt Luckeyer to be made.	
2nd December /15	Went round winter horse standings of 152 & 153 Bde, and fresh billets for D.A.C. at L'ETOILE owing to scarcity of water at VILLERS.	
3rd December	Decided on all winter horse standings. 154th Bde arriving Staff Capt during the night 3/4 Capt Hope went sick & leaves for England tomorrow.	
4th December	Went round horse standings with R.E. officer. Lt Krohn was attached to R.A. H.Q. as acting A.D.C.	

(73989) W4141—463. 400,000. 9/14. H.&J.Ltd. Forms/C. 2118/10.

Army Form C. 2118.

WAR DIARY
or
INTELLIGENCE SUMMARY.
(Erase heading not required.)

Instructions regarding War Diaries and Intelligence Summaries are contained in F.S. Regs., Part II. and the Staff Manual respectively. Title pages will be prepared in manuscript.

Hour, Date, Place	Summary of Events and Information	Remarks and references to Appendices
5th December.	Nothing to report.	
6th December.	Moved to CHATEAU DE PAS, COCQUEREL. Conference re Whites at Div. H.Q. 5:30 pm. Lieut S.G. Hartnell R.F.A. joined R.Q. as a/Staff Captain. Conference of Brigade Commanders at 10 a.m.	
7th December.		
8th December.	Lt H.F. Lockyer's Courtmartial 2:30 pm.	
9th December.	D.A.C. moved to L'ETOILE. Bde. Am. Col. 173. moved to VILLERS. Went round with have been with G.O.C. R.A.	
10th December.	Went round all Horse standings with Divisional Commander. General Lecky came to see General Birch in the afternoon.	

Army Form C. 2118.

WAR DIARY
or
INTELLIGENCE SUMMARY.
(Erase heading not required.)

Instructions regarding War Diaries and Intelligence Summaries are contained in F.S. Regs., Part II. and the Staff Manual respectively. Title pages will be prepared in manuscript.

Hour, Date, Place	Summary of Events and Information	Remarks and references to Appendices
11th December	Nothing to report. A conference of Bde Commanders at 4.30 pm. Brig Gen J.G. Rotton 7th D.A. came to the Reveal Park.	
12th December	Nothing to report.	
13th December	Nothing to report.	
14th December	General Leakey R.A. 13th Corps inspected "C" Battery 153rd Bde and "A" & "B" Batteries 172nd Bde and D.A.C. Billets at 3rd Army HQ in the afternoon.	
15th December	Inspection of 153rd Brigade Billets.	
16th December	Inspection of 172nd Brigade Billets. Inspected all Horse Lines.	
17th December	Inspection of 173rd Brigade Billets. Inspected 153rd Bde Horse Lines.	

Army Form C. 2118.

WAR DIARY
or
INTELLIGENCE SUMMARY.
(Erase heading not required.)

Instructions regarding War Diaries and Intelligence Summaries are contained in F.S. Regs., Part II. and the Staff Manual respectively. Title pages will be prepared in manuscript.

Hour, Date, Place	Summary of Events and Information	Remarks and references to Appendices
18th December	Inspection of D.A.C. billets at L'ETOILE.	
19th December	Went to FONTAINE to inspect ground for Staff Ride. Worked out scheme for Staff Ride on the high ground S of LIERCOURT. Two Zeppelin Telegrams received 9.10 and 9.20 pm. from 50th Inf Bde and 9th Div Arty.	
20th December	Tactical Scheme taking up Battery positions with 153rd & 173 Brigades	
21st December	Very wet. Scheme postponed	
22nd December	Wet. Scheme with 173 4154 Brigades. G.O.C.R.A. went round Bde Div. Commander.	
23rd December	Inspection of Billets 154th Bde. Inspected Horse lines	

(73989) W4141—463. 400,000. 9/14. H.&J.Ltd. Forms/C. 2118/10.

Army Form C. 2118.

WAR DIARY
or
INTELLIGENCE SUMMARY.
(Erase heading not required.)

Instructions regarding War Diaries and Intelligence Summaries are contained in F.S.Regs., Part II. and the Staff Manual respectively. Title pages will be prepared in manuscript.

Hour, Date, Place	Summary of Events and Information	Remarks and references to Appendices
24th December	General lately inspected 173rd Bde & 172nd Bde at DOUCITON. Visited Colonel regarding their bivs.	
25th December	Holiday.	
26th December	13th Corps Commander inspected Horse Standings, decided that bricks were not to be used.	
27th December	Went over ground S. of River for a tactical scheme.	
28th December	G.O.C. R.A. went round horse lines. Dr Lockyer again put in arrest for "Drunkenness".	
29th December	Went over ground S. of River for tactical scheme. G.O.C.R.A. visited Div Comdr re move in afternoon.	

(73989) W4141—463. 400,000. 9/14. H.&J.Ltd. Forms/C. 2118/10.

Army Form C. 2118.

WAR DIARY
or
INTELLIGENCE SUMMARY.
(Erase heading not required.)

Instructions regarding War Diaries and Intelligence Summaries are contained in F. S. Regs., Part II. and the Staff Manual respectively. Title pages will be prepared in manuscript.

Hour, Date, Place	Summary of Events and Information	Remarks and references to Appendices
30th December	G.O.C. R.A. went to BOULOGNE to look for Training Ground.	
31st December.	Nothing to report. G.O.C. R.A. still at BOULOGNE.	

31.12.15

J. Mforth
Brig Gen.
Comdg 36th (Ulster) Div Artillery

Army Form C. 2118.

WAR DIARY
or
INTELLIGENCE SUMMARY.
(Erase heading not required.)

H.Q. 36th Divisional Artillery

Instructions regarding War Diaries and Intelligence Summaries are contained in F.S. Regs., Part II. and the Staff Manual respectively. Title pages will be prepared in manuscript.

Hour, Date, Place	Summary of Events and Information	Remarks and references to Appendices
1st January 1916.	Nothing to report. General Brock returned from BOULOGNE after inspecting Training Grounds.	
2nd January.	Visited I.B.C. with reference to Training Grounds. Lecture to Inf. Officers on Ammunition Supply.	
3rd January.	Motored to LE CROTOY - ST VALERY - CAYEUX on the Coast to look for drill grounds.	
4th January.	Field day 173rd Bde RFA 109 I.Bde. Staff Captain billeted the area round CAYEUX.	
5th January.	G.O.C. R.A. visited BERCK to find Training ground.	
6th January	General Seely went round all Horse lines with G.O.C.R.A. G.O.C.R.A. went to visit Div H.R.	

Army Form C. 2118.

WAR DIARY
or
INTELLIGENCE SUMMARY.
(Erase heading not required.)

Instructions regarding War Diaries and Intelligence Summaries are contained in F.S. Regs., Part II. and the Staff Manual respectively. Title pages will be prepared in manuscript.

Hour, Date, Place	Summary of Events and Information	Remarks and references to Appendices
7th January.	Visited 153rd Bde. Saw D Batty on drill order. A Batty Gun drill and B & A.C horses. General Jackson G.O.C R.A. 14th Corps came with Gen. Brock. Went to a lecture on fighting at LOOS by Major A CON R.T given by Col. Tudor R.H.A.	
8th January	Visited 173rd Bde. Saw the horses of A.B.C.D Batteries. In the afternoon visited 157th Bde, saw the horses of A.D. & Am. Col. General Jackson K.O.C.R.A. 14th Corps came to see General Brock.	
9th January.	G.O.C. R.A. visited Div: H.Q.	
10th January.	Saw D. Bty 153rd Bde at drill. Visited Horses of B.C & Am. Col. 173rd Bde	

WAR DIARY or INTELLIGENCE SUMMARY.

Army Form C. 2118.

(Erase heading not required.)

Instructions regarding War Diaries and Intelligence Summaries are contained in F. S. Regs., Part II. and the Staff Manual respectively. Title pages will be prepared in manuscript.

Hour, Date, Place	Summary of Events and Information	Remarks and references to Appendices
11th January.	Saw C. A's, 172 re Bde Order and afterwards. Saw horses of C.D. Am Col 172. Major W. Graham joined D.A.C.	
12th January.	Saw B. A's 154 Bde on Route March. Saw horses of A A/S after 172. G.O.C. R.A visited 1. A.C.	
13th January.	Brigade day 172nd Bde. Saw horses B & C 154th Bde. Halted went to see Major Hutton I.G.C. also nore.	
14th January.	Brigade and Battery Staffs 173rd Bde. G.O.C R.A went to Calais to watch wire cutting.	
15th January.	Cols and Adjs of 153, 172, 173 Bdes and Adj of 154 Bde went up to the front line to see attached to 4. 37. 4/8. & 4/4 div respectively. G.O.C. R.A Came back from Calais	

WAR DIARY
or
INTELLIGENCE SUMMARY.
(Erase heading not required.)

Army Form C. 2118.

Hour, Date, Place	Summary of Events and Information	Remarks and references to Appendices
16th January.	Bde Major went to visit 7th Corps HQ and then on to P.A.S. (37th Div.) to visit Corps line, with G.S.O.2. Nothing else to report.	
17th January.	Lecture at III rd Army HQ. by General Budworth "Artillery at Loos". Visited Kennels of D.A.C.	
18th January.	Saw A.C. & A/C 154th Bde at firing drill. Visited Hnrs of A.C. D 153 in the afternoon. O.C. 153, 172, 173 + Adjutants returned from Front line.	
19th January.	Saw C. Battery 153rd Bde at Drill. Probable date of move 23rd January.	

WAR DIARY
or
INTELLIGENCE SUMMARY.

(Erase heading not required.)

Army Form C. 2118.

Hour, Date, Place	Summary of Events and Information	Remarks and references to Appendices
20th. January.	Went to BEAUVAL for lectures on "Ammunition" and "Wire cutting". Orders received for move to CAYEUX.	
21st January.	Motored to inspect positions for the defence of Corps line between LA CAUCHIE and COIGNEUX. Visited 7th Corps III Army & 37th Div HQs, in connection with above. Stayed night at DOULLENS.	
22nd January.	Inspected all the gun positions on above line. Arrived back at HQ RA about 4 pm.	
23rd January.	153, 154, 172 Bdes marched to CAYEUX area for training. Shell Coyte also left here for that area.	

WAR DIARY
or
INTELLIGENCE SUMMARY.
(Erase heading not required.)

Army Form C. 2118.

Instructions regarding War Diaries and Intelligence Summaries are contained in F. S. Regs., Part II. and the Staff Manual respectively. Title pages will be prepared in manuscript.

Hour, Date, Place	Summary of Events and Information	Remarks and references to Appendices
24th January	173rd Bde marched to BOISMONT and MONS. G.O.C.R.A arrived at HQR at CAYEUX 172 Bde marched to CAYEUX from BOISMONT and MONS	
25th January	173rd Bde arrived in billets round N-veu BRIGHTON. Brigades situated as under — 153 Bde { WURT, WATHPHURT, SAILENELLE and BRUTELLES 1st Bde (Hero Bt) CAYEUX 172 Bde (Rem Gt) CAYEUX 173 Bde { NOUVEAU BRIGHTON, MOLIÈRES	
26 January	G.O.C.R.A rode over to AULT to find out about Practise ground. Went to ABBEVILLE in the afternoon for same purpose	

Army Form C. 2118.

WAR DIARY
or
INTELLIGENCE SUMMARY.
(Erase heading not required.)

Instructions regarding War Diaries and Intelligence Summaries are contained in F. S. Regs., Part II. and the Staff Manual respectively. Title pages will be prepared in manuscript.

Hour, Date, Place	Summary of Events and Information	Remarks and references to Appendices
27th January	Motored to EU and gave the plans of the Practising Area.	
28th January } 29th January }	Visited HQ RA 18th Div. in connection with IVth Army Scheme.	
30th January	Nothing to report	
31st January	Nothing to report.	

H. J. Howell. Brig General R.A.
Chief 36th Div Artillery

31.1.16.

WAR DIARY or INTELLIGENCE SUMMARY.

Army Form C. 2118.

36 Div Arty

Hour, Date, Place	Summary of Events and Information	Remarks and references to Appendices
1st February.	The G.O.C. R.A inspected the proposed battery positions for firing on the range, with the M.O.R.E.	
2nd February.	Visited all the proposed battery positions and target positions in the morning. Saw the horses of 172 in the afternoon.	
3rd February.	G.O.C. R.A rode out to watch 173rd Bde at drill. Bde Major made a sketch of firing positions + targets for practise. G.O.C R.A visited horses of 153 Bde in afternoon.	
4th February.	Chose observation Stations for the gunnery practise. G.O.C. R.A visited horses of 153rd Bde	
5th February	Watched 'A' Batty 173rd Bde at drill.	

Army Form C. 2118.

WAR DIARY
or
INTELLIGENCE SUMMARY.
(Erase heading not required.)

Instructions regarding War Diaries and Intelligence Summaries are contained in F.S.Regs., Part II. and the Staff Manual respectively. Title pages will be prepared in manuscript.

Hour, Date, Place	Summary of Events and Information	Remarks and references to Appendices
6th February	Nothing to report.	
7th February	Watched 'A' Battery 153 Bde at Drill. Inspection of 153rd Bde Ammunition. G.O.C. R.A noted horses of C & 173 Bdes.	
8th February	G.O.C. R.A returned to BOULOGNE. Inspection Smaller 154 Bde.	
9th February	G.O.C. R.A 17th bde visited 36th Div Arty.	
10th February	G.O.C. R.A visited D. 173 at Drill. Inspection of 173rd Signallers. T & C Staff officer visited & taken off lengthy found.	

Army Form C. 2118.

WAR DIARY
or
INTELLIGENCE SUMMARY.
(Erase heading not required.)

Instructions regarding War Diaries and Intelligence Summaries are contained in F.S. Regs., Part II. and the Staff Manual respectively. Title pages will be prepared in manuscript.

Hour, Date, Place	Summary of Events and Information	Remarks and references to Appendices
11th February.	G.O.C. R.A went up to the 4th Div. Arty.	
12th February.	Nothing to report.	
13th February.	G.O.C. R.A. returned from 4th Div Arty.	
14th February.	A & B Btis 172 Bde & A. [ ] & 173 Bde fired on the Ranges. Too stormy to fire any more	
15th February.	C & D Bties 172 Bde & B.C. D 173rd Bde fired on the Ranges. Very stormy and wet. Staff Captn went up to Mr Grimson	
16th February.	Too stormy to shoot all day.	

(73989) W4141—463. 400,000. 9/14. H.&J.Ltd. Forms/C. 2118/10.

Army Form C. 2118.

WAR DIARY
or
INTELLIGENCE SUMMARY.
(Erase heading not required.)

Hour, Date, Place	Summary of Events and Information	Remarks and references to Appendices
17th February	A.B.C.D. 153rd Bde practised.	
18th February	No firing, too wet. Staff Capt returned from attachment to 4.D.A.	
19th February	A.B.C.D. 154th Bde practised.	
20th February	Nothing to report.	
21st February	A.B.C.D. 172 Bde and A.C.D 173rd Brigade shot on the ranges.	
22nd February	A.B.C.D. 173rd Bde fired in ranges. 154 Bde A.C. marched to PUCHEVILLERS 172nd Bde marched to PONT REMY. 172nd Bde A.C. marched from PUCHEVILLERS to D.A.C. marched to la Vicogne nr [illegible]	

WAR DIARY
or
INTELLIGENCE SUMMARY.
(Erase heading not required.)

Army Form C. 2118.

Hour, Date, Place	Summary of Events and Information	Remarks and references to Appendices
23rd February	Bde Major and Staff Captain motored to ACHEUX & Div. HQ. Staff Captain remained at ACHEUX. Div Am Cn moved to LA VICOGNE and VAL DE MAISON. 172nd Bde RFA marched to PERNOIS. 172nd B&A. Cn to ACHEUX. A. Battery 154 Bde stuck on the ramps.	
24th February	154 Bde RFA B.C.D. Batteries stuck on the ramps (No. 1 battery). 173rd Bde RFA & marched to PONT REMY. 172nd Bde RFA marched to PUCHEVILLERS.	
25th February	Staff Captain returned to ACHEUX. 172nd Bde moved to ACHEUX. 173rd Bde (less 1 Batty) moved to PERNOIS. 154th Bde RFA to PONT REMY. Men slopped.	

Army Form C. 2118.

WAR DIARY
or
INTELLIGENCE SUMMARY.
(Erase heading not required.)

Instructions regarding War Diaries and Intelligence Summaries are contained in F.S. Regs., Part II. and the Staff Manual respectively. Title pages will be prepared in manuscript.

Hour, Date, Place	Summary of Events and Information	Remarks and references to Appendices
26th February.	Bde Major and Staff Captain moved to ACHEUX.	
27th February.	Nothing to report.	
28th February.	G.O.C. R.A arrived at ACHEUX. 172nd Bde R.F.A. B. Battery into action. Sections of C & D Batteries into action. Triplane sections of 68th & 88th Batteries. 154th Bde R.F.A (less A Battery) to FRANQUEVILLE (join 46th Div) moved to PERNOIS. 153rd Bde R.F.A 10 ett, 173rd Bde R.F.A 173rd Bde (less A battery) moved to PONT REMY. to ACHEUX.	

Army Form C. 2118.

WAR DIARY
or
INTELLIGENCE SUMMARY.
(Erase heading not required.)

Hour, Date, Place	Summary of Events and Information	Remarks and references to Appendices
29th February	Remaining sections of C.D. Batteries 172nd Bde RFA into action 6:15 pm. Section of A.C.D. Batteries 173rd Bde into action 6:15 pm. Return of Bde 27th, 134th, 135th Batteries. Return of 154th Bde RFA to LOUVEN COURT. 153rd Bde RFA } to PERNOIS. 1 Batty 173rd Bde } 29.2.16. H.J. Birch Brig Gen. C.R.A. 36th Div	

CRA
36 D 3
Vol 6

Army Form C. 2118.

WAR DIARY
or
INTELLIGENCE SUMMARY.
(Erase heading not required.)

36th Division Artillery

HEADQUARTERS,
36TH DIVISIONAL
ARTILLERY.
Army Form C. 2118 4 D/
pages 3/4/16

Hour, Date, Place	Summary of Events and Information	Remarks and references to Appendices
1st March.	172nd Bde RFA HQ. relieved 14th Bde RFA HQ. and the Brigade took over the line. Section of the 36th D.A.C. relieved a section of the 4th D.A.C. at ARQUEVES. Sections of B. & D. Batteries 152nd Bde RFA relieved sections of 126th & 86th Batteries RFA.	
2nd March.	B. Battery 173rd Bde moved to LOUVENCOURT. Orders received for the relief of the 49th Div by the 36th Division.	
3rd March.	Personnel of 1 section B. Bty 173 moved into action. Sections of A.C.D. 173rd Bde moved into action, & replaced	

(73989) W4141-463. 400,000. 9/14. H.&J.Ltd. Forms/C. 2118/10.

Army Form C. 2118.

WAR DIARY
or
INTELLIGENCE SUMMARY.
(Erase heading not required.)

Instructions regarding War Diaries and Intelligence Summaries are contained in F.S. Regs., Part II. and the Staff Manual respectively. Title pages will be prepared in manuscript.

Hour, Date, Place	Summary of Events and Information	Remarks and references to Appendices
4th March	Section of B/173 into action at AUCHONVILLERS. Heavy snow.	
5th March	Relieved HQ 4th Div Arty at 9.0. am. ADv parties of 153 Bde arrived at 130 h.m. 6 guns about 30 rounds. ACHEUX and were attached to 2nd W.R. Bde RFA whom they are relieving.	
6th March	F.O.C.R.A went out to observe new position for A/153. D.153 and 153 Am Col. arrived at ACHEUX. S.O.S reported in front of 107th Infy Bde at 9.13 pm. Further upon [illegible].	
7th March	Section of B.C.D 153 RFA relieved section of 4th 5th & 6th W.R Bdes 49th Div. Section of D/153 relieved section of B/173 at AUCHONVILLERS. B/153 went into action in new position. Quiet night.	

WAR DIARY
or
INTELLIGENCE SUMMARY.

(Erase heading not required.)

Army Form C. 2118.

Hour, Date, Place	Summary of Events and Information	Remarks and references to Appendices
8th March.	Quiet night. 153rd Bde completed relief with 2nd W.R.Brigade. D/154 completed relief with D/164. Hrs. A.5. A small bombardment of enemy transport was carried out about 7.30 pm.	
9th March	Quiet night. Very little retaliation for our bombardment. 1st Corps Commander came to see G.O.C.R.A. Antennae of Bde Commanders. G.O.C.R.A went round O. Stations.	Appendix A.
10th March.	Quiet night. Nothing to report. D.172 practiced wire cutting.	
11th March.	Enemy bombarded THIEPVAL WOOD about 11:30 pm 10/11th, we replied for about an hour. Otherwise quiet. Nothing to report.	

Army Form C. 2118.

WAR DIARY
or
INTELLIGENCE SUMMARY.
(Erase heading not required.)

Instructions regarding War Diaries and Intelligence Summaries are contained in F.S. Regs., Part II. and the Staff Manual respectively. Title pages will be prepared in manuscript.

Hour, Date, Place	Summary of Events and Information	Remarks and references to Appendices
12th March	Quiet night. Nothing to report.	
13th "	" " " "	
14th March	Quiet night. Carried out a bombardment with Heavy Howitzers and Field Guns on enemy trenches N. of THIEPVAL.	Appendix B
15th March	Nothing to report.	
16th "	Quiet night. Nothing to report.	
17th "	Bombardment of BEAUMONT HAMEL, THIEPVAL, N. of THIEPVAL - Fme de MOUQUET ROAD.	Appendix C
18th "	Nothing to report.	
19th "	do	
20th "	Capt. C.A.L. Brownlow joined as Trench Mortar Staff Officer.	
29th March	Normal Trench warfare. The 92nd Bde (Inf.) of the 31st Division took over the front occupied by the 108th Infantry Brigade.	
30th March	The 93rd Infantry Brigade of the 31st Division took over the front occupied by the 107th Infantry Brigade. The G.O.C. 31st Division assumed command of the fronts at 10 a.m.	
31st March	The relief of the artillery of these Centre and left Group completed. One Section of Each unit being retained.	

Commanding (Signed) H. Brock. Brig Genl
31st March/1st April. CRA 36th Division

Heavy artillery of 31st Division

(73089) W4141—463. 400,000. 9/14. H.&J.Ltd. Forms/C. 2118/10.

Army Form C. 2118.

HEADQUARTERS,
36th DIVISIONAL
ARTILLERY.
B.M. No. 662
Date 30.4.17

36 Division Artillery. Vol 7

WAR DIARY
or
INTELLIGENCE SUMMARY.
(Erase heading not required.)

Instructions regarding War Diaries and Intelligence Summaries are contained in F.S. Regs., Part II. and the Staff Manual respectively. Title pages will be prepared in manuscript.

Hour, Date, Place	Summary of Events and Information	Remarks and references to Appendices
1st April	The reliefs of remaining Sections was completed on the night 1/2 April.	
2nd April	The CRA handed over control of Centre and left groups Artillery to C.R.A. 31st Division. Bde Major took over from Major Murray R.F.A.	
3rd April	Moved R.A. H.Q. to HARPONVILLE. Conference with B.G.R.A. 10th Corps at Heavy Group HQ. Took Crps R.A.B.G. round batteries & forward positions at HAMEL.	
4th April	Nothing to report.	
5th April	Nothing to report.	
6th April	Nothing to report.	

Army Form C. 2118.

WAR DIARY
or
INTELLIGENCE SUMMARY.
(Erase heading not required.)

Instructions regarding War Diaries and Intelligence Summaries are contained in F.S. Regs., Part II. and the Staff Manual respectively. Title pages will be prepared in manuscript.

Hour, Date, Place	Summary of Events and Information	Remarks and references to Appendices
7th April.	About 9 – 10.30 pm on the evening of the 6/7 April the enemy shelled MESNIL and HAMEL and about 2.30 pm the C position of B/153 at R.34.b.3.8 and damaged a gun.	Ref Sheet 57 D.
8th April.	Nothing to report.	
9th April.	Nothing to report.	
10th April.	Nothing to report.	
11th April.	Nothing to report.	
12th, 13th, 14th, 15th April	Nothing to report.	

(73989) W4141—463. 400,000. 9/14. H.&J.Ltd. Forms/C. 2118/10.

WAR DIARY
or
INTELLIGENCE SUMMARY.
(Erase heading not required.)

Army Form C. 2118.

Instructions regarding War Diaries and Intelligence Summaries are contained in F. S. Regs., Part II and the Staff Manual respectively. Title pages will be prepared in manuscript.

Hour, Date, Place	Summary of Events and Information	Remarks and references to Appendices
16th April	Nothing to report	
17th April	C/173 and B/152 moved into action.	
18th April	D/173 moved into action.	
19th April	Nothing to report	
20th April	Div HQ and Div Arty HQ moved to HEDAUVILLE.	
21st April	Nothing to report	
22nd April	Bombardment in conjunction with a minor enterprise carried out by 32nd Div. Major R.G. Thomson RFA joined to Command 153rd Bde RFA	
23rd April	Nothing to report.	
24th April		
25th April	D/172 moved into action.	
26th April	Nothing to report. Major H.C. Simpson D.S.O. joined to Command 173rd Bde RFA	

Army Form C. 2118.

WAR DIARY
or
INTELLIGENCE SUMMARY.
(Erase heading not required.)

Instructions regarding War Diaries and Intelligence Summaries are contained in F.S. Regs., Part II and the Staff Manual respectively. Title pages will be prepared in manuscript.

Hour, Date, Place	Summary of Events and Information	Remarks and references to Appendices
27th April.	Single gun C/172 into action at HAMEL. Bomb store at FORCEVILLE burnt out.	
28th April.	Nothing to report.	
29th April.	Bombardment in connection with Raid by 29th Division. MESNIL RIDGE and A.153. heavily shelled during the day. Trench mortars very active during the night on THIEPVAL WOOD.	Reference 57 D. S.E.
30th April.	Nothing to report.	

30.4.16.

H. Marsh
Brig Gen
Cmdg. 36th Divl Arty

Army Form C. 2118.

C.R.A. 36 Do
Vol 8

HEADQUARTERS,
36th DIVISIONAL
ARTILLERY.
B.M. No. 475
Date. 1/6/16

WAR DIARY
or
INTELLIGENCE SUMMARY.
(Erase heading not required.)

Instructions regarding War Diaries and Intelligence Summaries are contained in F.S. Regs., Part II. and the Staff Manual respectively. Title pages will be prepared in manuscript.

Hour, Date, Place	Summary of Events and Information	Remarks and references to Appendices
1st May.	Enemy attempted raid on MARY REDAN which failed.	
2nd May.	Nothing to report.	
3rd May.	" "	
4th May.	" "	
5th May.	" "	
6th May.	" "	
7th May.	Raid by the 36th Division at 11.45pm. (See Appendix I). The Raid was successfully carried out and the enemy lines entered but no prisoners were taken. A raid on the junction of the 32nd and our fronts took place simultaneously with our own and the Germans effected an entry. The German Bombardment was very heavy.	

Army Form C. 2118.

WAR DIARY
or
INTELLIGENCE SUMMARY.
(Erase heading not required.)

Instructions regarding War Diaries and Intelligence Summaries are contained in F.S. Regs., Part II. and the Staff Manual respectively. Title pages will be prepared in manuscript.

Hour, Date, Place	Summary of Events and Information	Remarks and references to Appendices
8th May	Nothing to report	
9th May	"	
10th May	"	
11th May	"	
12th May	Major the Hon H.R.Scarlett DSO joined the Div Arty	
13th May	"	
14th May	"	
15th May	"	
16th May	Attempted Raid on the HAMEL Subsector stopped by Artillery fire, about 12.30 a.m.	
17th May	Nothing to report.	

Army Form C. 2118.

WAR DIARY
or
INTELLIGENCE SUMMARY.
(Erase heading not required.)

Instructions regarding War Diaries and Intelligence Summaries are contained in F.S. Regs., Part II. and the Staff Manual respectively. Title pages will be prepared in manuscript.

Hour, Date, Place	Summary of Events and Information	Remarks and references to Appendices
16th May – 23rd May	Nothing to Report.	
24th May – 28th May	Nothing to Report.	
28th May – 31st May	Nothing to Report.	
31.5.16	H.J. Mack Brig Gen Comdg 36th Div Arty	

36th Divisional Artillery

C. R. A.

36th DIVISION.

JUNE 1916

36 Div RA
Army Form C. 2118.

Vol 9 June

WAR DIARY
or
INTELLIGENCE SUMMARY.
(Erase heading not required.)

Instructions regarding War Diaries and Intelligence Summaries are contained in F.S. Regs., Part II. and the Staff Manual respectively. Title pages will be prepared in manuscript.

Hour, Date, Place	Summary of Events and Information	Remarks and references to Appendices
1st June	Nothing to report.	
2nd June	Enemy Artillery rather more active than usual.	
3rd June	A bombardment carried out by the left Group in conjunction with a Raid by the 25th Division, which was successful.	
4th June	Nothing to report.	
5th June	A raid by the 36th Division on the German Trenches N. of the Ancre river. The went on for 1½ hours when "Cease fire" was sent by the Infantry. Report received about 12.45 am that Raiding party had returned, some casualties, & no prisoners.	Appendix I.
6th June	Nothing to report	

Army Form C. 2118.

WAR DIARY
or
INTELLIGENCE SUMMARY.
(Erase heading not required.)

Instructions regarding War Diaries and Intelligence Summaries are contained in F.S. Regs., Part II. and the Staff Manual respectively. Title pages will be prepared in manuscript.

Hour, Date, Place	Summary of Events and Information	Remarks and references to Appendices
7th June	Nothing to report.	
8th June	Practice attack by 108 & 109 Inf. Bdes at CLAIRFAYE. Ammunition began to arrive for dumps.	
9th June	Field day by Some Brigades near WARLOY. 172 Bde less 1 Battery took part. Z.49 T.M Bty (2") arrived and went into bivouac in AVELUY WOOD.	
10th June	Raid on William Redan on North side of the Ancre by enemy. No prisoners taken and party forced out as soon as the leaders entered. 114 French (49th Division) arrived — 246 Bde.	
11th June	Nothing to report. Much rain.	
12th June	Nothing to report. More rain.	
13th June	246 Brigade and 172 Brigade into action. More rain.	

WAR DIARY
or
INTELLIGENCE SUMMARY.
(Erase heading not required.)

Army Form C. 2118.

Instructions regarding War Diaries and Intelligence Summaries are contained in F. S. Regs., Part II. and the Staff Manual respectively. Title pages will be prepared in manuscript.

Hour, Date, Place	Summary of Events and Information	Remarks and references to Appendices
14th June	Nothing to Report.	
15th		
16th		
17th		
18th	Three Batteries 20th Regt Artillery under Commandant de VARINE arrived	
19th	Nothing to Report	
20th	Nothing to Report	
21st }	Nothing to Report	
22nd }		
23rd }		

Army Form C. 2118.

WAR DIARY
or
INTELLIGENCE SUMMARY.
(Erase heading not required.)

Instructions regarding War Diaries and Intelligence Summaries are contained in F. S. Regs., Part II. and the Staff Manual respectively. Title pages will be prepared in manuscript.

Hour, Date, Place	Summary of Events and Information	Remarks and references to Appendices
24th June	'U' day. 4th Army Scheme commenced. Wire cutting by day. Shelling Communications by night. Gas discharge arranged but cancelled owing to lack of wind. German shelling very intermittent and of no volume. Very quiet during the night.	Orders and Instructions attached.
25th June	'V' day. Wire cutting by day. Light Howitzer Bombardment at 18 hrs. keeping wire open by light. Enemy Artillery after quiet on our front. Enemy T. Mortars active in shelling THIEPVAL WOOD, one of our 2" mortars knocked out. Three German 'Sausage' balloons brought down by aeroplane bombs & one FOKKER shot down by ours. Push Tree (R 13 d 0800).	
26th June	Bombardment of THIEPVAL in the morning. Gas discharge during the afternoon accompanied by Heavy Bombardment. Enemy seen reinforcing from the E. of GRANDCOURT. Enemy retaliation very poor. A raid carried out in THIEPVAL Subsector at 11.30 pm	Appendix 2

Army Form C. 2118.

WAR DIARY
or
INTELLIGENCE SUMMARY.
(Erase heading not required.)

Hour, Date, Place	Summary of Events and Information	Remarks and references to Appendices
27th June	Raid successful. One Officer and 12 men take prisoners. X day Concentrated Bombardments on different areas. Gunner fire feeble. Previous night the men had to ford for 3 days owing to our Barrage for the prevention of supplies to Trenches.	
28th June	Y day. Concentrated Bombardment and wire cutting as before. German Artillery not active. 'Z' day postponed 48 hours owing to weather.	
29th June	Y₁ day. Bombardment and wire cutting as before. German Artillery not so active as during previous 24 hours. Practically all the wire required to be cut is cut.	

Army Form C. 2118.

WAR DIARY
or
INTELLIGENCE SUMMARY.
(Erase heading not required.)

Instructions regarding War Diaries and Intelligence Summaries are contained in F. S. Regs., Part II. and the Staff Manual respectively. Title pages will be prepared in manuscript.

Hour, Date, Place	Summary of Events and Information	Remarks and references to Appendices
30 June	½ day. Bombardment and wire cutting as before. Hostile fire much more active during the night	
1st July.	Z day. A fine morning but very misty, nothing to be seen. Bombardment commenced at 6.25 am. Hostile Barrage opened at 6.40 am on NE & E of THIEPVAL WOOD, and on HAMEL at 6.57 am. Infantry leaving trenches 7.25 am. Infantry in sunken road no barrage there 7.27 am.	

H. J. Brooke Brig Gen
Cmdg. 36th Div Arty

S E C R E T. Appendix 1.
B.M. 890.

Bombardment Table for Night 3/4th June, 1916.

U N I T.	Time.	Task.	Ammunition.	Remarks.
1 Sec.8" How.				
One gun.	0.20 – 1.20.	Q.17.b.3545.	20.	
One gun.	"	Q.17.b.9010.	20.	
1 Bty.6" How.	"	Q.17.b.2012 – Q.17.b.7505.	60.	
1 Sec.60-pdr.	"	Communication Trench in Q.12.	40.	
1 Bty.4.5" Hows.		Junction Support & Communication Trenches Q.17.b.6222.	25.	
One gun.	"	" " " " Q.17.b.4628.	25.	
One gun.	"	" " " " Q.17.b.2830.	25.	
One gun.	"	" " " " Q.17.b.1240.	25.	
One 18-pdr Battery.	"	Q.17.b.6215 – Q.17.b.4212 & Communication Trenches to Support Line.	240.	
One 18-pdr Battery.	"	Q.17.b.6122 – Q.17.b.1240.	240.	Enfilades.
One 18-pdr Battery.	"	Q.17.b.4212 – Q17.b.1517. & Communication Trenches to Support Line.	240.	
One 18-pdr Battery.	"	Q.17.b.1517 – Q.17.b.1240 & Communication Trenches to Support Line.	240.	

Note. From 0.0 – 0.20 The Left Group will open a steady rate of section Fire on their night lines on the enemy parapet, changing at 0.20 into the above bombardment.
Zero time will be 12 midnight.

2nd June, 1916.

Major, R.A.,
Brigade Major, 36th Divl. Artillery.

R.A. 10th Corps.
H.A.G. 10th Corps.
29th Div. Artillery.
O.C. Left Group.

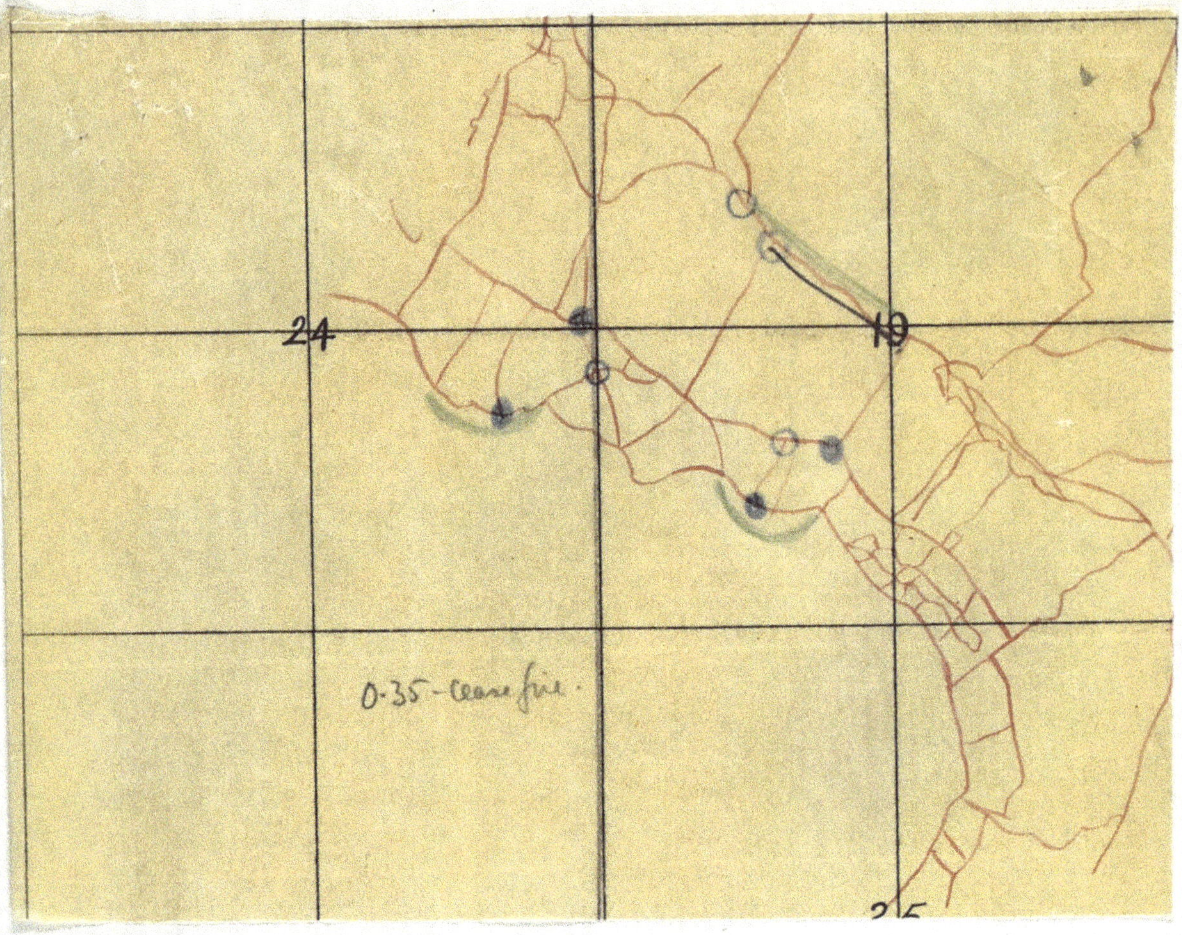

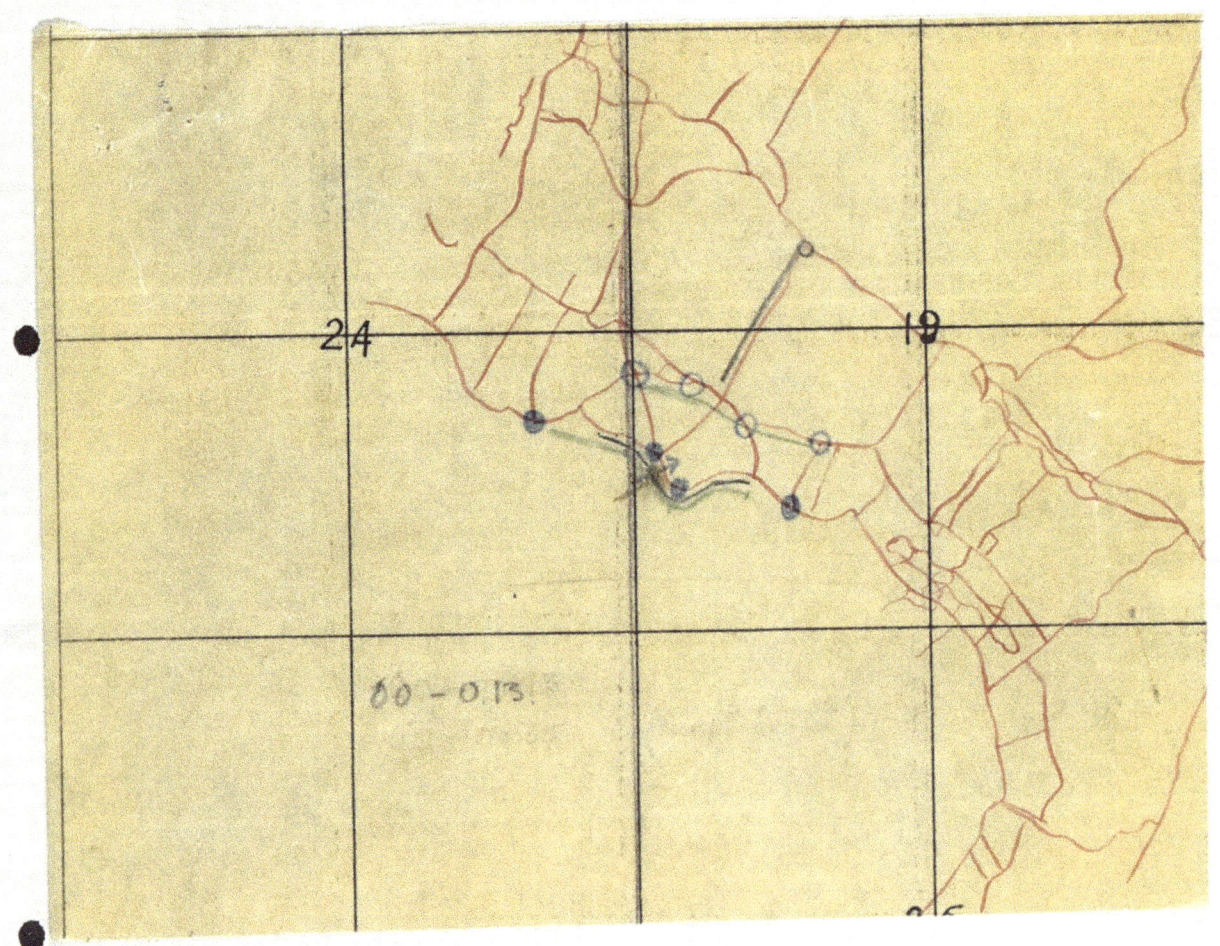

0.35 - cease fire.

00 - 0.13

S.E.C.R.E.T.

36th Div. Arty. No. B.M. 800/48
Appendix 2

Programme of Raid to be carried out on W/X night.

Point of Raid R.19.c. 1055.

Unit.	Time.	Task.	Ammunition.	Remarks.
8" How. Bty.				
One Gun.	0.0 – Cease fire.	R.19.c. 5540. (A.15).	20.	
One Gun.	0.0 – Cease fire.	Q.24.d. 6570 and Trench junctions.	20.	
One Gun.	0.0 – 0.13.	(R.19.c. 1545 (NEB).	20.	
	0.13 – Cease fire.	(R.19.c. 8060. (A.16).		
One Gun.	0.0 – 0.13.	(R.19.c. 1060. (A.18).	20.	
	0.13 – Cease Fire.	(Q.24.b. 9800. (A.19).		
6" How. Bty.				
One Gun.	0.0 – Cease fire.	R.19.c. 6.6. Trench Junction.	20.	
One Gun.	0.0 – Cease fire.	R.19.c. 0085.	20.	
One Gun.	0.0 – 0.35.	(R.19.c. 4068 (A.17).	20.	
	0.35 – Cease fire.	(R.19.c. 6028.		
One Gun.	0.0 – 0.35	(R.19.c. 2082.	20.	
	0.35 – Cease fire.	(R.19.c. 5040. (B.19).		
4.5" How. Bty.	0.0 – 0.13.	Bombard Front Trench.R.19.c. 4050 to Q.24.d. 8867.		
Three Guns.	0.13 – 0.25.	Lift & Bombard from R.19.c. 4068 to R.19.c. 0085.		
	0.25 – 0.35.	As for 0.0 – 0.13.		
	0.35 – Cease fire.	Bombard Reserve Trench R.19.d. 0595 – R.19.c. 6028.	160.	
One Gun.	0.0 – 0.35.	R.19.c. 6028 and walk back up Communication Trench to R.19.c. 3077.		
	0.35 – Cease fire.	As for the other 3 guns.		
2" T.M. Bty.	0.0 – 0.13.	Wire at R.19.c. 1055.		
	0.13 – 0.25.	Stop firing.		
	0.25 – 0.35.	Bombard Trench between R.19.c. 1545 & R.19.c. 1060.		
	0.35 –	Stop Firing.		

- 2 -

Unit.	Time.	Task.	Ammunition.	Remarks.
One 18-pdr.Battery.	0.0 - 0.13. 0.13 - 0.25. 0.25 - 0.35. 0.35 - Cease fire.	R.19.c. 4450 to R.19.c. 1060. Switch to trench R.19.c.7540 to R.19.c.4450. As for 0.0 - 0.13. As for 0.13 - 0.25.	160.	Two guns to cut wire at R.19.c.1055 if reported not cut on W day.(0"-013)
One 18-pdr.Battery.	0.0 - 0.13. 0.13 - 0.25. 0.25 - 0.35. 0.35 - Cease fire.	R.19.c. 1060 - Q.24.d. 7570. Switch to trench Q.24.d. 8075. to Q.24.d.4580. As for 0.0 - 0.13. As for 0.13 - 0.25.	160.	
One 18-pdr.Battery.	0.0 - 0.35. 0.35 - Cease fire.	Trench R.19.c. 6560 to R.19.c. 0085. Lift to Reserve Trench R.19.d. 0595 to R.19.d. 5040	160.	
One Section, 18-prs.	0.0 - 0.13. 0.13 - 0.25. 0.25 - 0.35. 0.35	Enfilade Q.24.d. 4580 - R.19.c. 1060. Enfilade Q.24.b. 8010 - R.19.c. 4068. As for 0.0 - 0.13. Stop.	80.	

Note. This raid will not be carried out on W/X night if the Gas Discharge takes place that night, but will come off the following night.

R.A. 10th Corps.
H.A.G., 10th Corps.
Centre Group. "G".
36th Division.
O.C. 13th R.I.R.,

P.Sheual

Brigade Major, R.A.,
Major, R.A.,
Brigade Major, 36th Divl. Artillery.

23rd June, 1916.

Fourth Army Scheme   Secret

HEADQUARTERS, 36th DIVISIONAL ARTILLERY.
B.M. No. 500/111
Date 9-6-16

Headquarters, R.A.,
Xth Corps.

The following is a list of Batteries of this Divisional Artillery, by Groups, including those Batteries of the 49th Divisional Artillery attached :-

RIGHT GROUP.

Commander - Lieut-Col. R.G. Thomson, D.S.O., R.F.A.,

    A)
    B) Batteries, 153rd Brigade R.F.A.,
    C)
    D)

    A   Battery, 246th Brigade R.F.A.,

CENTRE GROUP.

Commander - Lieut-Col. L.E.S. Ward, D.S.O., R.F.A.,

    A)
    B) Batteries, 172nd Brigade R.F.A.,
    C)   (Less 1 gun C Battery).
    D)

    B)
    C) Batteries, 246th Brigade R.F.A.,
    D)

    A   Battery, 154th Brigade R.F.A.,

LEFT GROUP.

Commander - Lieut-Col. H.C. Simpson, D.S.O., R.F.A.,

    A)
    B) Batteries, 173rd Brigade R.F.A.,
    C)
    D)

    B) Batteries, 154th Brigade R.F.A.,
    C)

    C   Battery, 172nd Brigade R.F.A., (1 Gun).

9th June, 1916.   Brigadier General,
Commanding 36th Divl. Artillery.

4th Army Scheme.   S E C R E T.   36th Div. Arty. No. B.M.500/156.

36TH DIVISIONAL ARTILLERY.

Battery Positions, shewing O.P's & Arcs of Fire.

- RIGHT GROUP -

No. of Position	UNIT	Position	No. of O.P.	Position	Arc of Fire
39.	A.153 Bde. R.F.A.,	Q.27.d. 6180.	109.	Q.23.c.1258.	40° -9
35.	B.153 " "	Q.34.b. 1250.	127.	Q.35.a.3662.	39° - 9
36.	C.153 " "	Q.34.b. 2884.	101.	Q.28.d. 8.6.	63°-94°
31.	D.153 " "	W.4.c. 3489.	101.	Q.28.d. 8.6.	26°-70°
37.	A.246 " "	Q.28.b.6104.	105.	Q.28.b.9587.	34°-94°

- CENTRE GROUP -

No. of Position	UNIT	Position	No. of O.P.	Position	Arc of Fire
41.	A.172 " "	Q.28.b.1049.	(111. (122.	Q.29.a.4542. Q.23.a.9995.	22°-99°
42.	B.172 " "	Q.28.b.0568.	(112. (123.	Q.22.d.9110. Q.29.a.8880.	30°-90°
46.B.	C.172 " " (3 guns)	Q.23.b.1585.	(124. (((	Q.23.b.0178.	95°-137° (1 gun) 95°-116° (2 guns)
32.	D.172 " "	W.4.a. 6379.	(102. (120.	Q.23.c.1090. Q.29.a.6572.	9°-96°
38.	B.246 " "	Q.28.b.5318.	110.	Q.22.d.8080.	35°-75°
40.	C.246 " "	Q.28.b.2830.	108.	Q.22.d.9437.	17°-77°
33.	D.246 " "	Q.34.c.7747.	103.	Q.29.a.6264.	30°-80°
48.	A.154. " "	Q.16.c.7148.	121.	Q.23.b.0770.	74°-126°

- LEFT GROUP -

No. of Position	UNIT	Position	No. of O.P.	Position	Arc of Fire
47.	A.173 " "	Q.22.a.2583.	(116. (126.	Q.22.d.9104. Q.22.d.9033.	63°-108°
49.	B.173 " "	Q.8.d. 0301.	118.	Q.29.a.5552.	67°-118°
44.	C.173 " "	Q.22.c.3032.	114.	Q.29.a.5250.	36°-8
34.	D.173 " "	Q.34.c.6581.	104.	Q.35.a.2590.	357°-62°
45.	B.154 " "	Q.22.c.0251.	115.	Q.23.c.1550.	31°-92°
46.A.	C.172 " " (1 gun)	Q.24.d. 3.1.			310°-337°
43.	C.154 " "	Q.22.d.3317.	113.	Q.23.c.1070.	33°-110°

18th June, 1916.   Major, R.A.,
Brigade Major, 36th Divl. Artill

SECRET. Copy No. 33

File

HEADQUARTERS,
36th DIVISIONAL
ARTILLERY.
B.M. No. 500/146
Date............

36TH DIVISIONAL ARTILLERY ORDER No. 1.

1. The 36th Division will attack the enemy trenches on their front in accordance with the attached 36th Division Order No. 34.

2. The period of the Preliminary Bombardment and wire-cutting will be 5 days, lettered U, V, W, X, Y, respectively.
    The date of U day will be notified later.
    Z day will be the day of attack.

3. Batteries will bombard in accordance with Schemes already submitted.

4. There will be one F.O.O. with the Headquarters of each Battalion actually attacking. These F.O.O's. will be under the sole orders of the Artillery Liaison Officers at Infantry Brigade Headquarters, and will only advance when told by him to do so. They should be accompanied by 3 telephonists (one a linesman), 2 miles of wire, 2 Telephones, flags, discs and lamps.

5. The Artillery Liaison Officer at Infantry Brigade Headquarters will have an Officer with him to send forward as he requires to obtain information of the progress of the attack.

6. If any 'Re-Bombardment' is ordered during 'Z' day or afterwards, it will last 30 minutes, the last 5 minutes of which will be intensive.

7. B/173 Brigade R.F.A., will be ready to advance to a position already chosen, by the fork roads at Q. 23. d. 6.0, on receiving orders from R.A.H.Q. This Battery will not be ordered to advance until the 'C' line has been reached and the Infantry have commenced consolidating it.
    If the advance of the Infantry against 'D' line is held up and a fresh attack has to be made against this Line, the following Batteries will be advanced to positions E of the River to cut the wire:-

    A/153; B/153; A/172; B/246; C/246;

    Officers from these Batteries should, if possible, be the F.O.Os. who are to be at Battalion Headquarters as laid down in para. 4.

    Attention is called to Paras. 7, 8, in 36th Division Order No. 34, Appendix A.

    C.E. Stranack
                                            Major, R.A.,
17th June, 1916.   Brigade Major, 36th Divl. Artillery.

Copy No. 1. to R.A., 10th Corps.   No. 29 to S.O., T.M.,
        2. " 36th Divn. "G".   30 " 107th Inf. Bde.
        3. " H.A.G., 10th Corps.   31 " 108th Inf. Bde.
        4.- 8 to 153rd Bde. R.F.A.,   32 " 109th Inf. Bde.
        9 -12 " 154th Bde. R.F.A.,   33, 34, 35, Filed.
       13 -17 " 172nd Bde. R.F.A.,
       18 -22 " 173rd Bde. R.F.A.,
       23 -27 " 246th Bde. R.F.A.,
          28 " 36th D.A.C.

SECRET.   36th Div. Arty. No. B.M. 500/:
193.

War Diary

O.C. Right Group,
  Centre "
  Left   "

INSTRUCTIONS FOR ARTILLERY DURING GAS DISCHARGE AND RAID.

1. Divisions will be ready to let off gas from the night U/V inclusive.

2. If the wind is favourable a wire will be sent by the Corps after 5 p.m. as follows - "WARN ROGER".

3. If the wind continues favourable a fixed hour will be sent by Corps giving Zero hour, at which gas will be discharged, as follows - "ROGER TONIGHT (Time)".

4. The Artillery programme as sent out by my B.M./500/146 is cancelled and a fresh programme is attached.

5. The Tasks will be as for the Intensive Bombardment on 'Z' day.

6. On conclusion of the Gas discharge a Raid will take place on each flank of the trench onto which the gas has been discharged and the Raiding parties will turn inwards along the gassed trench.

7. To support this Raid a barrage will be put up on each flank of the gassed trench, on the Right by the Right Group and on the left by the Centre Group.

8. As it is impossible beforehand to tell the two points on the German front trench between which the Gas will take effect, a message will be sent to each of the above Groups directly the exact direction of the discharge is known giving a point on each of the Front, Support and Reserve line trenches on each side of the gas.

9. Group Commanders will then work out their own barrage using 4 18-pdr. batteries and one 4.5" Howitzer Battery. The Front and Support lines between these points will not be fired on, but the Reserve line between these points will be barraged by one battery of each Group. The 4.5" Howitzer Battery should be used to block Communication Trenches.

10. The Barrage will commence at 2.15; i.e., 5 minutes after the Artillery programme mentioned in para. 4. has been completed and will continue till 5.20.

11. A steady rate of Fire will be used for this Barrage during the whole period of the Raid.

           Major, R.A.,
24th June, 1916.   Brigade Major, 36th Divl. Artillery.

R.A., 10th Corps.
36th Division, "G".
O.C. 154th Bde. R.F.A.,) For information.
  246th   "   "   )

SECRET.   Copy No. _____

                       AMENDMENT TO

           36TH DIVISIONAL ARTILLERY ORDER No. 1.

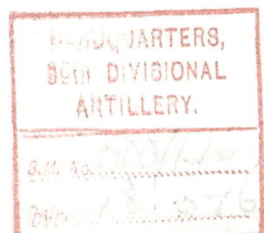

Para. 6.

           Any Commander requiring a Re-bombardment will state the
time he requires the Bombardment to begin.

           If the request does not arrive in time for the Bombard-
ment to begin at the time required, it will nevertheless cease
half an hour after that time, however late it may be beginning.

                                   C.E. Shanahan
                                                  Major, R.A.,
18th June, 1916.   Brigade Major, 36th Divl. Artillery.

Copy No. 1. to R.A. Xth Corps.   23-27 to 246th Bde. R.F.A.,
         2. to 36th Division, "G". 28 to 36th D.A.C.,
         3 to H.A.G., Xth Corps. 29 to S.O., T.M.,
     4 - 8. to 153rd Bde. R.F.A.,   30 to 107th Inf. Bde.
     9 - 12. to 154th Bde. R.F.A., 31 to 108th Inf. Bde.
    13 - 17. to 172nd Bde. R.F.A., 32 to 109th Inf. Bde.
    18 - 22. to 173rd Bde. R.F.A., 33, 34, 35 - Filed.

R.A.Xth Corps No.1504/124.
36th Div. Arty   B.M.500/194.

SECRET.

36th Division Artillery.

Table B.

The following ammendments will be made in Table B :-

(1). Gas may be used on night U/V if wind is favourable.

(2). Heavy Howitzers will fire during the concentrated periods only.

(3). The Divisional Artillery Time Table will be as follows in accordance with information received last night as to the latest procedure ordered by the enemy for dealing with a gas attack:-

Time	Guns	Rate
0.5 to 0.15	All guns	18 prs. 2 rounds per gun per minute. 4.5" Hows. 1 round per gun per minute.
1.35 to 1.45	All guns	18 prs. 1 round per gun per minute. 4.5" Hows. B.F. 30 seconds
At 1.55	All guns on front line lift to support line.	
1.55 to 2.0	All guns	18 prs. 1 round per gun per minute. 4.5" Hows. B.F. 30 Seconds.
At 2.0	All guns on support line lift back to front line.	
2.0 to 2.10	All guns	18 prs. 2 rounds per gun per minute. 4.5" Hows. 1 round per gun per minute.

(Sd) H. Whynter Major R.A.
24.6.16   Staff Officer R.A.Xth Corps.

O.C. Right Group.
O.C. Centre Group.
O.C. Left Group.
O.C. 154th Brigade R.F.A.) For information.
O.C. 246th Brigade R.F.A.)

                                              Major R.A.
24.6.16   Brigade Major 36th Divl. Artillery.

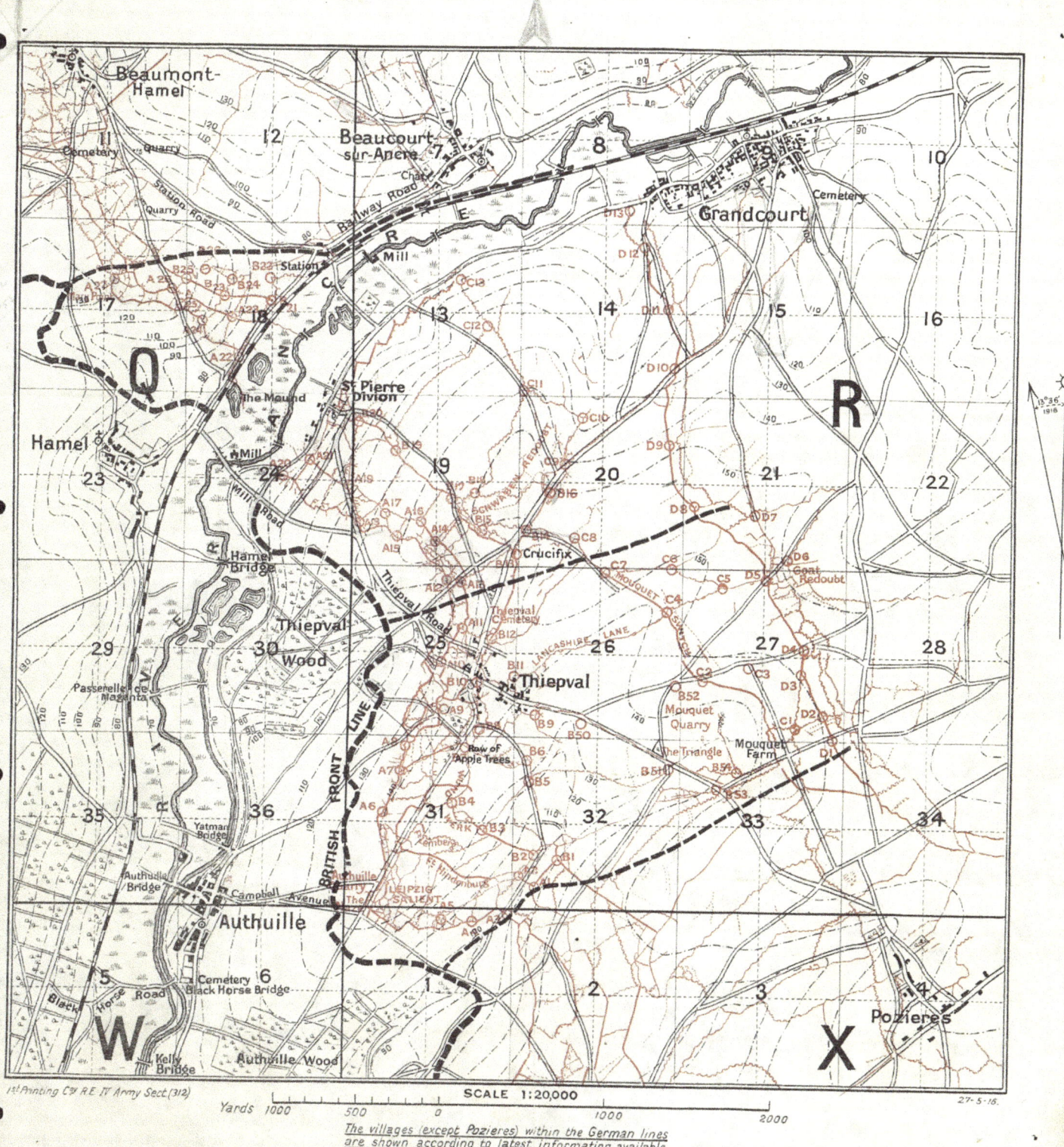

SECRET.

INTENSIVE BOMBARDMENT & TABLE OF LIFTS.
(HAMEL SUB- SECTOR)

Time.

-65 to 0.0	18-pdrs on all Trenches upto and inckuding the SUNKEN Road to Station and Station itself.
INTENSIVE BOMBARDMENT.	4.5" Hows. on Strong Points in above System. 9.45" T.M. on RAILWAY SAP in Q.18.c.
0.0. (0.0. - 0.3)	All fire Lifts off Front Line Trench and Communication Trenches between it and Support Trench. The Trench just N. of the Station comes under 18-pdr. fire. 4.5" How. on Special points. 9.45" T.M. ceases firing.
0.3. (0.3 - 0.8)	All fire lifts off Support Trench and Communication Trenches between it and Reserve Line to Reserve Line and E. of this line.
0.8. (0.8 - 0.13)	All fire lifts off Reserve Line to a line from Q.18.a.3035 to Station and E. of this line.
0.13. (0.13 - 0.33)	All fire lifts off above line to a line from Q.18.b.0075 running E along Trench to E of Station and E of this line.
0.33 (0.33 - 1.0)	All fire lifts off above line to a line from Q.18.b.5058 through the two houses and across the River to C.13 and C.12.
(1.0 - 1.12)	All fire lifts to a line from a point on Railway Road R.7.c. 5527, extending 100 yards N. of this point to C.12 and up the road from C.13 - D 13.
1.12 (1.12 - 1.18)	The above fire closes down to S. of the River.
1.18 (1.18 - 2.38)	All fire lifts on to "D" line and approaches to it from the E. A Section of 18-pdrs. and a Section of Hows. walk up the road from C.13 - D.13 at 100 yards per minute.
2.38	All fire lifts to form a Barrage 300^x E. of "D" line and approaches to this line from the East.
NOTE.	All 4.5" Howrs. and Trench Mortars Lift their fire in each case 3 minutes before the times laid down for 18-pr.

Major R.A.
20th June 1916.   Brigade Major 36th Divisional Artillery.

36th Div Arty.B.M.500/165

SECRET   APPENDIX "E"
INTENSIVE BOMBARDMENT AND TABLE OF LIFTS
(THIEPVAL SUB-SECTOR)

TIME	
-65 to 0.0.	18-pr Batteries on all Trenches (Fire and Communication) up to "C" Line inclusive.
INTENSIVE BOMBARDMENT.	4.5" Hows. Certain Trenches and Strong Points in "A" & "B" Lines.
	2".T.M. Bombarding Front Line Trench in THIEPVAL Sub-Sector.
	9.45" How.T.M. CRUCIFIX System M.Gs in Q 24b ST PIERRE DIVION RAILWAY SAP in Q 18c.
0.0. (0.0. -0.3.)	All fire lifts off the Front Trench and Communication Trenches, between Front F Support Trenches, to Support Trench and Trenches in rear (exclusive of "C" Line)
	2" T.M. Stop Firing.
	9.45" T.M. on ST PIERRE DIVION and Main CRUCIFIX REDOUBT.
0.3. (0.3.- 0.18.)	All Fire lifts off the Support Trench and Communication Trenches between Support and Reserve Trenches & Reserve Trenches to Reserve Line and Trenches in rear including "C" Line.
	9.45" T.M. on ST PIERRE DIVION up to 0.10 (Stops) The T.M. on CRUCIFIX REDOUBT stops firing.
0.18. (0.18- 028)	All fire lifts off Reserve Line to a parallel line about 400 yards East of Reserve Line and Trenches East of this Line.
	Sections of 18pr and 4.5" Hows walk up Communication Trenches between "B" & "C" Lines at 100 yards per minute and on reaching "C" Line commence bombardment of that Line.
0.28. (0.28 -1.18)	All fire lifts to "C" Line and appraches it to "D" Line.
1.18. (1.18-2.38.)	All fire lifts off "C" Line and approaches to it from the East.
	Sections of 18prs and 4.5" Hows walk up approaches between "C" & "D" Line at 100 yards per minute and on reaching "D" Line commence bombardment of that line.
2.38	All fire lifts to form a barrage 300 yards E of "D" Line and approaches to it from the E.
NOTE	All 4.5" Hows and Trench Mortars lift their fire in each case 3 minutes before the times laid down for 18 prs.

20th June 1916

Major.R.A.
Brigade Major 36th Divisional Arty

SECRET.

36th Div. Arty. No. B.M. 500/227.

4th Army Scheme.

O.C. Right Group,
    Centre "
    Left   "

AMENDMENTS TO APPENDIX E.

The following changes in the Lift at the taking of the 2nd Line are made owing to alteration in the Infantry Attack.

2.38
No fire S of a point R.20.b. 8090.
The Right Group will lift to Barrage 200^x E of Support line.

(2.38 – 2.55)
The Centre Group will switch until all fire is N of R.20.b. 8090 still keeping up the Bombardment on the 2nd Line.
The Left Group will continue to bombard the 2nd line.

2.55.
The Centre Group guns firing between R.20.b. 8090 and D.10 will lift to Barrage 200 yards E of Support Line.

(2.55 – 3.10).
All other guns as for 2.38.

3.10
The remaining Centre Group guns bombarding between D.10 and D.11 lift to Barrage 200^x E of Support Line.

(3.10 – 3.30.
Left Group continue to bombard the 2nd Line.

3.30.
The Right Battery of the Left Group ceases to Bombard 2nd Line and lifts fire 200^x E of Support Line.

(onwards)
The remaining Batteries of the Left Group continue Bombardment of 2nd Line to the River. Railway
All Batteries of Right and Centre Groups lift their Barrage to a line 200^x E of road from X Road at R.27 15.a. 8260 to R.21.a. 8200. No fire to be W. of this line for these Groups after 3.30 p.m.

Note.
4.5" How. Batteries should be put on to block approaches and roads.

After 3.30 p.m. all Batteries will fire in accordance with my B.M. 500/185 of the 24th inst.

27th June, 1916.

Major, R.A.,
Brigade Major, 36th Divl. Artillery.

O.C. 154th Bde. R.F.A.,)
O.C. 246th Bde. R.F.A.,) For information.
36th Division, "G".)

36th Divisional Artillery.

C. R. A.

36th DIVISION.

JULY 1916

Army Form C. 2118.

WAR DIARY
or
INTELLIGENCE SUMMARY.

(Erase heading not required.)

Instructions regarding War Diaries and Intelligence Summaries are contained in F.S. Regs., Part II. and the Staff Manual respectively. Title pages will be prepared in manuscript.

Hour, Date, Place	Summary of Events and Information	Remarks and references to Appendices
1st July.	Z day. During the night 1/2/2 the Div and RA HQ moved down to the thurrard report centre.	
6.25am	Bombardment commenced.	
6.45am	Hostile Barrage over the E and NE. face of THIEPVAL WOOD	
6.57am	Fire on HAMEL appears heavy, but observation difficult	
7.5am	Barrage on THIEPVAR WOOD hr heavy.	
7.15am	Barrage on THIEPVAR WOOD of 77mm with 150 m.m shelling the wood itself	
7.21am	Hostile fire on HAMEL diminishing, shot on THIEPVAR WOOD increasing. Our infantry have left their trenches.	
7.27am	Our Infantry massing in sunken road no holds Barrage there.	
7.40am	Infantry taken first line Trench in Centre and left attack	
7.42am	Infantry taken front and support Trenches & Centre and Left attack	

Army Form C. 2118.

WAR DIARY
or
INTELLIGENCE SUMMARY.
(Erase heading not required.)

Instructions regarding War Diaries and Intelligence Summaries are contained in F. S. Regs., Part II. and the Staff Manual respectively. Title pages will be prepared in manuscript.

Hour, Date, Place	Summary of Events and Information	Remarks and references to Appendices
7.45 am	Front and Support line taken by Right attack	
7.50 am	Left attack into B (Reserve) line.	
7.54 am	Right and Centre attack over the B (Reserve Line)	
	Left attack also over the B (Reserve Line)	
7.55 am	A line captured 7.45 am. (Summary)	(Liaison 109)
8.2 am	Infantry in HAMEL report that 29th Div are being pushed back.	(Liaison 108)
8.4 am	Field gun at ST PIERRE DIVION firing on PETERHEAD SAP.	(Liaison 108)
8.10 am	29th Division being pushed back and enemy have taken over first line. Supporting Infantry advancing with little loss (Right attack)	
8.15 am	Two supporting Battalions of Right Attack are in A (Support) Line	
8.25 am	32nd Division held up at Front Line.	
8.30 am	Occupying N.W. face of CRUCIFIX REDOUBT.	

Army Form C. 2118.

WAR DIARY
or
INTELLIGENCE SUMMARY.
(Erase heading not required.)

Instructions regarding War Diaries and Intelligence Summaries are contained in F. S. Regs., Part II. and the Staff Manual respectively. Title pages will be prepared in manuscript.

Hour, Date, Place	Summary of Events and Information	Remarks and references to Appendices
8.45 am	Our right and centre attacks have reached C lines at C 11.	(Division 108)
8.52 am	Red flare (We are here) seen at point 100× N of CRUCIFIX.	
8.54 am	Right Artillery Group (29th Div) report their infantry have reached sunken road (STATION road).	
8.55 am 8.57 am	Our infantry have reached C 11, but held up by M.G. fire. Left attacking infantry report being held up by M.G. fire in Railway Sap.	(Division 108)
9. am.	In contradiction to above 'C' report that our infantry are definitely in A front and support line.	
9.5 am	3rd of 32nd Division held up by Intermediate line and 5 extra divisions absent Our first line advised	(RA 10th Corps).
9.14 am	M.G. in THIEPVAL still firing into THIEPVAL WOOD	(Division 109)
9.16 am.	29th Division have taken whole front line duplicate	(RA 10th Corps).
9.12 am.	36th Division in possession of C8 B16 C9 C10 C11.	(Division 36 Div)

Army Form C. 2118.

WAR DIARY
or
INTELLIGENCE SUMMARY.
(Erase heading not required.)

Instructions regarding War Diaries and Intelligence Summaries are contained in F.S. Regs., Part II. and the Staff Manual respectively. Title pages will be prepared in manuscript.

Hour, Date, Place	Summary of Events and Information	Remarks and references to Appendices
9.23 a.m.	A.G. at Q17b 20 10 an hiding up 12th R.I.R.	(Liaison 10 B.) (RA 10th Corps.)
9.42 a.m.	Reinforcement arrived on Q17b 2010 from 9.50 – 10.20 a.m.	
9.45 a.m.	Heavy M.G. B13 and Consolidating between C18 and C12	(17th Hy.Arty. Bty)
9.47 a.m.	M.G.'s reported active at R2s e 9573 and 2030	
9.45 a.m.	Barrage about on Intermediate line between R20c73 and R27d 20 to continue till 10 a.m.	(RA 10th Corps)
10		
	Considerable M.G activity from THIEPVAL still firing on.	(10q Liaison)
9.52 a.m.	O.C. Cavalry Corps has sent forward F.O.O. to Crucifix Redoubt Q45 a.m.	
10.3 a.m.	Infantry of 107th Bde advancing towards D Line.	(10q Liaison).
10.16 a.m.	Barrage on D Line is to be lifted between R21c 4468 and sunken Road in R14d94. and N of sunken road as far as possible in conformity with artificial programme.	(RA 10th Corps)
10.17 a.m.	Hostile fire on HAMEL and THIEPVAL WOOD diminishing.	
10.29 a.m.	B19 and T20 not yet taken on account of M.G. in ST PIERRE DIVION	

WAR DIARY
or
INTELLIGENCE SUMMARY.
(Erase heading not required.)

Army Form C. 2118.

Instructions regarding War Diaries and Intelligence Summaries are contained in F. S. Regs., Part II. and the Staff Manual respectively. Title pages will be prepared in manuscript.

Hour, Date, Place	Summary of Events and Information	Remarks and references to Appendices
10.30 a.m.	Barrage appeared to cease at 11 a.m. on D line to be continued 200ˣ E. of then line. Slow bursts of fire.	(Refer to Appx.)
10.23 a.m.	Two m.g. near THIEPVAL CH. still doing considerable damage.	(chasm 107).
10.30 a.m.	25th Division are firing to retrenched German original front line from Q10 d 6.7 to Junction of 8th and 10th Corps from 12 noon – 12.20 p.m.	(RA Xth Corps)
10.40 a.m.	Artillery Barrage will now lift from BEAUCOURT Ridge till 11.50 a.m.	(29th D.A.)
10.50 a.m.	Barrage on Intermediate line in front of 32nd Div will now lift	(RA 10th Corps)
	till 11.30 a.m.	(" ")
10.55 a.m.	Barrage on 2nd line opp 36 Div will continue till further orders.	
11.3 a.m.	Hostile fire rather heavy on CRUCIFIX REDOUBT (NW face)	
11.4 a.m.	F.O.O. has just gone forward still at Bn. HQ	(to 8 Division)

WAR DIARY or INTELLIGENCE SUMMARY

Army Form C. 2118.

(Erase heading not required.)

Hour, Date, Place	Summary of Events and Information	Remarks and references to Appendices
11.20 a.m.	Men seen having about Mowing Point Tree, about 108. Probable German prisoners.	
11.23 a.m.	O.C. 108 Inf.Bde reports that transference of 29th Div. ammunition up to Q.17.b.9.1. (A.25) at 12 noon be entrusted to carrier parties.	(Lewin 108)
12.10 p.m.	Protective flank Barrage requested by 109th Bde on Ebew.	(36th Div. G.)
12.15 p.m.	Right.	(29th J.A.)
12.16 p.m.	29th Div attack at 12.45 p.m. instead of 12.30 p.m. Heavy hostile fire in B line from B12 – B17. Reported to RA Corps.	(Lewin 109)
12.35 p.m.	Suspected enemy Battalion advancing in R20.c.15.Rgd.	
12.45 p.m.	Counter attack from St PIERRE DIVION. Our guns D1/72 put out of action from shell fire.	
12.52 p.m.	Counter attack from SE Artipinock.	
12.54 p.m.	Right flank barrage intensified and hooked 200° true N.W.	

Army Form C. 2148.

WAR DIARY
or
INTELLIGENCE SUMMARY.
(Erase heading not required.)

Instructions regarding War Diaries and Intelligence
Summaries are contained in F. S. Regs., Part II.
and the Staff Manual respectively. Title pages
will be prepared in manuscript.

Hour, Date, Place	Summary of Events and Information	Remarks and references to Appendices
12.54 pm.	Trenches in R32c WI to bombarded from 12:15 pm - 1:30 pm.	(R.A. 11th Corps.)
1.13 pm.	French Batteries turned on to the Counter attack E of Courcoeur R26b. Enemy reported seen between the river and A.19.	
1.25 pm.	3/n Message 250 x E. of D Line dropped in to D line between D10 & D11 f Centre Coys left touch on to R 14d.	
1.27 pm.	Infantry at HAMEL report that no touch only 100 men holding an enemy front line. We are reported to have retired from D line	36 Div G.
1.38 pm.	Centre Coys retired Kpost up message to R14d 3.3 - R26b 2.8	
1.50 pm.	French Arabs turned on to a line from C.7 to R26 x 2.3 and C.4 to R26b 1.2.	

Army Form C. 2118.

WAR DIARY
or
INTELLIGENCE SUMMARY.
(Erase heading not required.)

Instructions regarding War Diaries and Intelligence Summaries are contained in F. S. Regs., Part II. and the Staff Manual respectively. Title pages will be prepared in manuscript.

Hour, Date, Place	Summary of Events and Information	Remarks and references to Appendices
2 pm	Column of Transport & with Eng. moving E. along IRLES - GREVILLERS road at 1.30 pm. Enemy still holding ST PIERRE DIVION and A20 and B20.	
2.15 pm	We are B19 - B13. Enemy advancing along Z15 Zey Trench to ST. PIERRE DIVION from C13. and from ST PIERRE DIVION - A21. M.G. and We fire from ST PIERRE DIVION	(108 Division)
2.20 pm	We are trenching along head from A19 - A21.	(109 Division)
2.50 pm	The Circular Trench between A19 and B19 though held by the enemy also has a h.f at A19.	(109 Division)
3 pm	Front and Support line trenches from R25C 8.3 - R25C 1.2 will be bombarded intensely from 3.30 pm - 4 pm when 49th Div. will attack THIEPVAL in cooperation with a battalion of 32nd Div.	(10th Corps)
3.20 pm	Message from 146th Inf Bde stating that they will attack THIEPVAL at 4 pm from the N. in cooperation with another formation.	(49 US Div.)

Army Form C. 2118.

WAR DIARY
or
INTELLIGENCE SUMMARY.
(Erase heading not required.)

Instructions regarding War Diaries and Intelligence Summaries are contained in F. S. Regs., Part II. and the Staff Manual respectively. Title pages will be prepared in manuscript.

Hour, Date, Place	Summary of Events and Information	Remarks and references to Appendices
3.25 pm	Counter attack from D 11. heavy crumping over the high ground in Thiepval Rise.	
3.43 pm	30 or 40 Germans seen at A 13 shooting into THIEPVAL WOOD, and hues heavily enfilading sunken road from R 25 c gap.	(109 Division)
3.47 pm	Germans seen in at A 20 and A 21.	
3.49 pm	Our infantry seen falling back from C line with prisoners.	
4 pm	Our infantry returning to our front line in THIEPVAL WOOD.	
4.7 pm	Counter attack coming up S.E. across R 26 a.	(R A 10th Corps)
4.24 pm	Germans in C line and thought also in B line.	
4.38 pm	Germans and British reported in A B & C lines.	

Army Form C. 2118.

WAR DIARY
or
INTELLIGENCE SUMMARY.
(Erase heading not required.)

Instructions regarding War Diaries and Intelligence Summaries are contained in F. S. Regs., Part II. and the Staff Manual respectively. Title pages will be prepared in manuscript.

Hour, Date, Place	Summary of Events and Information	Remarks and references to Appendices
5.10 pm.	Enemy Barraging E. of @ line. Feg shrapnelling between THIEPVAL WOOD and CRUCIFIX. He was holding top of hill.	
5.56 pm.	From Arm wrefgrs weapon or guns have entered TRUES from E.	
6.30 pm.	F.O.O.s report an left attack received and attacked. (marker A).	
6.45 pm.	German wptd advancing from R13 towards R19.	
7 pm.	R14 central.	
	A convoy of 23 wagons or guns entering TRUES from E.	
7.15 pm.	He was reported as holding C8 C9 C10 C11 B14 B15 B16 B17 B18 (HQ division).	
9.30 pm.	Three Red Rockets reported from the direction of Q16 (confirmed)	
9.40 pm.	Above reported to Corps RA - Ranger & 7th Queens Rockets.	
10 pm.	Report to Divisional Artill'y and from Civ on 27th Aug 15. Artillery Liaison Officer in HAMEL reported by Cr. Blacker that our Infantry were seen going towards GRANDCOURT from C line.	

Army Form C. 2118.

WAR DIARY
or
INTELLIGENCE SUMMARY.
(Erase heading not required.)

Instructions regarding War Diaries and Intelligence Summaries are contained in F. S. Regs., Part II. and the Staff Manual respectively. Title pages will be prepared in manuscript.

Hour, Date, Place	Summary of Events and Information	Remarks and references to Appendices
7.45 pm	Be held A and B line and C8 C9 C10 + (C11?). Enemy surrendering in considerable numbers coming in accompanied by our wounded.	108 Division
11.59 pm	We no longer hold C line but only parts of A & B lines.	109 Division
2nd July 1.20 am	Regts Section on us in front of our original line. Further feature in paper reports. A report about 1½ hour previous says 100 men of W Yorks Regt in B line about B17 awaiting orders.	(107 Division)
8.10 am	Our infantry reported in enemy front line trench about A18, also C.T. from A16 to B3 line. Orders issued to block A19 + B19 with trenchjine.	
8.15 am	Orders received as to relief of the 3rd Bg of the 36 Div by 45th Div Artillery to remain in.	(10th Corps.)

79/3298

Army Form C. 2118.

WAR DIARY
or
INTELLIGENCE SUMMARY.
(Erase heading not required.)

Instructions regarding War Diaries and Intelligence Summaries are contained in F. S. Regs., Part II. and the Staff Manual respectively. Title pages will be prepared in manuscript.

Hour, Date, Place	Summary of Events and Information	Remarks and references to Appendices
8.25 am.	About 50 of our Infantry seen round pt A.18 and THNEE.	
8.45 am.	Relief of 36th Div by 49th Div to commence as soon as possible. The Command of the 36th Div Arty passes to CRA 49th Div on completion of relief.	(10th Corps wire)
8.56 am.	A.G. still active on THIEPVAL. Infantry slowly seen at TS.19.	
9.20 am.	Red flare at A.19. (We or him?)	(RA19 to Corps)
11.22 am.	Our Front Line on edge of THIEPVAL WOOD being heavily shelled.	
1.10 pm.	Enemy left Corps turned on to cut all him in German Trenches N. of River opposite HAMEL Subsector.	(RA19 to Corps)
2.15 pm.	Supports sent across to A.15 and arrived without casualties.	
2.16 pm.	About 300 men seen on way to German Front and support line.	

Army Form C. 2118.

WAR DIARY
or
INTELLIGENCE SUMMARY.
(Erase heading not required.)

Instructions regarding War Diaries and Intelligence
Summaries are contained in F. S. Regs., Part II.
and the Staff Manual respectively. Title pages
will be prepared in manuscript.

Hour, Date, Place	Summary of Events and Information	Remarks and references to Appendices
3.15 pm.	Enemy being bombed out of C.T. from A.17 to B.19.	
5.20 pm.	Our infantry reported at A.17. A.16. A.15 from A.18 to Rest 2050.	HAIG.
5.30 pm.	Our infantry reported at Q.2.d.40.80 and a party of about 20 making for the X roads at Q.2.a.c.9.8.	
5.55 pm.	Attempted counter attack from N.W. face of CRUCIFIX REDOUBT stopped by artillery fire.	
6.40 pm.	Enemy seen in B line from B.19 to B.15.	
6.42 pm.	A yellow flag reported at A.18. Our infantry reported working along road from A.18 N.W. towards River. (Infantry reported out at 4.57)	(107 Rele.)
7 pm.	75 Germans seen going towards CRUCIFIX from THIEPVAL.	
7.40 pm.	Enemy seen moving up B line from CRUCIFIX and ST. P. DIVION.	

Army Form C. 2118.

WAR DIARY
or
INTELLIGENCE SUMMARY.
(Erase heading not required.)

Instructions regarding War Diaries and Intelligence Summaries are contained in F. S. Regs., Part II. and the Staff Manual respectively. Title pages will be prepared in manuscript.

Hour, Date, Place	Summary of Events and Information	Remarks and references to Appendices
7.44 pm	Enemy seen & moving up B line trench for B17 trenchworks. moving spiked hurdles.	
7.45 pm	Regun Corps report no few enemy in Administration or 2nd line.	
	Handed over Command of Artillery to B.G.C.R.A. 49th Div.	
3rd June	Nothing to report.	
4th June	Nothing to report.	
5th June	173 Bde and B + C 154 Bde ordered to join 12th Bri Artillery and taken out of action.	

Army Form C. 2118.

WAR DIARY
or
INTELLIGENCE SUMMARY.
(Erase heading not required.)

Instructions regarding War Diaries and Intelligence Summaries are contained in F.S. Regs., Part II. and the Staff Manual respectively. Title pages will be prepared in manuscript.

Hour, Date, Place	Summary of Events and Information	Remarks and references to Appendices
6th July	R.A. H.Q moved to RUBEMPRE	
7th July	Nothing to report	
8th July	"	
9th July	"	
10th July	S.A.A. section of DAC commenced move to ARE district with 36th Div.	
11th July	Nothing to report.	
12th July	Relief of 36th D.A. Batteries commenced on night 11/12	
13th July	Relief of Batteries finished. Orders received to proceed by road route begin drawn. 36th DA Order No 2 attached	

Army Form C. 2118.

WAR DIARY
or
INTELLIGENCE SUMMARY.
(Erase heading not required.)

Instructions regarding War Diaries and Intelligence Summaries are contained in F. S. Regs., Part II. and the Staff Manual respectively. Title pages will be prepared in manuscript.

Hour, Date, Place	Summary of Events and Information	Remarks and references to Appendices
14th July	moved HQ at 10 a.m. to AUTHEULE. Brigades as per hand Table	hand Table attached.
15th July	moved to CONCHY.	
16th July	moved to MONCHY	
17th July	moved to THEROUANNE	
18th July	moved to RECQUES and established HQ at Chateau.	
19th July	Orders received to move immediately and take over the position of the line covered by the 24th Div Arty. 172nd to 154th Bde moved to ST OMER; remainder of the Artillery moved to same.	Order No. 3 attached.

WAR DIARY
or
INTELLIGENCE SUMMARY.
(Erase heading not required.)

Army Form C. 2118.

Hour, Date, Place	Summary of Events and Information	Remarks and references to Appendices
20th July.	C.R.A. moved to BAILLEUL. Bdes moved as per hand Table	Hand Table Attached
21st July	Went round position of Right Group. 172 Bde took over infantry of Centre Group line.	
22nd July.	Took over responsibility of the line from 2nd D.A. at 6pm. Shelled HQ at BAILLEUL.	
23rd July	Arthur 15 report. 108th Infantry Bde took over line from 73rd	
24th July	Artillery Report. S.A.A. section joined up with D.A.C.	
25th July	Artillery report	
26th July	The 108th R.I.B. extended their left and took over trenches 141-C2 to Stes A14 and B14L came under orders of Right Group.	
27th July.	Section of B 154 and D173 moved to their positions. Cover front had taken over by 1 sec 173 de	36th Div A.C.O. No 6.

Army Form C. 2118.

WAR DIARY
or
INTELLIGENCE SUMMARY.
(Erase heading not required.)

Instructions regarding War Diaries and Intelligence Summaries are contained in F.S. Regs., Part II. and the Staff Manual respectively. Title pages will be prepared in manuscript.

Hour, Date, Place	Summary of Events and Information	Remarks and references to Appendices
28 July	Reviewing returns of B 173 and D 173 moved as in O.O. No.6. Completion of relief by 109th I.Rde.	
29 July	Instructions received to move Batteries to 50th Div area. Moves returned on	O.O. No. 7
30th July	Section of batteries moved as in Order No. 7.	
31st July	Remaining sections moved as in Order No. 7.	

H. J. Brock
Brig Gen
Cmdg 36 Div Arty

S E C R E T.   Copy No. 12

Reference Maps -

1/100,000 LENS 11.
1/100,000 HAZEBROUCK 5.A.

36TH DIVISIONAL ARTILLERY ORDER No. 2.

1. The 36th Divisional Artillery will march to the 2nd Army Area in accordance with attached March Tables.
   The move will be carried out in columns not larger than one Battery, and each column will move off at 15 minutes interval, which interval will be kept throughout the march.

2. Rations for the 15th will be drawn and carried.
   Rations for the 16th will be drawn at FREVENT.
   Further orders will be issued for subsequent days.

3. Trench Bridges will not be carried but will be handed in to the nearest R.E. Dump.

4. No extra transport is available, and Brigades must march as laid down in War Establishments.

5. Billeting parties from each Brigade and the D.A.C., will be sent on in advance each day.

6. Brigades and D.A.C., will wire R.A.H.Q., tonight the amount of Ammunition they are taking with them. Ammunition Echelons will march full.

7. Orders re Billeting for the nights 16/17th, 17/18th, and 18/19th July, will be issued in due course.

8. R.A.H.Q., will be at AUTHIEULE at 3 p.m. on the 14th instant, and at CONDHY at 3 p.m. on the 15th instant.

                                            C.E. Shanach
                                            Major, R.A.,
13th July, 1916.   Brigade Major, 36th Divisional Artillery.

Copy No. 1 to 153rd Bde. R.F.A.,   Copy No. 6 to Detachment, 36th
    "   2 to 154th   "   "   Divl. Train.
    "   3 to 172nd   "   "   "   7 to 1st Army "Q") For
    "   4 to 173rd   "   "   "   8 to 2nd Army "Q")inform-
    "   5 to 36th D.A.C.,   "   9 to 3rd Army "Q")ation.
                                        " 10 to R.A., 10th Corps.
                                        " 11 a 12 File.

SECRET.

March Table July 14th.

Starting Time.	Unit.	Route.	Billet.	Remarks.
8.0 a.m.	153rd Brigade R.F.A.,	VARENNES - LEALVILLERS - MARIEUX - ORVILLE thence N. of River AUTHIE to DOULLENS and GROUCHES (not to go through ACHEUX).	GROUCHES.	
8.45 a.m.	173rd Brigade, R.F.A.,	MILLENCOURT - SENLIS - VARENNES - and as for 153rd Brigade, R.F.A.,	MILLY & LEMARAIS.	
9.0 a.m.	172nd Brigade R.F.A.,	As for 153rd Brigade R.F.A.,	GROUCHES.	
10.0 a.m.	154th Brigade R.F.A., 'A' Battery.	As for 153rd Brigade R.F.A.,	AUTHIEULE.	B & C.154 Brigade, R.F.A., will follow 173rd Brigade, R.F.A., at 15 minutes interval.
12.15 p.m.	36th D. A. C.,	LEALVILLERS and as for 153rd Brigade R.F.A.,	AUTHIEULE.	March in Sections at 15 minutes interval.

P. T. O.,

SECRET.

March Table July 15th.

Starting Time.	Unit.	Route.	Billet.
7.0 a.m.	172nd Brigade R.F.A.,	GROUCHES - BOUQUEMAISON - BONNIERES.	FILLIEVRES.
8.0 a.m.	153rd Brigade R.F.A.,	- do -	AUBROMETZ.
8.45 a.m.	173rd Brigade R.F.A.,	- do -	MONCHEL.
9.15 a.m.	154th Brigade R.F.A.,	- do -	CONCHY.
10.0 a.m.	36th D. A. C.,	- do -	VACQUERIE DE BOURG.

[signature]
Major, R.A.,
Brigade Major, 36th Divisional Artillery.

13th July, 1916.

SECRET.

March Table July 16th.

Starting Time.	Unit.	Route.	Billet.	Remarks.
7.0 a.m.	172nd Brigade R.F.A.,	LINZEUX - CROISETTE - CROIX - WAVRANS.	BERCUENEUSE.	ST.POL is to be avoided.
7.45 a.m.	153rd Brigade R.F.A.,	- do -	ANVIN.	-do-
8.45 a.m.	173rd Brigade R.F.A.,	FLERS - CROISETTE - CROIX - WAVRANS.	MONCHY.	-do-
9.45 a.m.	154th Brigade R.F.A.,	- do -	MONCHY.	-do-
10.45 a.m.	36th D. A. C.,	CONCHY - FLERS - CROISETTE - CROIX.	WAVRANS.	-do-

R.A.H.Q., at MONCHY CHATEAU.
All men must be in billets by 9 p.m.
O.C. Detachment, 36th Divl. Train will draw rations from R.S.O., AIRE.

153rd Bde. R.F.A., 36th D.A.C.,
154th   "   "   1st Army "Q.",
172nd   "   "   36th Divn. "Q".
173rd   "   "   Detachment, 36th
                    Divl. Train.

15th July, 1916.

Major, R.A.,
Brigade Major, 36th Divisional Artillery.

SECRET.

March Table July 17th.

Starting Time.	Unit.	Route.	Billet.
7.0 a.m.	172nd Brigade R.F.A.,	FONTAINE - FEBVIN PALFART - FLECHIN - ENGUINE GATTE.	CLARQUES.
7.45 a.m.	153rd Brigade R.F.A.,	- do -	THEROUANNE.
8.30 a.m.	173rd Brigade R.F.A.,	- do -	THEROUANNE.
9.30 a.m.	154th Brigade R.F.A.,	- do -	DELETTE.
10.15 a.m.	36th D. A. C.,	- do -	DELETTE.

R.A.H.Q., at THEROUANNE.
All men must be in billets by 9 p.m.
O.C., 36th Divl. Train will draw Rations from R.S.C., WATTEN.

```
153rd Bde. R.F.A.,     1st Army "Q".
154th    "    "        2nd Army "Q".
172nd    "    "        36th Divn.
173rd    "    "        Detachment, 36th
36th D. A. C.,         Divl. Train.
```

15th July, 1916.

Major, R.A.,
Brigade Major, 36th Divisional Artillery.

SECRET.

March Table 18th July.

Starting Time.	Unit.	Route.	Billet.	Remarks.
7.0 a.m.	154th Brigade R.F.A.,	DOHEN - WAVRANS - LUMBRES - QUERCAMP - BONNINGUES.	CLERQUES. & ANDREHEM.	(One mile off the map & 2 miles W of BONNINGUES. (One mile off the map & 2 miles W of BOIS de CONDETTES.
7.45 a.m.	36th D. A. C.,	- do -	GUEMY and TOURNEHEM.	
7.0 a.m.	153rd Brigade R.F.A.,	HERBELLES - ESQUERDES - QUELMES - MENTQUE - TOURNEHEM.	BONNINGUES les ARDRES.	
7.0 a.m.	173rd Brigade R.F.A.,	BLENDECQUES - ST. OMER - TILQUES - NORDAUSQUES.	RECQUES and POLINCOVE.	
8.30 a.m.	172nd Brigade R.F.A.,	ECQUES - BLENDECQUES - ST. OMER - TILQUES.	NORDAUSQUES.	

R.A.H.Q., at CHATEAU, one mile W of RECQUES.

C.S.Marsh

Major, R.A.,
Brigade Major, 36th Divl. Artillery.

17th July, 1916.

SECRET.   Copy No. _____

Reference Map -

1/100,000 HAZEBRUCK, 5.A.

36TH DIVISIONAL ARTILLERY ORDER No. 3.

1.   The March Table for the 18th July is cancelled and Brigades and D.A.C., will march as per attached March Table.

2.   Battery Billeting Parties will go direct to billeting areas and not to TILQUES.

3.   The Section of the Divisional Train will be at NORDAUESQUES.
      Refilling point on TOURNEHEM - NORDAUSQUES Road; West of turning to Ford.

4.   All Baggage wagons will be sent to Road turning N thro second S in NORDAUSQUES for inspection by O.C., 36th Divl. Train at 2.30 p.m. 19th instant.

5.   Brigades will report arrival to Divisional Artillery H.Q., (Chateau one mile W of RECQUES).

                                                                  Major, R.A.,

17th July, 1916.   Brigade Major, 36th Divl. Artillery.

O.C. 153rd Bde. R.F.A.,
     154th "   "
     172nd "   "
     173rd "   "
    36th D.A.C.,
    Detachment, 36th Divl. Train.
    36th Division, "Q", (For information).

SECRET.

Reference Map,
1/100,000,
HAZEBRUCK, 5A.

Copy N° 8

36TH DIVISIONAL ARTILLERY ORDER No. 4.

1. The 36th Divisional Artillery will relieve the Artillery of the 24th Division, coming under the orders of the 5th Corps.

2. The 154th and 172nd Brigades R.F.A., will move to ST. OMER this afternoon under orders of Brigade Commanders concerned.

3. Billeting parties from these two Brigades will meet the D.A.A. & Q.M.G., at the MAIRIE, ST. MARTIN au LAERT, about 1 mile W. of ST. OMER, at 5.30 p.m.

4. The remainder of the Artillery, less the S.A.A. section of the D.A.C., will be ready to move at 8 a.m. tomorrow morning.

5. Refilling Point for the whole of the Divisional Artillery tomorrow, will be on road midway between ST. OMER and ARQUES; at 6 a.m. for 154th and 172nd Brigades R.F.A., moving to ST. OMER today and in the afternoon for remainder.

6. Acknowledge.

19th July, 1916.

Major, R.A.,
Brigade Major, 36th Divl. Artillery.

Copy No. 1 to 153rd Bde. R.F.A.,
   2 " 154th " "
   3 " 172nd " "
   4 " 173rd " "
   5 " 36th D. A. C.,
   6. " T.M.S.O.,
   7. " 36th Division, "G".
   8 " War Diary.
   9 & 10. Filed.

SECRET.   Copy No. 12

36TH DIVISIONAL ARTILLERY ORDER No. 5.

1. The March Table for 20th July is attached; that for the 21st and 22nd July will be issued later.

2. Billeting parties will go on in advance each day to arrange billets.

3. A motor lorry will be at each Brigade Headquarters at 7.0 a.m. tomorrow morning to take one officer, one batman and two telephonists per Battery of the 153rd and 173rd Brigades R.F.A., to the Square at BAILLEUL where they will be met with orders.
   A motor lorry will be at HOTEL DU COMMERCE, ST. OMER and one at ARQUES, at 7.0 a.m. tomorrow morning to take one Officer, one batman, and two telephonists per battery of the 154th and 172nd Brigades R.F.A., to BAILLEUL where they will be met with orders.

4. R.A.H.Q., 21st July, will be notified later.

5. Trench Mortar Batteries will remain at NORLAUSQUES till further orders and will be rationed by 36th Division.

6. Brigades will report arrival each day to R.A.H.Q.,

                                   B. Shanach
                                        Major, R.A.,
19th July, 1916.   Brigade Major, 36th Divl. Artillery.

Copy No. 1 to 153rd Bde. R.F.A.,
         2 " 154th Bde. R.F.A.,
         3 " 172nd Bde. R.F.A.,
         4 " 173rd Bde. R.F.A.,
         5 " 36th D.A.C.,
         6 " T.M.S.O.,
         7. " 36th Division, "G".
         8 " 36th Division, "Q".
         9 " R.A., 5th Corps.
        10 " 5th Corps, "Q".
        11 " O.C. 36th Divl. Train.
        12 " War Diary.
        13 & 14 - Filed.

SECRET.

March Table 20th July.

Starting Time.	Unit.	Route.	Billet.	Remarks.
8.0 a.m.	154th Bde.R.F.A.,	EBBLINGHEM.	CAESTRE-METEREN Area.	On arrival comes under orders of 5th Corps.
9.0 a.m.	172nd Bde.R.F.A.,	-do-	-do-	-do-
8.0 a.m.	173rd Bde.R.F.A.,	ST.MARTIN AU LAERT - ARQUES.	EBBLINGHEM - RENESCURE Area. WALLON CAPPELL EBBLINGHEM	-do-
9.0 a.m.	153rd Bde.R.F.A.,	NORDAUSQUES - ST.MARTIN AU LAERT - ARQUES.	-do- RENESCURE	-do-
10.0 a.m.	R. A. H. Q.,	-do-	-do- RENESCURE	-do-
10.15 a.m.	D. A. C., (Less S.A.A. Section).	-do-	-do-	-do-

July 21st.

| 8.0 a.m. | S.A.A. Section, D. A. C., | NORDAUSQUES - WATTEN. | VOLKERINGKHOVE. | |

July 22nd.

| 8.0 a.m. | S.A.A. Section, D. A. C., | ESQUELBECQ - HERZEELE. | WATOU. | |

(S.S.Shaw..h..) Major, R.A.,
Brigade Major, 36th Divl. Artillery.

19th July, 1915.

SECRET.   Copy No.

War Diary

AMENDMENT TO

36TH DIVISIONAL ARTILLERY ORDER No. 6.

Para. 1.   The 109th Brigade relieves the 122nd Brigade in the trenches, from Trench 128 (inclusive) to the River DOUVE, and not Trench 127, as stated.

[signature]

Major, R.A.,

28th July, 1916,   Brigade Major, 36th Divl. Artillery.

Copy No. 1. to 153rd Bde. R.F.A.,   Copy No. 7. to 109th Inf. Bde.,
        2. to 154th Bde. R.F.A.,   8 & 9. to 41st Div. Arty,
        3 to 172nd Bde. R.F.A.,   10. to R.A., 5th Corps,
        4 to 173rd Bde. R.F.A.,   11. to 36th D.A.C.,
        5. to 36th Division, "G".   12.   War Diary,
        6. to 108th Inf. Bde,   13 & 14. Filed,

Copy No. 11.

S E C R E T.

36TH DIVISIONAL ARTILLERY ORDER No. 6.

1. The 109th Brigade is to relieve the 122nd Brigade, 41st Division, in the trenches from Trench 127 (inclusive) to the River DOUVE (trench 133 inclusive), on the nights of the 27th/28th and 28th/29th July.

2. The boundary for defence between the 36th and 41st Divisions will be as follows :-

   From junction of trenches 126 and 127 to PROWSE POINT (U.14.d.9.9.) - to POOLES COTTAGES (U.14.d.2.3.) - to OXFORD FORT (U.19.b.3.2.) (all inclusive to 36th Division with exception of left branch of C.P. Railway which is retained by 41st Division) - thence in a straight line to the moat south of GRANDE MUNQUE FARM at T.24.d.5.5. - thence west to road junction at T.22.d.4.2. and G.H.Q. 2nd line at T.22.c.4.2. - To G.H.Q. 3rd line at S.24. Central.

3. The Artillery to cover the 109th Infantry Brigade will be composed as under :-

   C Battery, 183rd Brigade R.F.A., 41st Division.
   B Battery, 190th Brigade R.F.A., 41st Division.
   B Battery, 154th Brigade R.F.A., 36th Division.
   D Battery, 173rd Brigade R.F.A., 36th Division.

4. The two guns of B/154th Brigade R.F.A., at present out of action will move into action on the night 27/28th July, at T.17.d. 4.2.
   The remaining Section of B/154th Brigade R.F.A., at present in action about T.24.a. 2595 will be withdrawn on the night 28/29th July, and will join -its- other Section in action at T.17.d. 4.2.
   One Section of D/173rd Brigade R.F.A., will be withdrawn from action about N.26.c.8.7. on the night 27/28th July, and will move into action about T.23.b.5.5.
   The remaining Section of D/173rd Brigade R.F.A., consisting of one gun at N.26.c.8.7. and one gun at T.5.c. 3.9. will be withdrawn on the night 28/29th July and will join -its- other Section in action about T.23.b.5.5.
   In each of the above cases the guns will be withdrawn from the emplacements.
   No moves will take place before 10 p.m. each night.

5. The O.C. 153rd F.A. Group will take over command of the above 4 Batteries of Artillery and will issue instructions as to night lines &c.,

6. O.C. Batteries will report to O.C. 153rd F.A. Group at T.21.d.3.1. as soon as possible for instructions.

P. T. O.

7.   On the night   28/29th July, the Artillery covering the 36th Division Front will be distributed as under :-

   Covering 109th Infantry Brigade (Trench 127 - R. DOUVE)

   C.183rd Brigade R.F.A.,
   B.190th Brigade R.F.A.,
   B.154th Brigade R.F.A.,   (Right Sub-Group).
   D.173rd Brigade R.F.A.,

   Covering 108th Infantry Brigade (R.DOUVE - Trench C.2).

   A.153rd Brigade R.F.A.,
   B.153rd Brigade R.F.A.,
   C.153rd Brigade R.F.A.,
   D.153rd Brigade R.F.A.,   (Left Sub-Group).
   A.172nd Brigade R.F.A.,
   B.172nd Brigade R.F.A.,

8.   The O.C. 153rd Brigade R.F.A., will be in command of both the above Sub-Groups until other arrangements can be made.

9.   Acknowledge.

                                              Major, R.A.,
27th July, 1916.   Brigade Major, 36th Divl. Artillery.

Distribution -

   Copy No.1. to 153rd Bde. R.F.A.,
        2 to 154th Bde. R.F.A.,
        3 to 173rd Bde. R.F.A.,
        4 to 36th Division, "G".
        5. to 109th Inf. Bde.
        6. to 108th Inf. Bde.
      7 & 8 to 41st Div. Arty.
        9 to 50th Div. Arty.
        10 to R.A., 5th Corps.
        11   War Diary.
        12,13 & 14 - Filed.

SECRET.

Reference Map –
1/20,000 Sheet 28.S.W.

Copy No.

War Diary

36TH DIVISIONAL ARTILLERY ORDER No. 7.

1. The Batteries of the 36th Divisional Artillery at present covering the front held by the 50th Division will be relieved by Sections on the nights 30/31 July, 31st July/1st August, and will move to fresh positions in accordance with Table of Reliefs which will be issued later.

2. The Officer Commanding, 173rd Brigade R.F.A., will take over Command of the Right Group from Officer Commanding, 153rd Brigade R.F.A., on completion of relief under arrangements between Group Commanders concerned.

3. All reliefs by the 50th Divisional Artillery will take place in accordance with 50th Divisional Artillery Operation Order No. 22 of the 28th instant.

4. Ammunition handed over and received by Batteries and D.A.C., will be reported on completion of relief.

5. Completion of Reliefs each night will be reported by wire.

6. Acknowledge.

Major, R.A.,
Brigade Major, 36th Divl. Artillery.

30th July, 1916.

Distribution:-

No. 1. to 153rd Bde. R.F.A.,
2 to 154th Bde. R.F.A.,
3 to 172nd Bde. R.F.A.,
4 to 173rd Bde. R.F.A.,
5 to 36th D. A. C.,
6 to 36th Division, "G".
7 to 36th Division, "Q".
8 to 36th Divl. Train.
No. 9 to 108th Inf. Bde.
10 to 109th Inf. Bde.
11 to 50th Div. Arty.
12 to 41st Div. Arty.
13 to R.A. 5th Corps.
14 to R.A. Signal Officer.
15 to War Diary.
16, 17 & 18 – Filed.

SECRET.

36TH DIVISIONAL ARTILLERY.

Table of Reliefs, 30/31 July.

UNIT.	Time.	New position at.	Remarks.
H.Q. 173rd Brigade, R.F.A.,	12 noon 30th July.	T.21.b. 2.7.	
One Section, A/173 Battery, R.F.A.,	After dark.		Goes to wagon lines
One Section, B/173 Battery, R.F.A.,	-do-	T.24.c. 1590.	Relieves one section of C/183 Battery, R.F.A., 41st Div. Arty.
One Section, C/173 Battery, R.F.A.,	-do-		Goes to wagon lines.
One Section, C/172 Battery, R.F.A.,	-do-	T.18.a. 0050.	Position at present unoccupied.
One Section, A/154 Battery, R.F.A.,	-do-		-do-

SECRET.
O.O.907

36TH DIVISIONAL ARTILLERY.

Table of Reliefs, 31st July,/1st August, 1916.

UNIT.	Time.	New Position at	Remarks.
H.Q. 154th Brigade R.F.A., Trench Mortar Batteries.	Any time during 31st July.		
One Section, A/173 Battery, R.F.A.,	After dark.	S.23.a. 7.6.	To Wagon Lines.
" " B/173 "	-do-	T.14.c. 1590.	Relieves remaining Section of C/183 Battery, 41st Div. Arty.
" " C/173 "	-do-	T.23.a. 7.3.	Position at present unoccupied. Remaining Section may move in on night 1/2nd August.
" " C/172 "	-do-		To Wagon lines.
" " A/154 "	-do-	T.18.a. 2040.	Complete Battery moves in.
" " C/154 "			Remains in present wagon lines.
H.Q. 172nd Brigade R.F.A.,	After handing over.	T.15.d. 0.3.	Original Headquarters.

(signature)
Major, R.A.,
Brigade Major, 36th Divl. Artillery.

30th July, 1916.

36. Div only

Vol II

Army Form C. 2118.

WAR DIARY
or
INTELLIGENCE SUMMARY.
(Erase heading not required.)

Instructions regarding War Diaries and Intelligence Summaries are contained in F.S. Regs., Part II. and the Staff Manual respectively. Title pages will be prepared in manuscript.

Hour, Date, Place	Summary of Events and Information	Remarks and references to Appendices
1st August	Nothing to report	
2nd August	—	
3rd August		
4th August	Order received to take over an entire portion of the line fm 50th Div. Order No 8 issued	Order No 8 attached.
5th August	⎫	
6th August	⎬ Move as per Order No 8 took place. Very quiet.	
7th August	⎭	

Army Form C. 2118.

WAR DIARY
or
INTELLIGENCE SUMMARY.
(Erase heading not required.)

Instructions regarding War Diaries and Intelligence Summaries are contained in F.S. Regs., Part II. and the Staff Manual respectively. Title pages will be prepared in manuscript.

Hour, Date, Place	Summary of Events and Information	Remarks and references to Appendices
8th – 14th August	Nothing to report, lines very quiet all this week.	
15th August.	IXth Corps took over from Xth Corps at 12 midnight.	Operation Order No. 9.
	Section of B & C 154th Bde withdrawn from action	
16th – 19th August	Nothing to report.	
20th – 23rd August	Nothing to report.	
24th August	B & C 154 handed over to 14th Div	
25 – 28 August	Nothing to report	
29th August	Nothing to report	
30 August	Gas discharge along Div Front	
31st August	"	Instructions attached

H. J. Brock
Brig Gen.
Cmdg. 36th Div Arty

Army Form C. 2118.

CRA
36th Division Vol 12

WAR DIARY
or
INTELLIGENCE SUMMARY.
(Erase heading not required.)

Instructions regarding War Diaries and Intelligence Summaries are contained in F.S. Regs., Part II. and the Staff Manual respectively. Title pages will be prepared in manuscript.

Hour, Date, Place	Summary of Events and Information	Remarks and references to Appendices
1st September.	Nothing to report. RAHQ moved fm BALLEUL to ST JANS CAPPEL. Nothing to report.	
2nd September.	Nothing to report.	
3rd September.	Nothing to report.	
4th September.	Took over Right Group. 15th Div Arty moved to reserve.	attached
5th September.	Information received that since 23rd Corps Appendix our front has altered. Intermittent Bombardment ordered	attached
6th September.	Bombardment in accordance with order No 12	attached
7th September.	Relief of 86th Bde RFA by 36th Div Arty. Order No. 13.	attached

Army Form C. 2118.

WAR DIARY
or
INTELLIGENCE SUMMARY.
(Erase heading not required.)

Instructions regarding War Diaries and Intelligence Summaries are contained in F.S. Regs., Part II and the Staff Manual respectively. Title pages will be prepared in manuscript.

Hour, Date, Place	Summary of Events and Information	Remarks and references to Appendices
8 September	Moves according to R.A. Order No 13 in progress	Order No 14. Order No 15
9 September	Moves completed. Orders issued for reorganization	
10 September		
11 September	Holding to front. Reorganization in Progress.	List of Battery positions attached.
12 September		
13 September		
14 September	Orders issued regarding raids and bombardment	Order No 16 & 17
15	Two successful raids carried out by 107th & 105th Bde	

Army Form C. 2118.

WAR DIARY
or
INTELLIGENCE SUMMARY.
(Erase heading not required.)

Instructions regarding War Diaries and Intelligence Summaries are contained in F. S. Regs., Part II. and the Staff Manual respectively. Title pages will be prepared in manuscript.

Hour, Date, Place	Summary of Events and Information	Remarks and references to Appendices
16th September	Two Instruments carried out according to the attached order. Very little retaliation from the enemy.	
17th September	Nothing to report	
18th September	Nothing to report	
19th September	Order No. 19 issued for gas discharge. Cancelled owing to wind.	No. 18.
20th September	Nothing to report	

Army Form C. 2118.

WAR DIARY
or
INTELLIGENCE SUMMARY.
(Erase heading not required.)

Instructions regarding War Diaries and Intelligence Summaries are contained in F. S. Regs., Part II. and the Staff Manual respectively. Title pages will be prepared in manuscript.

Hour, Date, Place	Summary of Events and Information	Remarks and references to Appendices
21st September	Nothing to report.	O.O. No. 19.
22nd September	T.M Bombardment. Adv attacked.	
23rd September	Nothing to report.	
24th September	} Nothing to report.	
25th September		
26th September		
27th September	Enemy Observation Balloon brought down near KEMMEL HILL	O.O. No. 20.
28th September	T M Bombardment.	

Army Form C. 2118.

WAR DIARY
or
INTELLIGENCE SUMMARY.
(Erase heading not required.)

Instructions regarding War Diaries and Intelligence Summaries are contained in F.S. Regs., Part II. and the Staff Manual respectively. Title pages will be prepared in manuscript.

Hour, Date, Place	Summary of Events and Information	Remarks and references to Appendices
29th September	Nothing to report. Orders issued for a Coup de Main from 16th Division	Order No 21.
30th September	Three raids took place at 10 pm 108(right) Brigade did not go out owing to an accident with bomb close - 107th (centre) & 109 (left) Brigades attacked and were most successful - 109(left) Brigade entered the enemies trenches and returned with captured rifles and a m/c gun - no prisoners were taken.	

H. J. Brock
Brig Gen RA.
Comdg. 36th Divl. Arty.

1.10.16.

WAR DIARY
or
INTELLIGENCE SUMMARY.
(Erase heading not required.)

Army Form C. 2118.

Vol 13

Headquarters
36th Div. Arty.

Instructions regarding War Diaries and Intelligence Summaries are contained in F. S. Regs., Part II. and the Staff Manual respectively. Title pages will be prepared in manuscript.

Hour, Date, Place	Summary of Events and Information	Remarks and references to Appendices
Oct 1st '16	Simpson's Group commence taking over from 2nd Canadian Div.	Order No 21
Oct 2nd '16	Completion of above relief took place night 2/3rd	
Oct 3rd 16	Nothing to report	
Oct 4th 16	Enemy registered our front near DURHAM R¹ & FARM STRETCHER LANE and KING'S WAY, also W³, W⁴ & W⁵ FRONT LINE with 105 c.m. and 77 m.m. during m.g. of afternoon. A heavy bombardment of M.G. line started in the evening about 8 p.m. & was most intense. Took place in the evening about 8 p.m. Front mortars went very actively on our front line. We allotted for Z. bombardment - enemy did about 9 p.m.	
Oct 5th	O.K. Group bombarded the enemy's trenches by (Hermes) H.M.S. How? 15 p.r. also 2 M.G. (Heavy machine guns) (6" How)	Order No 22

Army Form C. 2118.

WAR DIARY
or
INTELLIGENCE SUMMARY.
(Erase heading not required.)

Instructions regarding War Diaries and Intelligence Summaries are contained in F.S. Regs., Part II. and the Staff Manual respectively. Title pages will be prepared in manuscript.

Hour, Date, Place	Summary of Events and Information	Remarks and references to Appendices
Oct 6th '16	Nothing to report	
" 7th '16	— " —	
" 8th '16	Nothing to report	
" 9th '16	At 1.a.m. gas was emitted by 107 - 108th 109th Brigades — A henerade raid put from Lewis at 2.45am. A patrol sent out to ascertain the damage done. Brigade to ascertain the damage done. 107 succeeded in bringing back some rifles and a machine gun and some equipment. The other Bdes were unsuccessful — Simpson Camp relieved by Selina	Order No 24
" 10th '16	Nothing to report. Relief of Simpson Camp completed.	Order No 25
" 11th '16	Raid carried out at 2½ am night 11/12 th.	Order No 26

Army Form C. 2118.

WAR DIARY
or
INTELLIGENCE SUMMARY.
(Erase heading not required.)

Instructions regarding War Diaries and Intelligence Summaries are contained in F.S. Regs., Part II. and the Staff Manual respectively. Title pages will be prepared in manuscript.

Hour, Date, Place	Summary of Events and Information	Remarks and references to Appendices
Oct 12th September.	Artillery Support.	
" 13th September	Heavy enemy Bombardment about 2 a.m. & enemy attempted Raid which was repulsed	
" 14th September	Heavy enemy Bombardment about 3 p.m. Very little damage done. T.M. Bombardment arranged for has Cancelled	Order by O. Consulted.
" 15th September	Nothing Important.	
" 16th September		
" 17th September	T.M. Bombardment very bad & had to cease	Order No 28.
" 18th September	Nothing to report.	
" 19th September	Nothing to report.	
" 20th September	Major Stewart temporarily to R.A. 1X Corps.	
" 21st September	T.M. Conference 153 H.Q. Demonstration of Fullerphone 1X Corps Signals.	
" 22nd September.	Nothing to report.	

WAR DIARY
or
INTELLIGENCE SUMMARY.
(Erase heading not required.)

Army Form C. 2118.

Instructions regarding War Diaries and Intelligence Summaries are contained in F.S. Regs., Part II. and the Staff Manual respectively. Title pages will be prepared in manuscript.

Hour, Date, Place	Summary of Events and Information	Remarks and references to Appendices
Oct 23rd September	Conference Inf. Bde Commanders & CRA at Div. H.Q. re Minor Enterprises – Demonstration of 6" Newton T.M. at 2nd Army School at Boltren.	
" 24th September – Boltren –	Demonstration of 2" Trench Mortar firing from trolley on Beaurille track – Not successful	
" 25th September	Y.36 T.M.Bty. (Centre Group) carried out bombardment of trenches and wire in N.36.d.-(28.S.W.) Hampered by rifle mechanisms –	
" 26th September	Y.36. carried out further bombardment 170 rounds but had further trouble owing to Rifle Mechanisms blowing out –	
" 27th September	Nothing to report –	
" 28th September	X.36 T.M. Bty carried out bombardment of enemy's wire and retaliation on enemy mortars. 62 rounds fired.	
" 29th September	Conference at 153 Bde H.Q. on Trench Mortars and Minor Enterprises – 16th Div. raided near PECKHAM 7.P.m. – 173 Brigade Co-operated – 3 prisoners captured	

WAR DIARY
or
INTELLIGENCE SUMMARY.
(Erase heading not required.)

Army Form C. 2118.

Hour, Date, Place	Summary of Events and Information	Remarks and references to Appendices
29th September (contd) October	one of whom gave information that reliefs were taking place at 11 pm on WYTSCHAETE - KRUISTRAAT - CABARET Road. 173 swept the road accordingly.	Order 29.—
30th September October	107th Brigade raided at U.1.a. 27.68. Raid into unsuccessful. — 153 Bde were not called on to fire at all. Raiding party lost their way at first and did not reach German trenches for some time after this, starting out when they got in they found them occupied and were bombed out and forced to return.	"
31st September October	108 Brigade raided at U.2.c. 55.95. Raid was unsuccessful owing to a false parapet with wire behind it under camouflage deceiving the raiding party.	"
	109 Brigade raided on front N.36a. 56.63 to N.36.a. 56.80. unsuccessful — left party penetrated but found enemy expecting them, Right party failed to cut the wire with the Ammonal tube and did not penetrate.	

1/11/16.

A. J. Prot

Brig. Gen. R.A.
Commanding 36th Div. Artillery

War Diary.

Simpsons Group.
36

October 1st to 10th.
1916.

WAR DIARY of Simpson's Group. RFA

Army Form C. 2118.

Instructions regarding War Diaries and Intelligence Summaries are contained in F. S. Regs., Part II. and the Staff Manual respectively. Title pages will be prepared in manuscript.

INTELLIGENCE SUMMARY.
(Erase heading not required.)

Place	Date	Hour	Summary of Events and Information	Remarks and references to Appendices
	OCTOBER			
	1st & 2nd		Simpson's Group was formed in order to take over the front of the centre and right groups 3rd Canadian division - namely N30c.10.72 to N15b20.55 - pending the arrival of the 16th Divisional Artillery. The Group is composed of three 18 pdr (6 guns) and one 4.5 How (4 guns) batteries as follows:- C/153, B/173, C/173 and D/172 (How). The relief was carried out on the nights of the 1st/2nd and 2nd/3rd October in accordance with table Appendix (i). On coming into action the batteries of the Group were disposed as shown in Appendix (ii) para 2 and cover fronts as shown in Appendix (ii) para 3 - The Group comes under the 16th Division for tactical purposes.	Appendix (i) Appendix (ii)
E M M E L	3rd		Batteries were unable to register owing to mist - Quiet.	
	4th		Operations Nil - Dull and rainy.	
X	5th		The 36th Division - on our right - carried out a bombardment of the enemy trenches chiefly by medium and light T.Ms at 8.30 am. We co-operated with a section of C/153 who fired 60 rounds. Enemy's retaliation was feeble.	

T.131. Wt. W708-776. 500000. 4/15. Sir J. C. & S.

Army Form C. 2118.

WAR DIARY
or
INTELLIGENCE SUMMARY.
(Erase heading not required.)

Instructions regarding War Diaries and Intelligence Summaries are contained in F. S. Regs., Part II. and the Staff Manual respectively. Title pages will be prepared in manuscript.

Place	Date	Hour	Summary of Events and Information	Remarks and references to Appendices
KEMMEL	OCTOBER 6th		Operations nil. – Quiet. weather fair. In order to show the rapidity of cooperation, in the event of the front of any one Battery being attacked, a comprehensive defence scheme was made out showing the duties of each battery when any particular section of trench was attacked. Vide Appendix (iii)	Appendix (iii)
	7th 8th 9th		Quiet. Operations nil – Snipers & machine guns active on our front. At 1.30 am gas was discharged by the 36th Division, on our right, we did not cooperate – Quiet day. The relief of Simpsons Group by 16th Divisional Artillery commenced and was carried out on the 9th and 10th October as per table attached Appendix (iv)	Appendix (iv)
	10th		Hostile artillery and trench mortars shewed rather more activity than usual – Relief of Simpsons Group was completed and the batteries comprising it returned to their former groups	

H.C. Rep.
Lt Col RGA
O.C. 173rd Br. Ap.

Appendix (j).   Relief of the 3rd Canadian Divisional Artillery

36 Division Batteries	Canadian Division Batteries	Position
	Night of 1/2nd October 1916	
One section C/153 Battery relieves One Section 30th Battery at		N 16 c 7.3
" " C/153 " " " 31st " "		N 15 d 2½.2
" " B/173 " " " 33rd " "		N 10 a 3.8
" " B/173 " " " 45th " "		N 10 a 2½ 3½
" " C/173 " " " 32nd " "		N 15 b 2.7
" " D/172 " " " 43rd " "		N 26 c 8.7
	Night of 2/3rd October 1916	
" " C/153 " " One Section 30th Battery		N 15 d 2½.2
" " B/173 " " " 33rd " "		N 10 a 3.8
" " C/173 " " " 32nd " "		N 15 b 2.7
" " C/173 " Moves into unoccupied position		N 16 c 0.8
" " D/172 " relieves one Section 43rd Battery		N 14 c 9.9

N.B. These Batteries have one section detached from the main gun position. These sections must be connected to it by telephone —

Appendix (j)

Appendix ii

Defence Scheme — Simpsons Group.

1. The defence of the line held by the 16th Div. will be taken over by Simpsons Group on the completion of reliefs ordered in 36th Div. Arty Order No 21.

2. The batteries of the group will be in action as follows:—

C/153	4 guns	N 15 d 2½ 2
C/153	2 guns	N 16 a 7.3
C/173	4 guns	N 15 b 2.7
C/173	2 guns	N 16 c 0 8
B/173	4 guns	N 10 a 3 8
B/173	2 guns	N 10 a 2½ 3½
D/172	2 guns	N 26 c 8.7
D/172	2 guns	N 14 c 9½ 9

3. For defensive purposes the batteries will cover the line as follows:—

    C/153 from N 30 c 10 72 — N 24 c 83.33
    C/173 from N 24 c 83.33 — N 24 a 70.88
    B/173 from N 24 a 70.88 — N 18 b 20.55

    Right Section D/172 1 gun will block trench junction N 24 d 73 08
        1 "   "   "   Communication trench O 19 c 20.80
        1 "   "   "   "   "   N 24 b 95 08
        1 "   "   "   "   "   N 18 d 85.25

4. All batteries will be connected by telephone to the battalion HQ in the section they cover and also to group HQ.

5. Liaison officer will be found with each battalion in the front line.

1-10-16

Appendix (iii)   Copy No

Simpson Group

Supplement to reference scheme

The following arrangements will be made for the defence of the front if any point is attacked:-

1. If the front covered by B/153 is attacked one section of Left Group 21st D.A. will barrage from N30c 10.72 – N30a 15.02

   B/153 will barrage from   N30a 15.02 – N30a 42.75
   4 guns of C/173   —   —   N30a 42.75 – N24c 85.25
   Left Section C/173 —   —   N24c 85.25 – N24b 25.10
   One section of D/173 —   —   N24d 25.10 – N24c 70.88
   4 guns D/173   —   —   N24a 70.88 – N18b 20.55

   D 172 will block following points:-
       N30c 50.80   N30b 05.78
       N30a 70.20   N30a 70.76

2. If the front covered by C/173 is attacked

   1 Section B/153 will barrage from   N24c 65.10 – N24c 80.55
   C/173   —   —   N24c 80.55 – N24a 97.32
   1 Section D/173 —   —   N24a 97.32 – N24a 70.88
   4 guns D/173   —   —   N24a 70.88 – N18b 20.55

   This arrangement will remain in force till the Australian Artillery commence firing, when

   1 Section B/153 will barrage from   N30c 42.75 – N24c 65.10
      C/173   —   —   N24c 65.10 – N24d 25.70
      D/173   —   —   N18c 80.00 – N18b 20.55

   D 172 will block following points
       N24d 25.24   N24b 60.13
       N24a 83.65   N24b 62.60

   If the front covered by D/173 is attacked
   4 guns D/173 will barrage from N24a 70.85 – N18d 20.60
      B/173   —   —   N18d 20.60 – N18b 20.55
   also 4 guns B/153 —   —   N30c 10.72 – N24c 83.33
   1 section C/153 —   —   N24c 83.33 – N24d 25.55
   1   "   C/173 —   —   N24b 25.65 – N24a 70.85

   This arrangement will remain in force as the Australian Artillery commence fire, when

C/153 will barrage   N30c 10.72 – N24c 83.33
C/173   "   "   N24c 83.33 – N24a 80.60
D/173   "   "   N18d 20.60 – N18b 20.55

D/172 will block the following points:-
    N24b 62.60   N18d 68.12
    N18d 85.25   N18a 95.95

In case the front of the Group on our right is attacked

1 Section C/153 will barrage   N30c 52.15 – N30c 10.7
4 Guns C/153   "   "   N30c 10.72 – N30a 42.72
C/173   "   "   N30a 42.72 – N24a 95.45
D/173   "   "   N24a 95.45 – N18b 25.55

2 Guns D/172 will block following points:-
    N30c 50.60   N30c 50.85

5. In case the front of the group on the left is attacked:-
    1 Section C/173 will barrage support line N18b 80.15 – D13a 40.80
         C/153   N30c 10.72 – N24D 25.70
    4 Guns C/173   N24D 25.70 – N24a 70.85
         D/173   N24a 70.85 – N18b 20.55

    D 172 will block the following points
        N24b 60.60   G 13c 3.9
        N18d 85.25   G 7d 5.3

6. Battery Commanders will report to Group Headquarters immediately the threatened front is known giving location as exactly as possible.

    These orders come into force when S.O.S. signal is sent.

7. Acknowledge

        Copies to
    No 1. D/173
     2. C/173
     3. C/153
     4. D/172
     5. 16th Div
     6. 4th Australian Div
     7. 48th Inf Bde
     8. 47th   "
     9. 49th   "
     10. File
     11. Left Group 31 Div
     12. 36th D.A.

6.10.16

                            (sd) Simpson
                             Lt Col
                         Commanding Northern Group

Appendix (iv) Reliefs at Kindmann group by 164th Div. artillery

164th Div. Batterien.   **36th Div. Batts.**   **Destination of 36th Div. Batts.**   **Remarks.**

night of 9th/10th Oct. 1916

One sect. B/180	Relieves one sect. B/173	N10a 3.8.	N32d 7.9
"	B/177	C/173 N15d 2.7	N33a 7.8
"	C/177	C/153 N15d 2½.2	T17a 12.45

night of 10th/11th Oct. 1916

One sect. C/180	" one sect. B/173	N10a 3.8	N32 6.7.9
One sect. A/180	"	B/173 N10a 2.3.3½	wagon line
One sect. B/77	"	C/173 N15d 2.7	N33a 7.8
"	C/177	"	C/153 N15d 2½.2	T17a 12.45
One sect. A/177	"	C/153 N16a 7.3	T17a 12.45
"	D/177	"	D/172 N14d 9.9	T18d 0.4
"	D/177	"	D/172 N26d 7.7	T18d 0.4

One sect. C/173 at N16a 1.1 will be withdrawn at 8 pm and will march to wagon line. This section will not be relieved by 164th D.A.

Appendix (iv)

Nov 1916

HQ O^c
36 750 Bde
Vol 14

Army Form C. 2118.

WAR DIARY
or
INTELLIGENCE SUMMARY.
(Erase heading not required.)

Hour, Date, Place	Summary of Events and Information	Remarks and references to Appendices
1st – 5th Nov^r	Ordinary Trench Warfare, nothing unusual to report.	
5th – 14th Nov^r	Nothing to report. Enemy activity below normal.	O.O. N° 30 & 31
15th Nov^r	T.M. Bombardment. Very little retaliation from the enemy.	O.O. N° 30.
16th Nov^r	Raid at 10 pm in Left Sector.	
17th Nov^r	Last nights raid successful. Three prisoners taken and many Germans killed.	
18th Nov^r	Nothing to report	
19th Nov^r	Nothing to report.	
20th – 22nd Nov^r	Nothing to report	
23rd Nov^r	Very successful T.M. Bombardment carried out in accordance with Order attached.	O.O. N° 32.

Army Form C. 2118.

WAR DIARY
or
INTELLIGENCE SUMMARY.
(Erase heading not required.)

Instructions regarding War Diaries and Intelligence Summaries are contained in F.S. Regs., Part II. and the Staff Manual respectively. Title pages will be prepared in manuscript.

Hour, Date, Place	Summary of Events and Information	Remarks and references to Appendices
24th Nov.	The enemy were very active with T.M's about 10.30 p.m and finally the S.O.S call was replied to by the Artillery. This turned to be false.	
25th Nov.	Nothing to report.	
26th 27th Nov.	Nothing to report.	
28th Nov.	Nothing to report.	
29th Nov.	T.M. Bombardment in accordance with order attached. The weather was foggy + observation difficult, but a great deal of damage apparently done to enemy trenches.	O.O. No 32.
30th Nov	Nothing to report.	

H. J. Brock
Brig Gen
Cmdg. 36 Div Arty.

December 1916   WAR DIARY   of   C.R.A.   Army Form C. 2118.
INTELLIGENCE SUMMARY   36th Division

Instructions regarding War Diaries and Intelligence
Summaries are contained in F.S. Regs., Part II
and the Staff Manual respectively. Title pages
will be prepared in manuscript.

Vol 15

Hour, Date, Place	Summary of Events and Information	Remarks and references to Appendices
1st December	Nothing to report.	
2nd December	Nothing to report.	
3rd December	Orders issued with reference to the change in the Trenches of the 36th Div.	OO No 34.
4th December	Nothing to report	
5th December	A 5.0.S. alarm started in the DOUVE Sector, otherwise nothing to report.	
6th December	At 10 am 173rd Bde. R.F.A. came under Tactical orders of 16th D.A. and 113 Bde 25th Div., under 36th D.A. I.e. Completed the take over of the DOUVE Sector.	

Army Form C. 2118.

WAR DIARY
or
INTELLIGENCE SUMMARY.
(Erase heading not required.)

Instructions regarding War Diaries and Intelligence Summaries are contained in F.S. Regs., Part II. and the Staff Manual respectively. Title pages will be prepared in manuscript.

Hour, Date, Place	Summary of Events and Information	Remarks and references to Appendices
7th December	Nothing to report.	
8th December	Nothing to report.	
9th December	Nothing to report.	
10th December	Nothing to report.	
11th December	Nothing to report.	
12th December	Nothing to report.	
13th December	Nothing to report.	
14th December	Nothing to report.	

Army Form C. 2118.

WAR DIARY
or
INTELLIGENCE SUMMARY.
(Erase heading not required.)

Instructions regarding War Diaries and Intelligence Summaries are contained in F.S. Regs., Part II. and the Staff Manual respectively. Title pages will be prepared in manuscript.

Hour, Date, Place	Summary of Events and Information	Remarks and references to Appendices
15th December	The T.M. + Gun Bombardment in accordance with attached Order 37 took place at 10.30 a.m. The fire was very effective and a l/v of damage was done to the enemy trenches. The enemy retaliation was feeble. At 7 p.m. a round of gun fire for each battery was fired at the same target in order to catch enemy working parties.	O.O. N° 37
16th December	At 5 a.m. a round of gun fire from all batteries was fired at PETITE DOUVE Salient. Nothing to report	O.O. N° 38
17th December	Nothing to report	
18th December	The Army Commander visited our position.	

(73989) W4141—463. 400,000. 9/14. H.&J.Ltd. Forms/C. 2118/10.

Army Form C. 2118.

WAR DIARY
or
INTELLIGENCE SUMMARY.
(Erase heading not required.)

Instructions regarding War Diaries and Intelligence Summaries are contained in F.S. Regs., Part II. and the Staff Manual respectively. Title pages will be prepared in manuscript.

Hour, Date, Place	Summary of Events and Information	Remarks and references to Appendices
19th December	Nothing to report	During the last fortnight & present, the activity of hostile artillery greatly increased. Considerable shelling taking place practically every day.
20th December	Commander-in-Chief inspected the Divisional Artillery. Forty men & 40 men each Section D.A.C. paraded.	
21st December	Nothing to report	
22nd December	Nothing to report	
23rd December	Nothing to report	
24th December	Nothing to report	
25th December	Nothing to report	
26th December	Nothing to report	
27th December	Relief of 173rd Bde: by 180th Bde: 16th Div: commenced. Relief of A, B, & D Batteries 113th Bde: 25th Div: by C/173, A/172 & C/172 commenced.	Div Arty Order No. 40
28th December	Reliefs as above completed. Div: Artillery regrouped into two groups from night 28/29 December.	Div: Arty: Order No: 41

WAR DIARY
or
INTELLIGENCE SUMMARY.

(Erase heading not required.)

Army Form C. 2118.

Hour, Date, Place	Summary of Events and Information	Remarks and references to Appendices
29th December	173 Bde: RFA Commenced move to Training area "A" less C/173	Div: A/Q Order No: 42
	AUDINGHEM near WISSANT. Billet at WALLON CAPPEL	
	Night 29/30 Dec: 108th Inf: Bde: withdrawn from	
	the line which was distributed between 109 Bde.	
	(on right) & 107 Inf. Bde.	
	Div: Arty, Right Group, 172 Bde plus C/173 covering 109 & 7/Bde.	
	Left Group, 153 Bde covering 107 Inf. Bde.	
30th December	173 Bde: RFA. Continued march Billet at YPRES	
31st December	173 Bde: RFA. Continued march Billet GOLDENBERG	

A. J. Parsch
Maj: Sr RA.
Cmdg 36th Div: Arty;

WAR DIARY *or* **INTELLIGENCE SUMMARY.**

Army Form C. 2118.

HQrs 36th 15th Artillery

(Erase heading not required.)

Hour, Date, Place	Summary of Events and Information	Remarks and references to Appendices
1st January	No Return to report in connection with operations. List of Honours & Awards to the Divisional Artillery to be dated January 1st is attached.	Operation Order No 43
2nd January	Centered T.M. & gun bombardment of enemy front, support & reserve line in vicinity of MORTAR FARM N36d 70 25 - Bombardment reported effective. Fire Cooperation of 7/36 T.M. Battery was carried, also 2 & X/36 T.M. Battery into new co-operating with the 6" Mortars in the DOUVE Section.	
3rd January	1/36 2nd T.M. Battery withdrawn from the line & went Order No: 44 into rest in the vicinity of 2nd Army T.M. School.	

WAR DIARY
or
INTELLIGENCE SUMMARY.

(Erase heading not required.)

Army Form C. 2118.

Hour, Date, Place	Summary of Events and Information	Remarks and references to Appendices
4th January	Nothing to report	
5th "	Nothing to report	
6th "	Nothing to report	
7th "	Nothing to report on Divisional Front. Attempted enemy raid 4am on front of right brigade of 16th Division. Raid failed	
8th "	Nothing to report	
9th "	Nothing to report	
10th "	Nothing to report	
11th "	X/36 2" T.M Battery relieved in the line by Y/36 2" 7.m. battery, the former going into rest	Order No 45

Army Form C. 2118.

WAR DIARY
or
INTELLIGENCE SUMMARY.
(Erase heading not required.)

Instructions regarding War Diaries and Intelligence Summaries are contained in F.S. Regs., Part II. and the Staff Manual respectively. Title pages will be prepared in manuscript.

Hour, Date, Place	Summary of Events and Information	Remarks and references to Appendices
January 12	173 Bde. RFA Ammunition column moved from Toney aux Boulles/Villes at ESCOEUILLES & QUESQUES	Order No 47. Order No 46 cancelled
January 13	March continued to CAMPAGNE	
January 14	RA C QUINGHEM. Horses detailed by D/153, completed to 6·9 guns. 1 Section D/173 Rest. March continued to BORRE & PRADELLES	
January 15	Completion of march. Relief of B/172 & C/172 by A/173 & D/173 commenced	Order No. 48
January 16	Relief of B/172 & C/172 as above completed. Command of Right Group taken over by O.C. 173 Bde. Right Group consisting of A, C & D/173, A/172 & 1 Section of D/172 attached to D/173	

Army Form C. 2118.

WAR DIARY
or
INTELLIGENCE SUMMARY.
(Erase heading not required.)

Instructions regarding War Diaries and Intelligence Summaries are contained in F. S. Regs., Part II. and the Staff Manual respectively. Title pages will be prepared in manuscript.

Hour, Date, Place	Summary of Events and Information	Remarks and references to Appendices
January 17th	Ten minute bombardment of enemy trenches & communications S. & S.W. of MESSINES, on occasion of probable enemy relief	Order no. 49.
January 18th	Nothing to report	
January 19th	Nothing to report	
January 20th	2/36 2"T.M. Battery relieved in the line by 1/36. The former going into rest billets	Order no. 60.
January 21st	Nothing to report	
January 22nd	From 2 p.m. till about 6 p.m. enemy bombarded our trenches in Right Group area near ANTON'S FARM & also part of 25 Division with both H.T. Mortars & artillery. About 5.30 p.m. S.O.S. Call was sent by our own Right Battalion, an S.O.S. rocket having	

(73989) W4141—463. 400,000. 9/14. H.&J.Ltd. Forms/C. 2118/10.

WAR DIARY or INTELLIGENCE SUMMARY

Army Form C. 2118.

Hour, Date, Place	Summary of Events and Information	Remarks and references to Appendices
January 23rd	previously (5.15 pm about) have sent up on 25th Division front. Enemy worked in his places on 25th Division front & also at ANTON'S FARM. The lead party quickly left our trenches but returned a 2" T.M. with bad. of X/36 T.M. Battery. Few casualties amongst the infantry, 3 men wounded of X/36 Battery. Detachments had been withdrawn as those guns were out of action with trench rifle mechanism. Barrage by Right Group put down. Some 2,000 rounds in all being fired. Bombardment of trenches & Dumps in MESSINES carried out by Div. Artillery & Corps H.A. on account of nightly bombs $2500.	Order No. 52

Army Form C. 2118.

WAR DIARY
or
INTELLIGENCE SUMMARY.
(Erase heading not required.)

Instructions regarding War Diaries and Intelligence Summaries are contained in F.S. Regs., Part II. and the Staff Manual respectively. Title pages will be prepared in manuscript.

Hour, Date, Place	Summary of Events and Information	Remarks and references to Appendices
January 24th	Nothing to report.	
January 25th	Enemy Artillery very active, one gun of A172 knocked out of action & destroyed.	
January 26th	Enemy Artillery still very active, one gun of T152 destroyed.	
January 27th	Enemy Artillery active as in the previous two days & registering with aeroplanes.	
Jan. 28, 29, 30	Nothing to report.	
Jan. 31st	Enemy Artillery very active, shelling B173 & D153 at positions T13.c. A few casualties.	

31.1.17.

H.E. Piper
Lieut. Col.
R.A. 36 Div. Arty

Army Form C. 2118.

CRA
36" Division
Vol 17

WAR DIARY
or
INTELLIGENCE SUMMARY.
(Erase heading not required.)

Instructions regarding War Diaries and Intelligence Summaries are contained in F.S. Regs., Part II. and the Staff Manual respectively. Title pages will be prepared in manuscript.

Hour, Date, Place	Summary of Events and Information	Remarks and references to Appendices
1st February	D173 + D153 front line heavily shelled again.	
2nd February	D173 round 15 pounder Trench 9.5.	
3 – 4 February	Enemy Artillery very quiet, hardly a shot being fired.	
5th February	A withdrawal of the enemy lines in Conjunction with 25th D.A. carried out. Enemy Retaliation nil.	O.O. No 57 (36 Canadian by 18)
6th February	Nothing to report	
7th February	"	
8th February	"	

Army Form C. 2118.

WAR DIARY
or
INTELLIGENCE SUMMARY.
(Erase heading not required.)

Instructions regarding War Diaries and Intelligence Summaries are contained in F.S. Regs., Part II. and the Staff Manual respectively. Title pages will be prepared in manuscript.

Hour, Date, Place	Summary of Events and Information	Remarks and references to Appendices
9th February.	T.M. Bombardment awaits [attached] Order. Practically no retaliation.	O.O. 59.
10th February	Repetition of C153 and A153 by S.G. Guns with artillery observation. Major Gaul + Lieut Brown wounded. Y/36 relieved X/36 in the Battery line.	O.O. 60 & 61.
11th – 13th February	Nothing to report.	
14th February	Enemy attempted raid opposite ONTARIO FARM at about 1 am, [frustrated] and again at 6 pm. 2nd Raid unsuccessful. B/173 relieved from 8th Corps and attached 25th Division. Nothing to report.	O.O. 62
15th February		

(73989) W4141—463. 400,000. 9/14. H.&J.Ltd. Forms/C. 2118/10.

Army Form C. 2118.

WAR DIARY
or
INTELLIGENCE SUMMARY.
(Erase heading not required.)

Instructions regarding War Diaries and Intelligence Summaries are contained in F.S. Regs., Part II. and the Staff Manual respectively. Title pages will be prepared in manuscript.

Hour, Date, Place	Summary of Events and Information	Remarks and references to Appendices
16th February.	Nothing to report	
17th February.	Bombardment in connection with a raid by the 25th Div.	O.O. 63.
18th February.	Nothing to report. Enemy Artillery rather more active than usual	
	Relief of Z/36 T.M. Battery by X/36 T.M. Battery.	O.O. 65.
19th February.	Bombardment in connection with a raid carried out by 16th Div.	O.O. 64.
		O.O. 66
20th February	T.M. Bombardment.	
21st February.	Raid by 109th Brigade. Enemy front line found full of wire and	O.O. 67
	trenches were not entered. A.172 (Pop. 51.) shelled during day —	
	About 50 shells. 10. Solton including a few Lachrymators.	
	Reorganisation into Army Brigades completed. 172 Brigade	
22nd February	disbanded. 113 Army Brigade attached for administration.	
	B.73 relieves I section A.172 (now C.77). Enemy raid on 25th front.	O.O. 68.
23rd February.	Relief completed. Intelligence lecture by Lt Col Mitchell at	
	2nd Army H.Q.	

Army Form C. 2118.

WAR DIARY
or
INTELLIGENCE SUMMARY.
(Erase heading not required.)

Hour, Date, Place	Summary of Events and Information	Remarks and references to Appendices
24th February	Conference at RAHQ IXth Corps 10.30 am — Ditto Group Commanders 2.30 pm —	
25th February	Nothing to report —	
26th February	Nothing to report —	
27th February	C.R.A. visits Magnum Opus position —	
28th February	Nothing to report —	

1.3.17.

H.J. Cark
Brig. Gen.
Commanding 36th Divl Artillery.

WAR DIARY
or
INTELLIGENCE SUMMARY.
(Erase heading not required.)

Headquarters
36th Divl. Artillery

Army Form C. 2118.

Vol 18

Instructions regarding War Diaries and Intelligence Summaries are contained in F.S. Regs., Part II. and the Staff Manual respectively. Title pages will be prepared in manuscript.

Hour, Date, Place	Summary of Events and Information	Remarks and references to Appendices
1st March	B/153 very heavily shelled about 500 shells in all fell in & near the position. Three casualties wounded	
2nd – 4th March	Artillery Report. Night firing on thoroughfares	O.O. 69.
5th March	Nothing to report	
6th March	Bombardment of Trenches in accordance with attached order. No enemy retaliation	O.O. 71 (O.O.70 cancelled)
7th March	Bombardment of Trenches in accordance with attached order. Very little retaliation.	O.O. 72.
8th March	Enemy fired on 16 Bde Front. On left front heavily Bombarded. Night firing carried out in accordance with O.O. 69.	

Army Form C. 2118.

WAR DIARY
or
INTELLIGENCE SUMMARY.
(Erase heading not required.)

Instructions regarding War Diaries and Intelligence Summaries are contained in F.S. Regs., Part II. and the Staff Manual respectively. Title pages will be prepared in manuscript.

Hour, Date, Place	Summary of Events and Information	Remarks and references to Appendices
9th March	Enemy Raid on 16th Div front. Heavy Bombardment of & on left sector. B/173 heavily shelled by hostile artillery.	
10th March	Nothing to report.	
11th March	B.173 & B.153 heavily shelled by 150 hun How. Casualties B.153. Three killed one gun damaged.	
12th March	B.173 & A.153 shelled. One Inf. Officer wounded on latter position. Artillery to keep very active during last few days	
13th March	Very quiet day. Nothing to report.	

Army Form C. 2118.

WAR DIARY
or
INTELLIGENCE SUMMARY.
(Erase heading not required.)

Instructions regarding War Diaries and Intelligence Summaries are contained in F. S. Regs., Part II. and the Staff Manual respectively. Title pages will be prepared in manuscript.

Hour, Date, Place	Summary of Events and Information	Remarks and references to Appendices
12th March	Orders issued regarding Relief of Artillery by N.Z.D.A. + relief of 16 D.A. by 36th D.A.	O.O. 72. 74.
13th March	Relief of the Infantry Bde of 16th Div by 36. Div. Complete.	
16th March	113th Army F.A. Bde moved to EECKE area.	O.O. 75.
17th March	Scheme Relieved in the line by N.Z.D.A. & relieved batteries of 16 D.A.	
18th March	Took over Command of the Artillery covering 36th Division on the Front between WULVERGHEM – WYTSCHAETE road and number of bunkers N24. N.2. at 9 a.m. Remaining batteries relieved & were reliened on the nights 17/18th.	
19th March	Nothing to report.	
20th March	Orders issued regarding the move of 153rd Bde R.F.A. to Training Area.	C.O. 76

Army Form C. 2118.

WAR DIARY
or
INTELLIGENCE SUMMARY.
(Erase heading not required.)

Instructions regarding War Diaries and Intelligence Summaries are contained in F.S. Regs., Part II. and the Staff Manual respectively. Title pages will be prepared in manuscript.

Hour, Date, Place	Summary of Events and Information	Remarks and references to Appendices
21st March.	A & C 153 relieved in the line by D 153. On the night 20/21. w.t. 0707b. 153 Bde marched in accordance with order.	
22nd March.	Nothing to report. 153 Bde arrived at LUMBRES.	
23rd March.	Nothing to report.	
24th March.	S.O.S. signal sent up by 2/N 2. Division on our right about 4 a.m. 36th D.A. supported. All quiet about 5.15 a.m.	
25th March.	Nothing to report.	
26th March.	Nothing to report.	

Army Form C. 2118.

WAR DIARY
or
INTELLIGENCE SUMMARY.
(Erase heading not required.)

Instructions regarding War Diaries and Intelligence Summaries are contained in F.S. Regs., Part II. and the Staff Manual respectively. Title pages will be prepared in manuscript.

Hour, Date, Place	Summary of Events and Information	Remarks and references to Appendices
27th March.	⎱	
28th March.	⎬ Nothing to report.	
29th March.	⎰	
30th March.	Schemes Cancelled MPH	
31st March.	The Section of A/143 at T.24.a.2.8. was relieved with S.g.s.	H. Powell. Lieut for Comdt 36 Div. Art

Army Form C. 2118.

WAR DIARY
or
INTELLIGENCE SUMMARY.

(Erase heading not required.)

Vol 19
H.Q. 36th Divn Artillery

Instructions regarding War Diaries and Intelligence Summaries are contained in F.S. Regs., Part II. and the Staff Manual respectively. Title pages will be prepared in manuscript.

Hour, Date, Place	Summary of Events and Information	Remarks and references to Appendices
April 1st	T.M. Batteries relieved on front of Battery withdrawn from the line for work at base employments. X & Z were the front, Y on the right, Z on the left at LUMBRES.	The Army Commander + BG, R.A inspected 153rd Bde R.A at LUMBRES.
April 2nd	Nothing to report	
April 3rd	Relief arranged to the trench track of 153rd Bde from training areas, and relief of Batteries going into action bombarded by D/172 (BAD rounds) in accordance with 153rd Div orders No. 3 at 5.30 pm to 6.30 pm	Div Art orders No 77
April 4th	Bombardment of trenches in 36th Div front at 5.30 pm - 6.40 pm (168 rounds by D/172) in accordance with above.	
April 5th	153rd Bde R.A R.H.A marched from LUMBRES to WARDRECQUES. Road by 16th Divn Ammn Trenches in N2 d 4 & d. 8.45 pm 173 & 182 arrived in main bivouac, outside of LUMBRES and power house.	In Rh.A with the 87th Bde Came under the Orders of B.G.R.A w/153rd Bde. R.A (SPANBROEK Group.)
April 6th	153rd Bde marched from WARDRECQUES to 1.4th Divl Area and spent the night at Bryan Line. Bivouacs occupied by him.	
April 7th	Conference at Divisional C.R.A & Brigade Commanders. The position of B/173 at N.15.b.3.5, 8.5 covered with 10.5 cm Hrs at N.15.b.3.3, 4.1.30pm 4.2/5 with 220 rounds. Some casualties & considerable damage to material was caused.	

(73989) W4141—463. 400,000. 9/14. H.&J.Ltd. Forms/C.2118/40. 10 + 11 am

Army Form C. 2118.

WAR DIARY
or
INTELLIGENCE SUMMARY.
(Erase heading not required.)

Instructions regarding War Diaries and Intelligence Summaries are contained in F.S. Regs., Part II. and the Staff Manual respectively. Title pages will be prepared in manuscript.

Hour, Date, Place	Summary of Events and Information	Remarks and references to Appendices
April 8th.	The section of C/173 at N15.6.3.5 P.S. was shelled at 4 pm & 2.45 pm by 10.5 cm & 15 cm How. Considerable damage was done & casualties occurred among men of C/153 Battery who had come up to the Battery room. (1 man killed, 3 wounded) 7.50 am & 9.05 am & at 11.30 am A/173 Battery was shelled at N73 a 8.8. with 10.5 cm & 15 cm Howitzers. The shooting was accurate but very little damage was done. The Mont of 153rd Bde R.F.A. was completed, except that A/153 did not go into action owing to damage done to the position at N15 b 35.95	
April 9th	Nothing to report.	
April 10th	Nothing to report.	
April 11th	Nothing to report.	

Army Form C. 2118.

WAR DIARY
or
INTELLIGENCE SUMMARY.
(Erase heading not required.)

Instructions regarding War Diaries and Intelligence Summaries are contained in F.S. Regs., Part II. and the Staff Manual respectively. Title pages will be prepared in manuscript.

Hour, Date, Place	Summary of Events and Information	Remarks and references to Appendices
April 12th	No section of A/153 brought into action at N15 b 35 85	
April 13th	Nothing to report.	
April 14th	⎫ Nothing of importance occurred otherwise.	
April 15th	⎪ Hostile artillery quiet and no deliberate shoots were carried out on our batteries.	
April 16th	⎬ Considerable trench mortar activity by no. 2" Batteries, principally on wire-cutting every	
April 17th	⎪ Trench mortars Confederately machine.	
April 18th	⎭ Groups concentrations in front/rear were fired nearly every day. These are replied to by a diameter to the very effective	

WAR DIARY
or
INTELLIGENCE SUMMARY.
(Erase heading not required.)

Army Form C. 2118.

Hour, Date, Place	Summary of Events and Information	Remarks and references to Appendices
April 25th	During the day the enemy's support line opposite the Divisional Front, and they front in front, were bombarded by the IX Corps Heavies. A programme of fire by 18 pdrs and 4.5" Hows was carried out in conjunction with this on Trench Junctions and communication Trenches being back from the Support line. The enemy's artillery ceased to reply, except our batteries, but a 16th Div Bde in N21a came very heavily shelled during this shelling.	Disp. to 79.
April 21st	From 11 midnight till 5.00am a bombardment of Turkish communication Trenches all known extended approach in the Debinand Road, and	

WAR DIARY
or
INTELLIGENCE SUMMARY.
(Erase heading not required.)

Army Form C. 2118.

Hour, Date, Place	Summary of Events and Information	Remarks and references to Appendices
April 21st	Carried out 1 x 60pdr H.E. concentration with a slow programme on the new nitrea ammunition. Fired about 2,000 rounds 18 pdr & 500 rounds 4.5" Hrs. were fired. A relief was expected to take place that night, confirmed by a wireless msg which stated it would be the relief of a couple during the evening. Late in the evening 227R Battery a number of batteries. There were fired into N 27 a. The 1x 60pdr H.H. continued the destruction programme till midday.	Wab G 78
April 22nd	There was nothing to report.	

WAR DIARY
or
INTELLIGENCE SUMMARY.
(Erase heading not required.)

Army Form C. 2118.

Hour, Date, Place	Summary of Events and Information	Remarks and references to Appendices
April 23rd, April 24th, April 25th	Wire cutting continued on the enemys front line with 2" T.M.S. The hostile artillery continued to be comparatively inactive. A slight increase of hostile T.M. activity was of previous days noted by groups concentrations	
	April 24th & 25th. A & B Batteries 153rd Bde went into action at 1.6 pm as follows. 156th A153 (already in action N15.b.25.25) 2 Section A153. N21.a.90.65. B153 N30.a.7.3. Emplacements to contain. covering for to A programme of 2" T.Ms, 18pr and 4.5" Hows was carried out on the SPANBROEK MOLEN between 3pm and 5pm to keep observation from the 16A. D/F Heavy T.M.s which have being fired in the PETIT Bois Sector and 6 crater V.36 Heavy Btty. Bdy. which fired 20 rounds with no fuse.	Col. Thomson took over command of the SPANBROEK Sub. during the absence of Col. Sampson on leave. A153 took over before to the wire. Divisional artillery order No.81.
April 26th		

Army Form C. 2118.

WAR DIARY
or
INTELLIGENCE SUMMARY.
(Erase heading not required.)

Instructions regarding War Diaries and Intelligence Summaries are contained in F.S. Regs., Part II. and the Staff Manual respectively. Title pages will be prepared in manuscript.

Hour, Date, Place	Summary of Events and Information	Remarks and references to Appendices
27th April	Horse artillery event	
28th April	Holts Trench Mortar Battery relieved in action entered by no 2" T.M.S.	
29th April	18 Pdr Bge "C" H.Q. carried out calibration work	
30th April	On the night of 29th April/1st May, Lyra firing was carried out by the Divisional artillery on our front against all communication trenches and known avenues of approach from 9 pm to 5 am.	Iso milling shot No P.O.
	Work on Battery positions at Magnum Opus went on continuously throughout the month.	

H.J. North, R.A.
Brig Gen
Cmdg. 36 ["]Div Art[y".]

Headquarters
36th Div Arty.

Army Form C. 2118.

WAR DIARY
or
INTELLIGENCE SUMMARY.
(Erase heading not required.)

Instructions regarding War Diaries and Intelligence Summaries are contained in F.S. Regs., Part II. and the Staff Manual respectively. Title pages will be prepared in manuscript.

Hour, Date, Place	Summary of Events and Information	Remarks and references to Appendices
May 1st	A daylight raid was carried out at dawn on the German trenches at N.30.c.35.50. and N.30.c.10.95. a barrage was put on before, but was not so effective. The enemy caught our & front 2d German and came back wounding casualties.	
May 2nd 3rd 4th	Normal activity on both sides. On account of Smoke Screen behind the German ridge by the enemy no changes apparently to enemy with our Artillery were noted. & three no new movements	
May 5th 6th	Throughout there two nights the enemy heavily shelled Chateau back area. on & wide front, including 28 LA CLYTTE, KEMMEL	

Army Form C. 2118.

WAR DIARY
or
INTELLIGENCE SUMMARY.
(Erase heading not required.)

Instructions regarding War Diaries and Intelligence Summaries are contained in F.S. Regs., Part II. and the Staff Manual respectively. Title pages will be prepared in manuscript.

Hour, Date, Place	Summary of Events and Information	Remarks and references to Appendices
May 7th	Neuve Eglise aux Camps and roads the receives attention - 77 pks & 10 cm guns and 10.5 and 15cm Howitzers were used.	
	All guns & Howitzers on 2nd army front (except 12" How) carried out two minutes bombardment of enemy trenches communications and back areas for 5 minutes and retaliated to a certain extent, gun at 8.45 pm and 11 pm. The enemy 18pr & 4.5" Hos concentration in reported. Fire was during the night.	Dw Arko S.O. No 82
May 8th	Salvoes 18pr balloons were put on from this date 18 am at 20 cm to intense 1/2 retaliation was 4 to 60 pr batteries.	

(73989) W4141—463. 400,000. 9/14. H.&J.Ltd. Forms/C. 2118/10.

Army Form C. 2118.

WAR DIARY
or
INTELLIGENCE SUMMARY.
(Erase heading not required.)

Instructions regarding War Diaries and Intelligence Summaries are contained in F.S. Regs., Part II. and the Staff Manual respectively. Title pages will be prepared in manuscript.

Hour, Date, Place	Summary of Events and Information	Remarks and references to Appendices
May 9th 4.18 pm	Nothing to report.	
May 11th	The enemy turned a battery fortune at No 2 8.1. (opp 3 Bde) 1 man was killed and 1 gun damaged.	
May 12th	(continued) The French watched normal actions in the front enemy study were active in enemy supported trenches, and work continues on all positions being sent up to No. Fortune.	
May 15th	a battery fortune at W 33 a 88 was heavily shelled (6/17s) one arm rest wire and damaged 2 more killed.	

Jr. 3 Ger. Jul. H.Q. and R.A.H.Q. moved up to ULSTER Camp P. DRANOUTRE.

Army Form C. 2118.

WAR DIARY
or
INTELLIGENCE SUMMARY.
(Erase heading not required.)

Instructions regarding War Diaries and Intelligence Summaries are contained in F.S. Regs., Part II. and the Staff Manual respectively. Title pages will be prepared in manuscript.

Hour, Date, Place	Summary of Events and Information	Remarks and references to Appendices
May 16th	A level line carried out by the 9th Div at the right (between N36d 50.60 and N36d 75.00) at 11.25 pm. 30th Div Batteries cooperated in the barrage & also in a fewer bombardment further east.	36 M Div Arty O.O No 83
May 19th to May 21st	Increased artillery activity on both sides. Fine weather continues.	
May 22nd	A silent raid 27 K place at 1.30 am. at N30 c 67.85 by the 14th J.R. 20 artillery support was required. & but enemy was prepared in caves.	
May 23rd	Intercepted wireless from Staff Capt in Ka Dalarn, to forwarded to their own lines, many units unless instructions from Staff Capt.	M 74 Brigades 76th FA Obe TCol Byal Chy 84th JA Obe l'Col Corran Jha 108 JA Be 2d Japh's 289 Jn Re Lt Col Park
	R.A. IX Corps.	

WAR DIARY
or
INTELLIGENCE SUMMARY.
(Erase heading not required.)

Army Form C. 2118.

Hour, Date, Place	Summary of Events and Information	Remarks and references to Appendices
May 24th	At 10.30 a.m. present took place at T N36a 5797 by the 15th R.D.R. 36th Div Artillery Conference between under orders from SPANBROEK. Maj's H.P. 32nd Div Arty, Brigades now came forward to areas in rear companies representatives to their forward positions. The enemy Brigades Shelled & came into action with bursting hung in action by the night of 9.10th all batteries being reported by the 20th inst. The 32nd Div artillery were all in action by 9 am, and carefully registration during the preliminary bombardment to be under the Spanbroek group the defence of the line continued to next.	161st Bde R.F.A. ELEVEN DAS 168th Bde R.F.A. Infantrymen B.M.O./133.
May 25th	an attack with projectors and artillery cooperation was considered firing "gas", due to unfavourable weather Conference of all Brigade Commanders at H.Q.	O.O. No 84.

WAR DIARY
or
INTELLIGENCE SUMMARY.
(Erase heading not required.)

Army Form C. 2118.

Instructions regarding War Diaries and Intelligence Summaries are contained in F. S. Regs., Part II. and the Staff Manual respectively. Title pages will be prepared in manuscript.

Hour, Date, Place	Summary of Events and Information	Remarks and references to Appendices
January 26th	Batteries busy putting into action and bringing up ammunition. The S.A. Battalions of the 82nd D.A. Division who pushed into the line making positions were pushed up by 26th D.I.V. dugouts to counter-attack and bring up the machine-gun carrying parties and making positions, the to the numbers of over 2000 men.	
January 27th	118th Camp Prisoners were Rested throughout. The supposed mile – 10 C.H. Prus. all Reds were wounded, located, and a considerable number of casualties occurred to enemy parties to enemy, of men.	

WAR DIARY
or
INTELLIGENCE SUMMARY.
(Erase heading not required.)

Army Form C. 2118.

Hour, Date, Place	Summary of Events and Information	Remarks and references to Appendices
May 28th	Heavy shelling par division lines up to Battn Head quarters on KEMMEL. (Ferme) Q branch moved to MILLE Oaten. Back areas were again shelled, from [illegible] the nights losses 9 killed and 38 wounded. Same 12 noon on 27th The Bn left covered in [illegible] Rifles and 39(?) Irish and came round by their Est[?] quarters. Col Dunston continued to carry on the defence of the line as O.C. Frontcote [?] Group and acted as Liaison Officer with 108th Bde Stands Brigade taking this time, to inform Headquarters with B Bn H.Q.	O.O. 85

Army Form C. 2118.

WAR DIARY
or
INTELLIGENCE SUMMARY.

(Erase heading not required.)

Instructions regarding War Diaries and Intelligence Summaries are contained in F.S. Regs., Part II. and the Staff Manual respectively. Title pages will be prepared in manuscript.

Hour, Date, Place	Summary of Events and Information	Remarks and references to Appendices
29th/30th June	Firing Carried on by Batteries of 153 & 173" Brigades, covering to programme. Vreuil. Peter rely, Machine firing up to 200 rounds a day.	
31st June	1st Day of Preliminary Bombardment. (see return with this getting details for action we to be touched in wording Friday)	

G. 6. 17.

H. J. Parth
Povi Gn. R.A.
Cmdg. 36th Div. Art.

Headquarters
36th Div. Artillery

WAR DIARY
or
INTELLIGENCE SUMMARY
(Erase heading not required.)

Army Form C. 2118.

Hour, Date, Place	Summary of Events and Information	Remarks and references to Appendices

The following artillery plan covers the operations
resulting in the capture of the MESSINES WYTSCHAETE Ridge.

The field artillery supporting the attack of the 36th Division against the Ridge
was comprised
of the 36th Divisional artillery Group — commanded by
Brigadier General Brock D.S.O. R.A.

It consisted of the following units:—

36th Divisional Artillery

153rd Bde R.F.A.   Lieut Col R.J. Newton DSO R.A.
173rd Bde R.F.A.   Lieut Col H.E. Simpson DSO R.F.A.

Army Field Artillery Brigades

96th   D.A. Brigade   Lieut Col J.C. Rogers C.M.G.   84th J.A. Brigade Lieut Col Gibb DSO
100th D.A. Brigade   Lieut Col B.H. Parke Ch.J. Rogers J.A. Brigade Lieut Col H.J. Prickle DSO

36th Divisional artillery
161st Brigade R.F.A. Lieut Col A.W. Cotton DSO R.F.A.
162nd Brigade R.F.A. Lieut Col R. Wynmauer DSO R.A.

324, 36th Field Mortar Batteries   144   18 pdrs   ? Heavy Hows
                                    46   4.5" Hows 24 medium Hows
making a total of

Army Form C. 2118.

WAR DIARY
or
INTELLIGENCE SUMMARY.
(Erase heading not required.)

Instructions regarding War Diaries and Intelligence Summaries are contained in F. S. Regs., Part II. and the Staff Manual respectively. Title pages will be prepared in manuscript.

Hour, Date, Place	Summary of Events and Information	Remarks and references to Appendices
Rest enfo France 5 Nov 98 S.W. 1915	Of the above the 160th Brigade R.F.A. were bivouacked and the brigade batteries of 32nd Div. were here for cover before going up to the eastern of the BLUE line now in Ham to the black line up to the the armor line, 3.10 pr. batteries were being run up to the front and were executed for covering behind rifle hole lines. The Division was arranged in 2 groups {right left each of these was divided into two sub groups, known as — A.B.C.D sub groups. The 32nd Div. artillery was kept inside this manoeuvre, and has known as E.F. sub groups. (161)(163) It furthermore was divided equally between the 2d mann groups and a flanking line back, to suit the Heliotropische.	To this is the 16th Div. 76 to 9. D.F. Bdr. were attached of Hon Blackline. OC 173rd Bde R.F.A. under OC 15. 3 rd Bde R.F.A. for — A.B.C.D. Sub groups. The Heliotropische the Division groups and the Lay bases

(73989) W4141—463. 400,000. 9/14. H.&J.Ltd. Forms/C. 2118/10.

Instructions regarding War Diaries and Intelligence Summaries are contained in F.S. Regs., Part II. and the Staff Manual respectively. Title pages will be prepared in manuscript.

WAR DIARY
or
INTELLIGENCE SUMMARY.
(Erase heading not required.)

Army Form C. 2118.

Hour, Date, Place	Summary of Events and Information	Remarks and references to Appendices

The Barrage to be created from N36.b.0.0.15 to N2.d.85 in the German Front Line (1000 yards app 10). There was reduced to 1000 yards on the Black Line and to 500 yards on the No Reserve Line.

However the were Lewis gunners acted as Liaison officers with the two attacking infantry brigades his G. Bush O.y.A. a 36th Dn H.Q.

acted as Liaison officer from the 1st Corps H.Q.

An officer from the 108th Bde R. Inf. acted as Liaison officer for the attack on the with the 30th Infantry Brigade Headquarters on the Reserve line.

There was a Liaison officer with each of the Original attacking battalions and there joined the Reserves which carried on the attack after the Blue Line when their failure, and remained with Their Battalions for the rest of the day.

Have met with much heavy Counterbattery & harass fire from the German Heavy artillery.

(73989) W4141-463. 400,000. 9/14. H.&J.Ltd. Forms/C. 2118/10.

Army Form C. 2118.

WAR DIARY
or
INTELLIGENCE SUMMARY.
(Erase heading not required.)

Instructions regarding War Diaries and Intelligence Summaries are contained in F.S. Regs., Part II. and the Staff Manual respectively. Title pages will be prepared in manuscript.

Hour, Date, Place	Summary of Events and Information	Remarks and references to Appendices
Preliminary action	From Zero minus 11 days all calibre ammunition were fused at light action. Batteries of 18" DH only were used. 500 rounds a higher were fired in addition to that number necessary to keep enfilade fire than the Bosch artillery had embossed during the day and night fires always to be mounted by machine Guns. Wire kites were accumulation	
	From zero minus 7 day to W day a 5 day bomb. element were carried over for the first 2 days for which with 18pdr fired 10 rounds per Gun for day including 300 per miles at 4.5" Hows fired 10 rounds per minute 4 in 7 rounds including 400 rounds at night.	
	In the last 2 days are 18pdrs fired 150 rounds per gun firing including 50 at night at 4.5" How fired 170 rounds per How firing including 50 at night. on 3 nights an Oil shot bombardment was carried out on an were allotted by 18 Corps O.M. fire being concentrated on the day net near Eouft in O.18.B.5. Trench	

(73989) W4141—463. 400,000. 9/14. H.&J.Ltd. Forms/C. 2118/10.

Army Form C. 2118.

WAR DIARY
or
INTELLIGENCE SUMMARY.
(Erase heading not required.)

Instructions regarding War Diaries and Intelligence Summaries are contained in F. S. Regs., Part II. and the Staff Manual respectively. Title pages will be prepared in manuscript.

Hour, Date, Place	Summary of Events and Information	Remarks and references to Appendices
	Practice Barrages 2 Corps and 2 army practice Barrages were fired, and in addition the right division staff fired 2 a.m. ranging & the 6" Howitzer and Corps Barrages. These Barrages for 6 to 10" Howitzers were included. Two days slow lifts, bombs were expended succeed fast rates were carried out by the 36th Division. Trench Mortars. From 2-11 days 2-2 minimum 7 days fired 205 rounds a day. Ian than minimum - 1000 rounds a day, dealing with the enemy's front and support lines, wire, dugouts and mine craters. The Heavy T. M. fired 1500 rounds in all, in the next line and strong points in rear. The Anglo-use Heavy Trench Mortar fires at Bufer Wood never mind farm. The French Mortars did not fire in Zero day.	

WAR DIARY
or
INTELLIGENCE SUMMARY.
(Erase heading not required.)

Army Form C. 2118.

Hour, Date, Place	Summary of Events and Information	Remarks and references to Appendices
Artillery O.P. for 3 Day.	A Creeping barrage was fired of 12.18 pm batteries (firing 1 gun to 20 rounds) Starting barrage at 9.17 pm Between S" — A.S" the interval. The lifts being so arranged as to synchronise with the IX Corps H.A. Heavies no trench line or strong point barrage was received up to the time the creeping barrage reached the first objective there were no closer than 150 yards of their creeping barrage. At 3.18 pm Barrage of 0.2 Heigen fired a protective, of Roche Pour another objective much shelling barrage. On 2 day the barrage came down not very heavy but after the [illegible] dressed up & time Zero without anything untoward. The [illegible] stormed and continued accordingly.	

Army Form C. 2118.

WAR DIARY
or
INTELLIGENCE SUMMARY.
(Erase heading not required.)

Instructions regarding War Diaries and Intelligence Summaries are contained in F. S. Regs., Part II. and the Staff Manual respectively. Title pages will be prepared in manuscript.

Hour, Date, Place	Summary of Events and Information	Remarks and references to Appendices
	Shortly after the capture of the Green Line orders were received from IX Corps R.A. for the advance of the 153rd and 173rd Bdes R.F.A. according to programme, as soon as the advance to the Mauve Line commenced, & positions previously reconnoitred for them.	
	Routes had previously been arranged and the move took place without any delay.	
	173rd Bde R.F.A. were ready to open fire in 2 hours from the time of starting. 153rd Bde were ready soon after.	
	Single guns had registered from these positions the previous day.	
	The Barrage from the Black to the Mauve line was planned as follows — a creeping barrage of 9 18 prs in front of which was another barrage arranged in depth of 2 18 pr Batteries and 6 4.5" How Batteries lifting with the creeping barrage three and four hundred yards ahead.	

WAR DIARY
or
INTELLIGENCE SUMMARY.
(Erase heading not required.)

Army Form C. 2118.

Hour, Date, Place	Summary of Events and Information	Remarks and references to Appendices
	an average of 100 yards unaccompanied with the 75th Division on the left. Their pace was 1 pm to 78 yards in the creeping barrage, and 1 pm to 25 yards in the standing barrage.	
	There was a neutral zone which ext by Tanks 33 2d Inf Bde of 11 & Division. This was fired to 3/10 pm for the attack on the Ootrowen accord to the 30th Div MG Coy. The barrage from the howr. a creeping barrage of 9 18pr Batteries and a standing Barrage of 4 K.A. How Batteries. The first 1 pm to 20 yards in the creeping barrage and 1 pm to 100 yards in the standing barrage, most Rum allowing at ranges varying from 5200 & 6400	

Army Form C. 2118.

WAR DIARY
or
INTELLIGENCE SUMMARY.
(Erase heading not required.)

Instructions regarding War Diaries and Intelligence Summaries are contained in F.S. Regs., Part II. and the Staff Manual respectively. Title pages will be prepared in manuscript.

Hour, Date, Place	Summary of Events and Information	Remarks and references to Appendices
June 1st.	2nd Day of Bombardment. Practice Barrage in IX Corps Front.	See War Diary. No. 87.
June 2nd.	3rd Day of Bombardment. Raids on 25th Division Front at 11 p.m. Continuation by Right Division Group as shown in order. Gas Bombardment by 4 5" Howitzers, repeated the damage inflicted. Right Division Group took Front in a Practice Barrage over C.T.s to the 2nd Army Corps.	See Diary. No. 88. " " 89. See Diary. No. 90.
June 3rd.	4th Day of Bombardment. Ordinary Practice Barrage was fired on the Front of the 2nd Army. Bombardment of Wytschaete by IX Corps Heavy Artillery and II Anzac Corps Heavy Artillery, Group artillery in which 36 & Divs.	See War Diary No. 91. See War Diary No. 93.

(73959) W.4141—463. 400,000. 9/14. H. & J. Ltd. Forms/C. 2118/10.

WAR DIARY
or
INTELLIGENCE SUMMARY.
(Erase heading not required.)

Army Form C. 2118.

Instructions regarding War Diaries and Intelligence Summaries are contained in F.S. Regs., Part II. and the Staff Manual respectively. Title pages will be prepared in manuscript.

Hour, Date, Place	Summary of Events and Information	Remarks and references to Appendices
June 3rd.	Practice Barrage and Oxford Group. Attack by a raid by 13th R.I.R. North of the Spanbroek Mohar, in which a 60 Barrage was fired by the 3rd Bde as Coy. A complete success, and 16 Prisoners were captured.	56th D. W. Ay O.O. No. 32. 36th D. W. Ay O.O. No. 94.
	A "bombardment" with all divisional Artillery right with co-operation by the Batys of main Group.	3 Can D W Ay O.O. No 95.
June 4th.	50th Dy of Bombardment. In messages to "B" army, C Corps the right main Group fired in a Practice Barrage.	3rd Div Art Ay O.O. No 90.
June 5th.	As army Practice Barrage were fired on the Similar Lines by a raid, the attack being arranged to carry the Spanbroek Mohar. F. S. Shot were used by the D.T.P. Spanbroek Mohar.	10th W Ay O.O. No 98.

(73989) W4141—463. 400,000. 9/14. H.&J.Ltd. Forms/C. 2118/10.

Army Form C. 2118.

WAR DIARY
or
INTELLIGENCE SUMMARY.
(Erase heading not required.)

Instructions regarding War Diaries and Intelligence Summaries are contained in F. S. Regs., Part II. and the Staff Manual respectively. Title pages will be prepared in manuscript.

Hour, Date, Place	Summary of Events and Information	Remarks and references to Appendices
June 6th (Y Day)	A bombardment with gas shell was carried out by 4.5" Howitzers. Items ranging from Zeppelins to Dugouts to Telegraph-like wires were set with, which the G.O.C. must have from our own hides, considering having informations?	30th Divl. O.O. 99.
June 7th Z Day	Zero Hour 3.10 a.m. at which time Mines were exploded and the barrage came down. The course of the battle was traced and up to the time of this, and worked in accordance with the programme previously arranged, as already stated. All arrangements were made for Division 2 Wing this was air. 8pm by wire to Corps.	2 Divl. artly O.O. No 96. No 97. No 102. and afterwards. B.M.G 71.

WAR DIARY
or
INTELLIGENCE SUMMARY.
(Erase heading not required.)

Army Form C. 2118.

Hour, Date, Place	Summary of Events and Information	Remarks and references to Appendices
June 8th.	76th & 70th Bde Ammn Brigades R.F.A. with crews to their wagon lines went into action by withdrawing.	
June 9th.	84th and 102nd Ammn J.B. Brigades and 3 AMk Div arty withdrew to their wagon lines. The 26th Div arty went forward into position in the southern sector of the divisione by relieving villages of Reaumont in reserve, the Div arty being actually relieved by 162nd Div Artillery. Became an the move.	36th Divarty O.O. No 101.
June 10th.		
June 11th.	C.R.A. 11th Div. left and Command of the Force taken by 11th Div with batteries of 168th J.M. and 36th J.M. in 2 groups. 5.8.A. and 179 M Bties 5.9.A. 153 M Bties. O.C. 58th Bde — 95 Bde O.C. 59th Bde — 96 Bde	

Army Form C. 2118.

WAR DIARY
or
INTELLIGENCE SUMMARY.
(Erase heading not required.)

Instructions regarding War Diaries and Intelligence Summaries are contained in F. S. Regs., Part II. and the Staff Manual respectively. Title pages will be prepared in manuscript.

Hour, Date, Place	Summary of Events and Information	Remarks and references to Appendices
June 12th.	H.Q. 36 in Div wkg sevres. Beck & Mc Ivor Cappel.	
June 13		
to	No Change & nothing to report.	
June 18		
June 19th.	All batteries of 36° D.A. withdrew from action to forward Wagon Lines	
June 20.	H.Q. 36° Div. Arty: moved from ST. JANS CAPPEL to DRANOUTRE.	
June 21st	153 Bde. & 173 Bde.: also Nos: 1 & 2 Sections DAC. moved to rest in No. 16 Sub. area.	

WAR DIARY
or
INTELLIGENCE SUMMARY.
(Erase heading not required.)

Army Form C. 2118.

Hour, Date, Place	Summary of Events and Information	Remarks and references to Appendices
June 22nd	Nothing to report.	
June 23rd	Nothing to report.	
June 24th	36th D.A.C. marched from No.16 Sub. area to relieve 11th D.A.C. in the line. Relief completed by 6 p.m. 36th D.A.C. established at DRANOUTRE. 7th Bn attached to H.Q. 36th DAC & moved with them.	36th D.A. Order No. 102.
June 25th	Nothing to report.	
June 26th	CRA 36 DA took over Command of the Dale Artillery (11 DA and 16 DA) at 10 am HQ at LesLes Grands Trembles, covering the Brigades on 36 in Defence of the Line	

Army Form C. 2118.

WAR DIARY
or
INTELLIGENCE SUMMARY.
(Erase heading not required.)

Instructions regarding War Diaries and Intelligence Summaries are contained in F. S. Regs., Part II. and the Staff Manual respectively. Title pages will be prepared in manuscript.

Hour, Date, Place	Summary of Events and Information	Remarks and references to Appendices
June 26th	The 15 & 16 Batteries arrived up to strength abreast Q.P.A. 17 & 18 Batteries & Ammunition returning the 11th D.A.	30th D.A. O.O. No 103.
June 27th	Relief completed between the 11th and 36th D.A. Batteries.	
June 28th	Recent Crumble by 9 gun between the 16th and 15th Divisional artilleries in Loops Salient.	36th DA OO No104.
June 29th		
June 30th	The enemy continued to shell arras, without any retaliation. Counter battery work. Enemy aircraft became very active over our lines. No French relief has into the line as yet, position for defence has been accounted. On delivery of S.O.S 18p' and 12 6045" Hos counter from the expanded on the front, (50% at night) being remarkably active, both tracks and powder. Known to be held by the enemy.	

(7.3989) W41441—463. 400,000. 9/14. H.&J.Ltd. Forms/C. 2118/10.

Army Form C. 2118.

WAR DIARY
or
INTELLIGENCE SUMMARY.
(Erase heading not required.)

Instructions regarding War Diaries and Intelligence Summaries are contained in F.S. Regs., Part II. and the Staff Manual respectively. Title pages will be prepared in manuscript.

Hour, Date, Place	Summary of Events and Information	Remarks and references to Appendices
June 30th	The weather became unsettled with heavy rain; poor visibility. Very little valuable information up to date as to 676th has been used by the Enemy.	

H. J. Forsyth.
Brig Gen. RA
Comdg. 36 Divl Art.

1.7.17

Jly - Sep 1917
Missing

WAR DIARY / INTELLIGENCE SUMMARY

Army Form C. 2118
HQ RA 36
October '17. Vol 25

36th Div. Arty.

Place	Date	Hour	Summary of Events and Information	Remarks
YTRES to WOOD	1/10/17 to 5/10/17		In consequence of many batteries positions of the Bn Artillery being effectually engaged by hostile counter batteries work, night firing of 18/25's the month was carried out by s.g.b. guns at debited positions. Two of those guns were almost immediately engaged by the enemy & one destroyed. TM batteries engaged enemy trenches & strong points and also carried out wire cutting on 2nd & 3rd lines. Discharge of gas projectors on enemy from right front trench.	
YTRES to WOOD	6/10/17 to 10/10/17		Two minor raids carried out on Right Front front resulted in the capture of a prisoner on each occasion. The shell bombardment of RIBÉCOURT on the night of 9/10 and the concentration against canal bridges on 8th was not carried out in consequence of suspected relief of this line by 12th (?) Div area (MONCHY LE PREUX) on 5th inst.	

X/36 TM battery

Army Form C. 2118.

WAR DIARY
INTELLIGENCE SUMMARY
(Erase heading not required.)

36⁰ Div: Arty.   October 17

Place	Date	Hour	Summary of Events and Information	Remarks and references to Appendices
YPRES WOOD	8/10/17 to 10/10/17		Wire cutting by T.M.s were carried out on 6⁰ & 10⁰ belts & narrow bombardments on 7⁰ and 8⁰ C.s.	
	11/10/17 to 15/10/17		Hostile aircraft active throughout the period Batteries of the Divisional Artillery redistributed on 12⁰ inst — Tks 153 Bde. R.F.A. (from 1 the Right Group comprising 1 107 Inf. Bde & 1 R Bde = 108 Inf. Bde. Tks 173 Bde R.F.A. forming the Left Group covering 109 Inf. Bde & 1 R Bde = 108 Inf. Bde & 109 C. Inf. Bde. 1/136 T.M. Battery took part in 12⁰ Divisional flanks on night of MOORCHY - LE - PREUX on 14⁰ inst. covering indirect machine gun fire Silence ruled to from 36⁰ Divisional Artillery to next day night/day heymnt carried out nightly Our hostile H.Q. moved to YPRES on 13⁰ inst.	
YPRES	16/10/17 to 20/10/17		I.C. Corps Areas bombarded on 17⁰ inst. Groups Concentrations by Right Group in areas to enemy T.m. activity on B.E. & F.S.B. coy.	

WAR DIARY
INTELLIGENCE SUMMARY

36th Div. Artillery   October 1917

Place	Date	Hour	Summary of Events and Information	Remarks and references to Appendices
YTRES	16/10/17 to 24/10/17		Wire cutting by our T.M. batteries was carried out on 18th inst. Night firing & harassing continued. Hostile shelling was slight during the period.	
YTRES	24/10/17 to 25/10/17		Group Concentration by Right Group against K.27.d on 2.5 inst IV Corps Concentration on K.23.c.7.9 on 2 s.d. inst. Gas projectors fired from left group area against trenches west of HAVRINCOURT. Thermit Shell series against HAVRINCOURT Sugar factory gave apparently disappointing results. Our T.M. batteries did active trench mortar work cutting & bombarding enemy posts. As a result of enemy mine cutting 4 a shot round from 2/36 & 7/36 respectively, two of the T.M. personnel were killed. Night firing as usual. Hostile counter battery work slight.	

WAR DIARY
or
INTELLIGENCE SUMMARY.

(Erase heading not required.)

36th Div. Artillery   October

Army Form C. 2118.

Place	Date	Hour	Summary of Events and Information	Remarks and references to Appendices
YTRES	29/9/17 to 31/9/17		Hostile artillery more active. Chiefly against forward area. Minor Bombardment carried out by batteries of 6th Bde on 29th inst. Wire cutting by own T.M. batteries on 28th, 29th & 30th inst. Hostile dumps & posts also engaged. Night firing programmes Entered.	

H. J. Powell
Brig Gen R.A.
Cmdg 36th Div Art'y.

War Diary
of
C.R.A.
36th Division.

November 1917.

1/7 D of W

CRA
36 DIV
Vol 26

WAR DIARY or INTELLIGENCE SUMMARY

Army Form C. 2118.

Place	Date	Hour	Summary of Events and Information	Remarks and references to Appendices
Ypres.	1/4/17		The Like out about 6.30 am. Artillery officers and observed hill of documents & records accumulated since the Division came in, to the paper sent from Bde office. Hostile artillery active more however in forward areas. Battery positions at Q1.a.32 heavily shelled by 10.5 cm how later No casualties.	
	2/4/17		Quiet enemy rifle snipers Aeroplanes & communication trenches kept under fire accordingly. L.K.30.c & K.36. Hostile encounters have begun Enemy attempt to hold post lines at Q.4.a.S.6. repulsed — one machine frames left in hands.	
	3/4/17		Artillery patrolled same by 3 3 46 20 & 74. OCA never lost horse who when enemy's P2 plan L.K.26.d. Box barrage busted 30 mins. Raid successful Infantry heavy casualties on enemy. 64 mass communicating trenches lyric.	

Army Form C. 2118.

WAR DIARY
or
INTELLIGENCE SUMMARY.
(Erase heading not required.)

Instructions regarding War Diaries and Intelligence Summaries are contained in F. S. Regs., Part II. and the Staff Manual respectively. Title pages will be prepared in manuscript.

Place	Date	Hour	Summary of Events and Information	Remarks and references to Appendices
YTRES	5/11/17		36 D.A.C. and 153rd Bde began busy Sunday in accordance with conditions normal. Usual programme of fire carried out & cups concentration from 10.15 a.m. on Enemy roads in HAVRINCOURT. Enemy's artillery quiet. Night tranquil.	36 D.A. Order No 134.
	6/11/17		Marked increase in hostile artillery activity — especially on forward area during the night.	
	7/11/17 to 9/11/17		Calibration shots carried out by 153 Bde in conjunction with 3rd Field Survey Company R.E. Results satisfactory.	
	10/11/17 to 12/11/17		Hostile artillery normal. Observation difficult owing to weather. Front quiet. Our T.M.s carried out important wire cutting shoots on K 20 C and have accurately & vigorously pushed hostile batteries.	
	13/11/17		F.A. received by C/153's position in Q 21 A Pilot was taken prisoner & machine removed by R.F.C. Pilot Plts7a to come from LAON, had lost his way in the mist & thought he had landed behind his own lines.	

Army Form C. 2118.

WAR DIARY
or
INTELLIGENCE SUMMARY.
(Erase heading not required.)

Place	Date	Hour	Summary of Events and Information	Remarks and references to Appendices
YTRES[?]	14/11/17		Preparations for an offensive with an extensive objective were hurried on. Within these limits forward battery positions were prepared for 173 Bgde in J30, J24 & J26* & for 280 Bgde RFA in DEMICOURT. Ammunition was cut down to a minimum in every precaution taken to hide activity. Ammunition was brought up by night - 700 rds. for gun for 18 pdrs and 450 rds. for 4.5" howitzers - including a proportion of smoke shell in both cases. Preparations were rendered of the easier to carry out by reason of the misty weather. The normal procedure of French battery meanwhile was maintained except that a limited amount of wire was cut at K.20.c. 5.9. by 18 pdrs and considerable gaps & lanes cut in wire in vicinity of the 6" Trench Mortars manning motor stations during the first phase of the offensive. Survey the wire in rear of the 62nd Divn and carried out protection between these chalks under the direction of this Division. Began being issued and to be published on the night of the 18th this re-stirring the battery moves	* Should be K26. 26 Div arty order No 1 36 Div Arty order No 2

WAR DIARY or INTELLIGENCE SUMMARY

Army Form C. 2118.

Place	Date	Hour	Summary of Events and Information	Remarks and references to Appendices
YPRES	14/11/17 19/11/17		Lt. Col. Hoskin and the remaining section of Mines in the night of the 19th showed no signs of supersession occupied their pepupation position of the 19th Inst under the care of a heavy barrage he moved on Frezen Berg dug in and Henry Fork O.R.S. were in the vicinity of J64a. There men belonged to the 1st R.I.F. a Battalion which normally should have moved up to the rest of the division to the rear division at know of the Canal. In addition I sent an occurrence pour a battalion of the Battalion had remained behind to man the outpost line and consequently the enemy's suspicions were not aroused by the identification of this new unit in this sector. In front preparation for the next days operation Lt. Col. Simpson D.S.O. moved to the Brigade H.Q. of the 109th Infantry Brigade at K.2.d.2.0. in the afternoon of the 19th and all telephone wires were laid to and from Brigade H.Q. but no scheme either from to Bde.	A. G. G. M. G. S. A. Shoone, 8.16 Runck A.L.R.G.A.R.G.A. (6/11.E.3.113) (O/C 156 HB) reported as H.A. Liaison Officer.

Army Form C. 2118.

WAR DIARY
or
INTELLIGENCE SUMMARY.
(Erase heading not required.)

Place	Date	Hour	Summary of Events and Information	Remarks and references to Appendices
YPRES	20/11		During the night & early morning the enemy phones increased artillery activity. The 173 Bgde had a gun and suffer a few casualties but as the whole of our new dispositions were complete before the shelling commenced no great inconvenience was caused. The 109 hy. Bgde was the pre divisional artillery. Bryan and handed its attack at 9.15am (Zero + 17.5) at the SPOIL HEAP in K20. The artillery covering the Brigade consisted of the 2/80 Bgde R.F.A. and the 173 Bgde R.F.A. + the 93 Army Bde R.F.A. The attack proceeded rapidly — the SPOILHEAP was quickly possessed and the trenches north westof the canal were cleaned up as far north as the	

WAR DIARY or INTELLIGENCE SUMMARY

Army Form C. 2118.

Place	Date 1917	Hour	Summary of Events and Information	Remarks and references to Appendices
YTRES	20/11		Pickets were during E.9.7.0. between E.26.a. & E.26.c. & E.26.b. where well known to T.C.B.'s had mid the 169 & Brigade on the left.	
			At 6 pm the 9 3rd Army Brigade R.J.A. moved to positions N.E. of HAPLINCOURT (K.27.C) ¼ ready to advance further next morning.	
			At 8.30 pm the 169 Brigade were ready & were ordered to move and held the command operations in K.8. & to be followed by the 170 Brigade. R.J.H.A. Batteries to be in action by dawn.	
	21/11		Brigades moved to their positions & with great difficulty owing to congestion of traffic and bad unstamped tracks. The 169 Brigade was held up by the 168th Brigade Infantry in the town with H.Q. at K.7.d.20. Close liaison was kept on our Rt close by the 3rd B.H. Brigade R.J.H. to keep in touch the begn to harass the K.A.C. Battery to be in action by 7.30 am but the foul weather nevertheless made the advance very difficult Communications with these Brigades & across very	

WAR DIARY
or
INTELLIGENCE SUMMARY.
(Erase heading not required.)

Army Form C. 2118.

Instructions regarding War Diaries and Intelligence Summaries are contained in F. S. Regs., Part II and the Staff Manual respectively. Title pages will be prepared in manuscript.

Place	Date 1917	Hour	Summary of Events and Information	Remarks and references to Appendices
YPRES	22/11		The 90th Brigade moved in relief	3(D.A. orders No 3,4,5, 6.
		11 a.m.	at 11 a.m. the 107th and 102nd Brigades renewed the attack supported by the Field artillery Brigades & a certain number of heavy artillery batteries. On the east bank of the Canal very little progress was made, on the west bank, MOEUVRES was captured but very stubborn battles in the day by the enemy.
			The resistance of the enemy stiffened considerably during the day.
	23/11		attacks were renewed by both Infantry Brigades. The 107th Bde M.G. Coy was hotly engaged by 12 tanks. neither attack gained much ground. Hostile artillery increased considerably during the day
			The 93rd Army Brigade relieved on two nights & the heavy G. forthcoming
			in K 15
			156th H Battery moved through A.N. Road Placed and then 2, 7 & 8 in S Batteries G.R.A. + 96 Div to F.O.O. and opened counterbattery support of the attack and were known as the ULSTER H.A.G.

A5534 Wt W4973/M687 750,000 8.16 D.D. & L. Ltd. Forms/C.2118/13.

WAR DIARY
or
INTELLIGENCE SUMMARY.
(Erase heading not required.)

Army Form C. 2118.

Place	Date	Hour	Summary of Events and Information	Remarks and references to Appendices
	23/11		H.Q. of this group were established at K 25 a 3.0.	
	24/11		The 109th Inf Bde. relieved the 108th Inf Bde. Fire was directed during the day on points where the enemy were reported massing for counter attacks, and help was rendered the division on the right who were counter attacked. Several runs for BOURLON VILLAGE and QUARRY WOOD passed thro' positions in BOURLONWOOD itself. The 107th Bgde. arranged & carry out an attack on the trenches in E15c and d and a bombardment and fire was carried out. Though the whole of the heavy artillery shells to Cover left flanks prep. firing to perimeter Curler attacked, rolling place up the line to both flanks in consequence the attack was not carried through.	36 D.H. orders not circulated No 10.

A 8831 Wt W4073/M687 750,000 8/16 D.D. & L. Ltd Forms/C.2118/13

Army Form C. 2118.

WAR DIARY
or
INTELLIGENCE SUMMARY.
(Erase heading not required.)

Instructions regarding War Diaries and Intelligence Summaries are contained in F. S. Regs., Part II. and the Staff Manual respectively. Title pages will be prepared in manuscript.

Place	Date 1914	Hour	Summary of Events and Information	Remarks and references to Appendices
YPRES	25/11		A Quiet day. The Division on our left has ordered attacks in the vicinity of POLYGON COPSE, and left the move by other on the left flank.	
	26/11		The Divisional artillery handed over to 2nd Division and Headquarters ceased to function. The organisation of the artillery before handing over was as follows:— Right Grp. Lieut. Col. STILLWELL R.H.A. 9 & 2 Army Brigades R.H.A. 17, 18 P Battery 1st Siege Bee R.G.A. 1 4.5" How. Battery 13th 2nd R.F.A. R.F.A. Left Grp. Lieut. Col. Simpson D.S.O. R.F.A. 17 3rd Bee R.F.A. 11/2 Batteries (16pr) 153rd 1st Bee R.F.A.	36 Dwa g for No 11. Crossing the Right attached to 13 Brigade Crossing the left Uh Infy Brigade

Army Form C. 2118.

WAR DIARY
or
INTELLIGENCE SUMMARY.
(Erase heading not required.)

Place	Date	Hour	Summary of Events and Information	Remarks and references to Appendices
LITTLE WOOD YPRES	29/11 to 30/11		Delivered R.A.H.Q. established near LITTLE WOOD, YPRES	

H.J. Moore
Major for RA
Comd. 36 - Div - Arty
12-12-17

WAR DIARY or INTELLIGENCE SUMMARY

Army Form C. 2118.

December 1917

Headquarters 36th Div Artillery

Place	Date	Hour	Summary of Events and Information	Remarks and references to Appendices
YPRES	1/12 to 5/12		36 D.A. H.Q. remained at YPRES, LITTLE WOOD R.E. CAMP. Wiring continuing. Prisoners taken are 108th and 109th Infantry Regts. put into the line S.W. of PASSCHENDAELE under the orders of the 6th and 61st Divisions respectively, were relieved by 3rd Corps. On the night of 7/8th December command of these Brigades passed to the G.O.C. 36th Division.	
			At the same time command of the artillery covering the front held by these Brigades should have passed to the B.G.R.A. 36th Div, but owing to lack of communication from the New Zealanders	
SOREL LE GRAND (R.H.N)			command did not pass from the C.R.A. of neighbouring divisions till Tuesday the 8th December.	
			The artillery taken over consisted of the 17th Bde R.F.A. 5th Army Bde R.H.A. 150th Army Bde R.F.A. 232nd Army Bde R.F.A.	Lieut Col Murray DSO R.F.A. Lieut Col West DSO R.H.A. Lieut Col Dickson DSO R.F.A. Lieut Col Graham CMG R.F.A.

Army Form C. 2118.

WAR DIARY
or
INTELLIGENCE SUMMARY.
(Erase heading not required.)

Place	Date	Hour	Summary of Events and Information	Remarks and references to Appendices
CORRIE 5 to 9 D	9/12		The artillery war proper according to the attached orders, in companies, each covering one of the Infantry Brigades holding the Front.	36 D.A. orders No 12 and 13
			The 267th Brigade R.F.A. (less OC's division) took over from the 15th A.M. A.D.A. order on 9/12 9.30 p.m. December and the 15th Bde Arty A.D.A. transferred to the 9th Division (Guns being exchanged).	36 DA ordr No 14
	10/12		A 60th Battery R.F.A. (Army Artillery) came under orders of C.R.A. 36 Div.	
			The 61st Division (Army artillery) relieved by 15th Div (Army artillery) on the left flks 36th Division	
	10/12		"O" Battery formed two reliefs by 402nd Battery R.F.A. personnel in the line 25th December and marched to the 3rd Army artillery school on 14th December.	

WAR DIARY or INTELLIGENCE SUMMARY

Army Form C. 2118.

Place	Date	Hour	Summary of Events and Information	Remarks and references to Appendices
SORRL 26 S2 N.W	14/12		The personnel of 173rd Bde R.F.A. (with 61st Div) exchanged with the personnel of 308 Bde R.F.A. (with 36th Div)	36 D.A. orders No. 15 and 16.
			The personnel of 153rd Bde R.F.A. (with 61st Div) exchanged with the personnel of 17th Bde R.F.A. (with 36th Div)	
			and the artillery arms then regrouped as follows —	
			Right Group under Lieut Col H. Simpson D.S.O. R.F.A.	
			H.Q. Q.12.a.2.6.	
			173rd Bde R.F.A.	
			232 " " "	
			462 " Battery R.F.A.	
			Left Group under Lieut Col E.J. Phillips D.S.O. R.F.A.	
			H.Q. K.30.d.11.	
			153rd Bde R.F.A.	
			2 Batteries @ 17 R.F.A.	
			462nd Battery R.F.A.	
			Both Groups covering and Infantry Brigade in the line.	

Army Form C. 2118.

WAR DIARY
or
INTELLIGENCE SUMMARY.
(Erase heading not required.)

Instructions regarding War Diaries and Intelligence Summaries are contained in F.S. Regs., Part II. and the Staff Manual respectively. Title pages will be prepared in manuscript.

Place	Date	Hour	Summary of Events and Information	Remarks and references to Appendices
SOREL LE GRAND	15/12		The 36th Division was transferred to the 5th Corps. In expectation of a relief by the 9th German Reserve Division just North of La Vacquerie, an increased programme of harassing was carried out on roads and tracks and assembly places.	
	16/12		63rd Div'n Infantry relieved the 36th Div'n Infantry on the night 15/16 +16/17	
	17/12		63rd H.Q. 63rd Division moved to LITTLE WOOD Camp YTRES and H.Q. 36 J.H. were situated at LITTLE WOOD R.E. Camp P.25.b.8.6. Command passed from G.O.C. 36th Div to G.O.C. 63rd Division at noon 17/12/17	
	20/12		The 63rd Division extended its right, relieving the 2nd Division and the relieving evening the portion of the line then over 1½ Bn 306th Bde 2m 179 R Bde R.T.M. were transferred to the Command of the C.R.A. 63rd Division and the artillery were again regrouped.	36 D.A.O No 17.

Army Form C. 2118.

WAR DIARY
or
INTELLIGENCE SUMMARY.
(Erase heading not required.)

Instructions regarding War Diaries and Intelligence Summaries are contained in F.S. Regs., Part II. and the Staff Manual respectively. Title pages will be prepared in manuscript.

Place	Date	Hour	Summary of Events and Information	Remarks and references to Appendices
LITTLE WOOD R.E. CAMP YPRES.	22/12		The 63rd Division extended its right and took over the remainder of the front held by the 61st Division. The artillery covering the front was increased by the 97th Army Bde R.F.A. 298th Army Field R.F.A. which had come into action under orders of the C.R.A. 61st Division prior to the relief. The line was then held by 3 Infantry Brigades, and the artillery was regrouped into 2 groups each covering a Brigade in the line	36 D.A. order No 18.
	25/12		A/D.C. Battalion 308 Bde R.F.A. came under the Command of the C.R.A. 61st Division	36 D.A. order No 19

Army Form C. 2118.

WAR DIARY
or
INTELLIGENCE SUMMARY.
(Erase heading not required.)

Place	Date	Hour	Summary of Events and Information	Remarks and references to Appendices
LITTLE WOOD R.E. CMPD YPRES			Throughout the above period, no offensive operations were undertaken by the Enemy, and away by our own infantry were carried out for the purpose of straightening our front line of the line, without artillery support. Enemy's counter battery work was not great and was confined mainly to the shelling of areas, but round BOAR COPSE (P 6 c) receiving most attention. Our artillery carried out harassing fire programmes by day and night each for battery firing an average of 125 rounds for 24 hours 1/5% at night and an average of 200 rounds per 24 hours 15/% at night. S.O.S. of 4" How battery firing	

Army Form C. 2118.

WAR DIARY
or
INTELLIGENCE SUMMARY.
(Erase heading not required.)

Instructions regarding War Diaries and Intelligence Summaries are contained in F. S. Regs., Part II. and the Staff Manual respectively. Title pages will be prepared in manuscript.

Place	Date	Hour	Summary of Events and Information	Remarks and references to Appendices
LITTLE WOOD RE CAMP YPRES	23/12		The 26th Divisional artillery was relieved by the 63rd (RN) Divisional artillery on the evening of 23rd and morning of 24th December. Guns being exchanged. Staffords. Ammunition passed to the CRA 63rd Div at 1 pm on 24th December.	
	26/12		Brigades and BHQ. on relieved marched via their respective to the BEAULENCOURT Staging area. The T.M. Battalion preceded by train direct to rest billets at HAMELET (near CORBIE)	
	27/12		Owing to the bad roads (blocked with snow) and congestion of traffic caused by other artillery moving, the 26th Divisional artillery bivouaced at BEAULENCOURT for this date.	

4.1.18

H. J. Brock
Cmd'g 26. Div: Art: Brig Gen RA.

Army Form C. 2118.

WAR DIARY
INTELLIGENCE SUMMARY.
(Erase heading not required.)

H.Q. 36th Div. Artillery

Vol 25

Instructions regarding War Diaries and Intelligence Summaries are contained in F. S. Regs., Part II. and the Staff Manual respectively. Title pages will be prepared in manuscript.

Place	Date	Hour	Summary of Events and Information	Remarks and references to Appendices
TREUX	1/4/18		The 36 Div Arty. moved from billets at BEAULENCOURT to TREUX area and were attached to XVIII Corps.	36 Div A.Ty. note No 22
CORBIE	2/4/18 to 6/4/18		The 36 Div. Arty. moved from the TREUX area to the CORBIE area. 153 + 173 Bgdes were billeted at HAMEL. 36 DAC at VAIRE. Div. Arty. H.Q. at CORBIE. This area was found quite unsuitable for artillery at rest - the billets were bad and watery [insanitary] in a degree.	36 Div A.Ty. note No 23
QUESNEL	7/4/18 to 11/4/18		The 36 Div A.Ty marched from CORBIE area to the QUESNEL area. Brigades + DAC see gained a great billets as follows:- 153 Bgde at HANGEST, 173 Bgde at QUESNEL and 36 DAC at HANGEST. Trench Mortar [personnel] (who rejoined the Divisional Artillery at CORBIE) at QUESNEL. 36 Div. A.Ty. HQ at Maison + QUESNEL	36 Div. Artillery Note No 24

Army Form C. 2118.

WAR DIARY
or
INTELLIGENCE SUMMARY.
(Erase heading not required.)

Place	Date	Hour	Summary of Events and Information	Remarks and references to Appendices
ROYE.	11/1/18 to 12/1/18		The 36 Div. Arty. marched from the billets at QUESNEL & HANGEST to the ROYE area. Brigades & Battery Commanders were taken round the front area opposite ST QUENTIN and reconnoitred the positions they were to occupy in the line returning to ROYE the same evening. The 36 Div. Arty. marched from the ROYE area to the French area where billets in accordance with attached artillery order N⁰ 27.	36 Div Arty order N⁰ 25. 36 Div Arty order N⁰ 27.
NESLE.	13/1/18		36 Div. Ark H.Q. remains at NESLE pending former taking over from 6th French Divisional Artillery to which meanwhile the artillery was attached. The 36 Div. Arty was reinforced by the 14th Army Field Bgde. and a Brigade of St John's S.O. One gun per battery was sent over the line relieving one gun per battery of the 6th French Divisional Artillery.	

WAR DIARY
or
INTELLIGENCE SUMMARY.
(Erase heading not required.)

Army Form C. 2118.

Place	Date	Hour	Summary of Events and Information	Remarks and references to Appendices
NESLE	14/1/18		The scheme put out in 36 Divisional Artillery order No 26 was complete & the Brigades were standing to take today in the frames until the arrival of the 6th Divisional (Heavy) Artillery. Infantry relays had already been completed and the line was being held by the 109 Infantry Bgde on the right and the 107 Infantry Bgde on the left. The Artillery was divided into Right & left group covering the Infantry Bgdes respectively. The right group consisting of 173 Bgde RFA & A+B batteries 14th Army Field Bgde under the command of Major Emerson. The left group consisting of 153 Bgde RFA & C batt'y 14th Army Field Bgde under the command of Major Collins M.C.	36 Divl Arty order No 26
OLLEZY	15/1/18 16/1/18		36 Divl Arty HQ marched from NESLE & occupied HQ of 6th French Divisional H.Q. at OLLEZY. Colonel de MIRIBEL & the staff of the French Division remained to give assistance until evening of 16th Jany. Command passed to B.G. R.A. 36 Division at 6 p.m. on the 15th inst.	

Army Form C. 2118.

WAR DIARY
or
INTELLIGENCE SUMMARY.
(Erase heading not required.)

Instructions regarding War Diaries and Intelligence Summaries are contained in F. S. Regs., Part II. and the Staff Manual respectively. Title pages will be prepared in manuscript.

Place	Date	Hour	Summary of Events and Information	Remarks and references to Appendices
OLLEZY	17/1/18 to 19/1/18		The policy of the XVIII Corps having been announced as mainly a defence one for the time being, very little activity was shown by the batteries. Guns were registered S.O.S lines carefully worked out & checked, and calibration proceeded with. Attention however was mainly directed towards improving battery positions, building alternate & reinforcing positions and perfecting O.P.s. The command Officer of the 14 A.F.A. Bgde, whose headquarters was at SERAUCOURT LE GRAND, was appointed to reconnoitre positions to cover the Battle Zone — a term employing a new system of country immediately in defence upon which the line might have to fall back in the event of an attack. S.O.S lines inclusive [?]system & comd. preparation arrangements were worked out & telephone communications adapted to suit the new groupings.	

WAR DIARY
or
INTELLIGENCE SUMMARY.

Army Form C. 2118.

Place	Date	Hour	Summary of Events and Information	Remarks and references to Appendices
OLLEZY	20/1/18 & 21/1/18		The situation remained very quiet. Hostile artillery was inactive & for except for one shooting on our forward trench systems. Hostile aircraft however, were continually crossing the line. Battline continued to report & calibrate & hostility & digging was habitual. Two 18 pdr Anti-tank guns sent from 179 Army Field Bgde were put into temporary positions at A.12.a.7.4 & B.14.c.4.7. — detachments being alongside in dug-outs. The D.T.M.O. was asked to take over these Anti tank guns & the Tank defences in the area.	
	22/1/18		At 9 pm a report reached Bge H.Q. that the enemy had effected a patrol raid on our line & were seen in trenches at the point of junction of the two infantry Bgdes. S.O.S lines were fired but at 9.30pm the situation was reported normal. It subsequently appeared that there had been much enemy patrol activity during the evening that an encounter had taken place & that no NCO & one officer were missing — but that no decent raid had been attempted	

Army Form C. 2118.

WAR DIARY
or
INTELLIGENCE SUMMARY.
(Erase heading not required.)

Instructions regarding War Diaries and Intelligence Summaries are contained in F. S. Regs., Part II. and the Staff Manual respectively. Title pages will be prepared in manuscript.

Place	Date	Hour	Summary of Events and Information	Remarks and references to Appendices
OLLEZY	23/1/18		Situation very quiet. New anti-tank position recommended & selected at B.22.a.22 & B.13.d.5.3. & S.7.n.0 orders to construct the emplacement.	
	24/1/18 25/1/18 26/1/18		Situation very quiet. Enemy throwing away heavy day mist's remaining. Weather improved. Work proceeded on battery position & O.P.	
	27/1/18		The 193 Labour Coy. was lent to the Divisional Artillery to assist in battery position. They are billetted at GRAND SERAUCOURT. S.O.S. rockets were tried out at SERAUCOURT LE GRAND with a view to testing the range of visibility & were found satisfactory.	

Army Form C. 2118.

WAR DIARY
or
INTELLIGENCE SUMMARY.
(Erase heading not required.)

Instructions regarding War Diaries and Intelligence Summaries are contained in F. S. Regs., Part II. and the Staff Manual respectively. Title pages will be prepared in manuscript.

Place	Date	Hour	Summary of Events and Information	Remarks and references to Appendices
OLLEZY	28/1/18 to 31/1/18		Situation remained quiet. On the 28th & 29th this enemy aeroplane formations came over lines & bombed HAM & villages in the vicinity including OLLEZY. The days were misty & on billets remained for the most part in check.	

J.C.B.
Lt. Col. R.F.A.
Commanding 36 Divisional Artillery

WAR DIARY or INTELLIGENCE SUMMARY.

Army Form C. 2118.

36th Div Artillery XVIII Corps Fifth Army

Place	Date	Hour	Summary of Events and Information	Remarks and references to Appendices
OLLEZY	1/2/18		In accordance with XVIII Corps Artillery Instructions, the Divisional Artillery adopted a defensive attitude, and work on positions took precedence of everything else. No harassing fire was carried out & no barrages were fired during the month. Towards the middle of the month Officers Observing Parties became so frequent in LE PIRE ALLER sector that special orders were issued that they were to be fired on. For purposes of defence the front was divided into three Zones. (1) The Forward Zone (consisting of the enemy's system of trenches, 1000 yards in depth) (2) The line of Redoubts or Strong Points (1500 yards in rear of the Forward Zone) (3) The Battle Zone (2000 yards in rear of the Strong Point Line and about 1200 yards in depth). Each Battery in the Forward Zone had orders to build an Alternative and a Reciprocal position, and at the same time	Ref MAP FRANCE 66cNW Ed 3.A. 1:20000 66 D.IVE Ed.2. 1:20000 ST. QUENTIN 1:100,000.

Army Form C. 2118.

WAR DIARY
or
INTELLIGENCE SUMMARY.
(Erase heading not required.)

Instructions regarding War Diaries and Intelligence Summaries are contained in F. S. Regs., Part II. and the Staff Manual respectively. Title pages will be prepared in manuscript.

Place	Date	Hour	Summary of Events and Information	Remarks and references to Appendices
OZZEZY	1/2/18		Positions had to be consolidated for the defence of the Battle Zone, in the land masses. Three Rifle O.P's had to be constructed inside the strong point defences for the forward zone and also for the Battle Zone. Two anti tank positions for the Lg. & 18pr. guns were also constructed.	
	6.14. 2.18.		Registration and calibration been carried out by all batteries. The hostile artillery activity has no object. No destructive shoots were carried out by either side during this period. Enemy aircraft displayed considerable activity whenever there was good visibility – but nowhere were they troubled any higher	
	15.2.18 – 17.2.18		The 14th Army Brigade R.F.A. was relieved in the line by the 179th Army Brigade R.F.A. on the nights 15/16 and 16/17. Lieut Col EBEY CMG DSO MC took over the duty of Superintendency work in the Battle Zone from Lieut Col M JOHN DSO MC	36 D A order No 29

A 5834. Wt. W4973/M687. 750,000 8/16 D. D. & L. Ltd. Forms/C.2118/13.

WAR DIARY
or
INTELLIGENCE SUMMARY.

Army Form C. 2118.

Place	Date	Hour	Summary of Events and Information	Remarks and references to Appendices
OLLEZY	1918			
	19.2. – 21.2		153rd Bde R.F.A. was relieved on the night 19/20 and 20/21 by 148th Bde R.F.A. 30th Div. proceeding to concentration area south of the 30th Division North of the River SOMME.) Taking over from Bde 26th Division thence British 92nd line held by them 152nd Brigade R.F.A. reverted to 2nd half at OFFOY and became "A" Reinforcing Brigade.	30 D.A. O. No 30
	22.2		D.232 Brigade R.F.A. was placed temporarily under the Command of the C.R.A. 36 Division and came into action in position 21/22 at A.21.d.8.3 in the anti-tank rôle. The 467 to battery 179 A.Bde R.F.A. forming the xiiith Corps Group, the remaining Batteries (see 18/2) being in the line for immediate defence	
	23.2.		at 6.0 am on 23rd Inst. the 30th Division took over the S.W. of the 36th Divisional front from the ST QUENTIN CANAL	

Army Form C. 2118.

WAR DIARY
or
INTELLIGENCE SUMMARY.
(Erase heading not required.)

Instructions regarding War Diaries and Intelligence Summaries are contained in F. S. Regs., Part II. and the Staff Manual respectively. Title pages will be prepared in manuscript.

Place	Date 1918	Hour	Summary of Events and Information	Remarks and references to Appendices
OUESSY	2.3.2		The 36th Divisional Front then extended from B 17 c 8 2 to the Canal exclusive and was held by 3 Infantry Brigades each with one Battalion in the Front Zone, one Battalion in the Battle Zone, and one Battalion in Reserve. The Divisional artillery was divided into two Groups, each with S.O.S. lines, rouline support zone, and counter attack areas, arranged in accordance with the standard rules.	36 D.A. Order No 32
			During this period the hostile artillery was slightly more active and his counter battery shoots were carried out against our field batteries, without causing damage.	
	28.2	at about 11 am. "A" Recuperating Bigade (no 86th R.F.A.) received the order "Prepare for attack". They moved up to their allotted positions in the Battle Zone, with one section per battery forward to assist in the defence of the line of strong points	

H. R. Buck
BRIG-GENERAL R.A.
Comd'g 36th Divisional Artillery

36th Divisional Artillery.

C. R. A.

36th DIVISION

MARCH 1918

Appendices attached:-
    Narrative of Operations 21st-31st March.
    Artillery Orders.

WAR DIARY or INTELLIGENCE SUMMARY

Army Form C. 2118.

H.Q. 36th Div. Artillery

Instructions regarding War Diaries and Intelligence Summaries are contained in F.S. Regs., Part II. and the Staff Manual respectively. Title pages will be prepared in manuscript.

(Erase heading not required.)

Place	Date	Hour	Summary of Events and Information	Remarks and references to Appendices
HLEZY	March 1st		Final arrangements were made for the defence of the line in expectation of an enemy attack on March 2nd. Special barrages were ordered to be put down in the event of the enemy penetrating the front line of resistance. At 8.30 p.m. during a heavy T.M. Bombardment/Training on the 14th Division front, the enemy evinced about half to the right defended by trigale & Captured line forwarks.	Reference Major Form G.B.C. 11/4000 McBardin 11/10000 AMIENS " BEAUVAIS "
	March 2nd		The situation remained quiet on the front.	
	March 3rd		A vigorous ship of harassing fire was ordered by XXII Corps by night and day. Single teams were put out to do harassing fire throughout the night, (entirely changing position). Barrels of fire were carried out by Groups (one Brigade per night) and Troops laid down by XXII Corps. The sun most artillery covered in Those shoots.	
	March 4th		Concentrations were drawn up for each Group — All available fires and Howitzer Battery parts / Enemy Battery were seemingly active in the light Group Sector Special once engaged promptly by artillery fire.	

A5834 Wt.W4973/M687 750,000 8/16 D. D. & L. Ltd. Forms/C.2118/13.

WAR DIARY
or
INTELLIGENCE SUMMARY

Army Form C. 2118.

(Erase heading not required.)

Instructions regarding War Diaries and Intelligence Summaries are contained in F. S. Regs., Part II. and the Staff Manual respectively. Title pages will be prepared in manuscript.

Place	Date	Hour	Summary of Events and Information	Remarks and references to Appendices
OMEZY	March 4th		Apparently the enemy believe that the French system had been evacuated, prisoners captured think, stating they had orders to verify them, & occupy the trenches if empty.	
	March 5th & March 11th		The front remained quiet — and nothing unusual occurred. Remained in Battle Zone position to work wire entrusted in Battle Zone Positions and O.P.S with all available labour. Defensive preparations were continued and a mobile defence scheme was carried across a training in Anti-Tank defence was stable at the artillery horse at ROYE and extended entrenchments were fought for a 4 days course of instruction.	
	March 12th & March 16th		The front remained quiet — the enemy's artillery making very little reply to our harassing fire and daily bombardment programmes. Special bomb of fire at times laid down by XVIII Corps were carried out every morning between 4 am & 7 am.	

Army Form C. 2118.

WAR DIARY
or
INTELLIGENCE SUMMARY.
(Erase heading not required.)

Instructions regarding War Diaries and Intelligence Summaries are contained in F. S. Regs., Part II. and the Staff Manual respectively. Title pages will be prepared in manuscript.

Place	Date	Hour	Summary of Events and Information	Remarks and references to Appendices
OLLEZY	March 17th		In consequence of the report from the V Corps that 4 enemy were shelling, further stringent measures were issued as a matter of precaution. Gloves were issued to the men. Of the Lewis & rifle men, anti-gas outfits etc as far as obtainable were procured. Certain batteries which we could not move out of the shelling belt in present positions were placed about 3000 back to alternative positions in present position in rear, on the nights 17/8/18th.	
			C/173 to 13de R to 6 F9. G6c60.00	
			D/173 to B26 R.M. 6 22. G46 30 vs	
			J22 to A Bee R24 to F24 A28 c 25 11	
	March 18th		Information received from a deserter, and several reinforcements, being revealed the presence of a large number of French motor transports to the enemy lines. The days bombardments were directed on to Maine & 4.5" Howitzer were returned to keep up continuous fire on certain areas containing	

A5834 Wt.W4973/M587 750,000 8/16 D.D.&L. Ltd. Forms/C.2118/13.

Army Form C. 2118.

WAR DIARY
or
INTELLIGENCE SUMMARY.
(Erase heading not required.)

Instructions regarding War Diaries and Intelligence Summaries are contained in F. S. Regs., Part II. and the Staff Manual respectively. Title pages will be prepared in manuscript.

Place	Date	Hour	Summary of Events and Information	Remarks and references to Appendices
OLLEZY	March 19th		There enforcements here contracted to us & amongst these certain a certain number of Diphtheria were caused by not brought parents. him be also being cut by 4.5" Hows until reported two received from deserters that they had arrived by a Pipe hole in their come by not his them in view of put these information of an impending offensive. Wire cutting was discontinued. Deserters stated that the enemy attack would take place on the morning of the 21st. turned to forward to forward fyre balloon barrel change. At 8.30pm a barrage was put down by 2 machineguns on our front searching certain another likely to be used as assembly of type places. 8.15 Sn R Sn turned 1 pm back to F10 A77a 58.55 a63 2d Battery moved 2 guns back to F27 A20 6 12.14.	

Army Form C. 2118.

WAR DIARY
or
INTELLIGENCE SUMMARY.
(Erase heading not required.)

Instructions regarding War Diaries and Intelligence Summaries are contained in F.S. Regs., Part II. and the Staff Manual respectively. Title pages will be prepared in manuscript.

Place	Date	Hour	Summary of Events and Information	Remarks and references to Appendices
OVILLERS	March 26th	4.30 am	a 15 minute bombardment was again carried out on a selected area (part of a Coy bombardment scheme) by all available guns.	
		10 pm	A similar bombardment to do similar was carried out during a raid further north by the 61st Division. This short bombardment the idea of an attack immediately impending, than the 4 different enemy divisions being found in the Trenches all preparations had been made observations looked not to the Divisional artillery. (including the Trench mortars of Inf'd groups) on the assumption that the enemy will attack, all however with a bombardment of some hours after his barrage on R. Time covered their Counter Prep task to zero positions after 10.30 pm as follows —	

B Tns Brigade D M to A27 a 58 35
C " " to B 56 60 00 } our subaltern having been wise
D " " to B 54 6 30 50   on ground.
463 c B5 # m
6 A20 b 12 14

WAR DIARY
or
INTELLIGENCE SUMMARY.

Army Form C. 2118.

Place	Date	Hour	Summary of Events and Information	Remarks and references to Appendices
05770	MARCH 21st		The German attack commenced —	
			A narrative of operations up to the 31st March	
			See APPENDIX A attached.	

22.4.18.

H.J. Brock
Brig. Genl. R.A.
Comd'g 36th Divl Artillery.

Colonel POTTER, D.S.O., R.F.A.,
Colonel ELEY, C.M.G., D.S.O., R.F.A.,
Colonel ERSKINE, D.S.O., R.F.A.,

The 36th Divisional Artillery will be divided into Groups as under :
CENTRE GROUP, under Colonel POTTER, D.S.O., R.F.A.,
    383rd Battery R.F.A.,
    D/91st Brigade R.F.A.,
    B/153rd "
    A/153rd "
    D/173rd "

LEFT GROUP, under Colonel ELEY, C.M.G., D.S.O., R.F.A.,
    463rd Battery R.F.A.,
    C/153rd Brigade R.F.A.,
    D/232nd Brigade R.F.A.,
    D/153rd "
    464th Battery R.F.A.,
    B/91st Brigade R.F.A.,

These Groups will take up positions forthwith to cover the Divisional Front, which will extend to FONTAINE LES CLERCS in the North to RIVER at L.16.c. in the South.
The CENTRE Group will take up positions at L.14.a. and c. and
The LEFT Group will take up positions at L.8.a., L.2.c. and a.

These positions will be reconnoitred at once under orders of the Group Commanders.
Batteries on the East of the River will cross by TUGNY BRIDGE at once.
The D.A.C., will move to the Railway Crossing at K.10.c.6.2. and Battery Wagon Lines will refill at this position, Battery Echelons can fill up when crossing the river at TUGNY with 18-pr. ammunition or at ST. SIMON Dump with B.X.

The CENTRE Group will cover 108th Infantry Brigade Front, and the LEFT Group the 107th and 109th fronts.
The fronts of the Infantry Brigades will be as follows :
108th Infantry Brigade : from L.16.a. to Cemetery in L.3.d.
107th Infantry Brigade : from LOCK in L.12.a. to the ROUPY - SERAUCOURT Road, inclusive.
109th Infantry Brigade : from the ROUPY - SERAUCOURT Road, exclusive to the right of the Battalion in the Battle Zone of E. South.

RIGHT GROUP, Lt. Col. ERSKINE, D.S.O., R.F.A., H.Q., OLLEZY.
   A/91st and C/91st Brigade R.F.A.,
   232nd Siege Battery.
will cover the front of the 61st Infantry Brigade, 20th Division, extending from L.22. to L.36.

ACKNOWLEDGE.

         (sd) G.T. NUGEE, Major, R.F.A.,
           for Major, R.A.,
21.3.1918.   Brigade Major, 36th Divisional Artillery.

NOTE on above Order.
The 36th D.A.C., moved at 4 p.m. 21st March from ST. SIMON to SOMMETTE EAUCOURT and established a Dump there.
The Instructions detailed in the above order for 36th D.A.C., were cancelled, and at 11 p.m. they were ordered to march to VERLAINES.

Copy of 36th Divisional Artillery Order, issued on 24th March.

1. The Artillery covering the 36th Divisional Front will be reorganised into Groups as follows, from 6 a.m. today 24th instant. The necessary communications will be arranged by that time.

ERSKINE GROUP: A/91st Bde.R.F.A.   B/91st Bde.R.F.A.(now at W.3.c.4.4.
                  C/91st   "   in the ELEY Group.
                  D/173rd   "

ELEY GROUP.   463rd Bty. R.F.A.,   464th Bty. R.F.A.
                  C/163rd Bde.R.F.A.   D/153rd Bde.R.F.A.
                  D/232nd Bde.R.F.A.

POTTER GROUP.   A/153rd Bde.R.F.A.   B/153rd Bde.R.F.A.
                  383rd Bty. R.F.A.   D/91st Bde.R.F.A.

2. Normal S.O.S. ZONES will now be as follows :
      ERSKINE GROUP   L.34.c.0.0.   -   L.32.c.0.0.
      ELEY GROUP   L.32.c.0.0.   -   K.36.c.0.0.
      POTTER GROUP   K.36.c.0.0.   -   K.34.c.0.0.

3. XVIII Corps H.A. are now attached to 36th Division as follows :
      36th H.A.G. (35th Heavy Battery & 145th Heavy Battery.)
      232nd Siege Battery.

S.O.S. Lines will be given as required from this office.

In case of advance batteries will support their infantry as closely as possible.
The 232nd Siege Battery R.G.A. will advance under orders from H.Q., 36th Divisional Artillery to a position about FLAVY LE MELDEUX (V.5).
The 35th and 145th Heavy Batteries will advance under orders from this office.
The ERSKINE & ELEY Groups will advance as arranged by G.Os.C. Infantry Brigades with whom these Groups are respectively working.
The POTTER Group will advance to a line about GOLANCOURT-BONNEUIL CHATEAU.

In case of a retirement, batteries will retire by sections.
The 232nd Siege battery will take up a position about V.21.a.5.7.
The 35th and 145th Heavy Batteries will remain in present positions until further orders.
The ERSKINE & ELEY Groups will retire to a line W.16.centl, V.12.centl.
The POTTER Group will cover the retirement of the above Groups and after these Groups are in action will retire to a line V.16.d.0.0., V.8. central, with H.Q., at FRENICHES.
The H.Q., of the ERSKINE & ELEY Groups will in all cases remain with the H.Q., of the Infantry Brigades they cover.
Further advanced or retired positions will be arranged for later as necessity arises.
In all cases advanced Mobile Wagon Lines will be established in the vicinity of gun positions to facilitate rapidity of movement.
The policy for todays operations are not yet definitely settled. The line held by the British troops as far as is known runs from S. of CUGNY-BROUCHY-MUILLEY VILETTE (?) -VERLANES-EPPEVILLE and thence along S. bank of River. The line held by the French Army runs through R.32.-Q.32.-V.5.
Some elements of our troops, including Cavalry, hold an intermediate line about Q.20.centl.-GOLANCOURT-Fme de BONNEUIL-P.23.c.0.0.
The information concerning dispositions contained in this order will not be distributed beyond Group H.Q.,

AMMUNITION SUPPLY. 36th D.A.C..   )
                   179th B.A.C.   ) are at AVRICOURT T.21.
                   462nd Battery   )
    A.R.P. is at Cross-roads T.29.a.1.5.
    O.C. D.A.C., (using 179th B.A.C.etc..) will forthwith create
FORWARD DUMPS :
    (a) At Cross-roads V.23.b.8.1. and
    (b) Between road junctions V.9.c.0.5. & V.8.c.8.6.
with an Officer in charge of each and an adequate dump party.
    These dumps will be maintained at -
    4000 rounds 18-pr. 1000 rounds 4.5" How. in each.

RATIONS.

If the situation permits rations for consumption 25th for all batteries and H.Qs. of 153rd, D/173rd, 179th and 91st Brigades R.F.A., will be at the road junction V.14.a.6.7. any time after 2 p.m. today (24th).

Batteries will send guides (or supply wagons if these are with units) there at that time prepared to await the arrival of the convoy. Rations for 173rd, D.A.C., 462nd and 36th T.Ms. will be delivered to AVRICOURT as today.

36th Divisional Train is at AVRICOURT.

(sd) H.F. GRANT-SUTTIE.

Major, R.A.,
24.3.1918.   Brigade Major, 36th Divisional Artillery.

DISTRIBUTION.

Col. ERSKINE, D.S.O., R.F.A.,
Col. ELEY. C.M.G., D.S.O., R.F.A.,
Col. POTTER. D.S.O., R.F.A.,
O.C. 232nd Siege Battery R.G.A.,
O.C. 35th H.A.G.,
H.Q., R.A., XVIII Corps.
H.Q., 36th Division, 'G'.
O.C. 36th D.A.C.,

Copy of 36th Divisional Artillery Order No. 33.

Ref: Map 70 E 1/40,000.

The 36th Divisional Artillery has come under the orders of the 77th French Division.

The Line held by the Infantry is as follows :
(a) An Outpost line running from N.12.c.8.0. - N.12.a.0.4. - H.35.c. 0.0. - H.34.a.0.5. - H.27.central. - H.21.c.0.0. - H.20.central. H.20.a.0.4. - H.13.a.0.0. - G.18.a.0.7. - G.4.central.

(b) A Line of Resistance in rear running from N.12.c.4.0. - N.11.central. - N.3.central. - H.33.d.6.0. - H.33.central - H.26.central - H.19.central - Cross roads G.18.c. - G.9. central - G.8.b.35.20.

The Line is held by three regiments of Infantry in the Front System, each regiment having two battalions in the Front Line and one in support.

The Field Artillery covering the front will be organised in two Groups as follows :

The POTTER GROUP. Headquarters, LA SENSE FARM.
               Consisting of A)
                              B)
                              C) 153rd Brigade R.F.A.
                              D)

The ELEY GROUP.   Headquarters, M.3.d.6.3.
               Consisting of
                    383rd Battery R.F.A.
                    463rd Battery R.F.A.
                    464th Battery R.F.A.
                    D/91st Brigade R.F.A.
                    D/232nd Brigade R.F.A.

The dividing line between Groups for S.O.S. purposes will be a line drawn through H.26.central.
                H.21.central.

Normal S.O.S. Lines in case of a general attack.
The barrage will be as follows :
RIGHT GROUP:
Southern and Western exits from CANNECTANCOURT & THIESCOURT.

LEFT GROUP:
The Southern and Western exits of LASSIGNY.
The Northern half of CANNY SUR MATZ.

In case of an enemy attack coming from the direction of one of these villages only, all available guns and howitzers will be turned on to the exits of the one which the attack is developing from.

In no case is a barrage to be put down without orders from the Divisional Infantry Commander.

The Right and Left Infantry regiments will send up Red S.O.S. Rockets till the barrage is put down. On the Right the Signal will be sent up from the direction of the line: on the Left - from GURY.

For the present the Centre Regiment will not fire Rockets, but send S.O.S. by telephone only.

Colonel SIMPSON, D.S.O.,R.F.A., will act as Liaison Officer with the Divisional Infantry Commander at G.5.c.0.7.
The POTTER GROUP is furnishing a Liaison Officer with the Right Infantry Regiment.
The ELEY GROUP is furnishing a Liaison Officer with the Centre Infantry ~~Brigade~~. Regiment.

Each Group will establish an O.P. to cover the Sector allotted to it to be manned continuously.

Batteries must also establish an O.P. each, if possible, and a system of Visual Communication must be arranged.

The 35th H.A.G.   Headquarters, F.3.d.5.2.
covers the front of the 77th French Division and consists of the
        35th Heavy Battery
        145th Heavy Battery
        232nd Siege Battery

with S.O.S. Lines as under :

One 60-pr. battery THIESCOURT and its Northern approaches.
One 60-pr. battery LASSIGNY and its Northern approaches.
One 6" How. Battery - 2 guns on the villages -
        CANNECTANCOURT.
        THIESCOURT.
        LASSIGNY.

AMMUNITION.

Sheet AMIENS 17.   D.A.C., is at ORVILLERS-SOREL (4 miles W. of GURY).

- do -   A.R.P. is at RESSONS Railway Station where there is

18-pr.	4.5" How.	60-pr.	6" How.
10,000	4,000	2,000	1,000 rounds.

(The 60-pr. and 6" How. had not reached the Dump at 8 p.m. tonight).

Sheet 70 E   Two Forward Dumps are being established at

		For	Capacity	
			18-pr.	4.5" How.
(a)	M.8.b.8.3.	Left Group	1800	300
(b)	M.29.d.9.2.	Right Group	1800	300

RATIONS.

Arrangements will be notified later.

        (sd)   H.F. GRANT-SUTTIE.

        Major, R.A.,
26.3.1918.   Brigade Major, 36th Divisional Artillery.

Mr Cordery

This is incomplete & is extracted from 36th Division G.S. for March 1918.

The whole narrative is attached to 36th Division Artillery for March 1918 which Major Mckey has.

NARRATIVE OF THE OPERATIONS CARRIED OUT BY THE
36TH DIVISIONAL ARTILLERY FOR THE PERIOD
MARCH 21st - MARCH 31st INCLUSIVE.

Reference Maps :
66 C N.W. 1/20,000)
66 D N.E. 1/20,000)
66 D   1/40,000)
70 E   1/40,000)

All details as to the organisation of the Artillery covering the 36th Divisional Front, and Arrangements for Defence prior to the enemy's attack on March 21st, are contained in the 36th Divisional Artillery Defence Scheme. The following modifications to the above are given herewith :

(a) On the 28th February the 'A' Reinforcing Brigade (153rd Brigade, R.F.A.,) had occupied its allotted positions for the defence of the Battle Zone on receipt of the order from XVIII Corps, R.A., "Prepare for attack".

(b) Owing to the intense Gas Shell bombardment by the enemy on the V Corps Front between 11th and 14th March, certain Batteries which had been carrying out most of the firing up to date were moved back to positions less likely to be located, and remained 'silent' in their new positions except for registration and concentrated bombardments.

On the night 17th/18th, 3 guns from each of -

C/173rd Brigade R.F.A., to F 9   G.6.c.60.00.
D/173rd Brigade R.F.A., to F 2   G.4.b.30.56.
D/232nd Brigade R.F.A., to F 24 A.28.c.25.11.

On the night 19th/20th -

B/173rd Bde.R.F.A., 1 gun to F 10 A.27.a.58.55.
463rd Bty. R.F.A., 2 guns to F 27 A.20.b.12.14.

On the night 20th/21st at 10.30 p.m. -

B/173rd Brigade R.F.A.,)
C/173rd Brigade R.F.A.,)
D/173rd Brigade R.F.A.,) completed their moves
463rd Battery R.F.A.,   )

all ammunition having been fired or removed.

The positions thus vacated by B, C & D/173rd Brigade, R.F.A., and 463rd Battery R.F.A., were reported to have been subjected to extremely heavy destructive fire, and Batteries would have been entirely neutralized if they had remained there.

The Location List of Units at the commencement of the Battle was as follows :

36th Divisional Artillery Headquarters,   OLLEZY,   P.1.b.

RIGHT GROUP.

Headquarters, 173rd Brigade R.F.A.,		G.8.a.8.4.
A/173rd Brigade R.F.A.,	F 5	G.5.d.69.34.
B/173rd "	F 10	A.27.a.58.55.
C/173rd "	F 9	G.6.c.60.00.
D/173rd "	F 2	G.4.b.30.56.
463rd Battery R.F.A.,	F 7	A.29.a.95.43.
464th "	F 3	G.5.c.82.73.

LEFT GROUP.

Headquarters, 179th Army Brigade, R.F.A.,		L.12.a.9.8.
383rd Battery, R.F.A.,	F 6	G.4.b.93.30.
463rd "	F 27	A.20.b.12.14.
D/232nd Brigade, R.F.A.,	F 28	A.21.d.82.27. 3 guns.
	F 24	A.28.c.25.11. 3 guns.

BATTLE ZONE GROUPS.

Headquarters, 153rd Brigade, R.F.A., ("A" Brigade R.F.A.,)

A/153rd Brigade R.F.A.,	7	G.8.d.78.55.	4 guns.
	7A	G.17.a.24.15.	2 guns.
B/153rd "	8	G.14.a.49.69.	2 guns.
	8	G.13.b.92.63.	2 guns.
	8A	G.10.c.61.19.	2 guns.
C/153rd "	19	L.4.a.29.28.	4 guns.
	19A	G.4.a.68.61.	2 guns.
D/153rd "	29	G.7.d.15.00.	4 guns.
	29A	G.9.b.49.48.	2 guns.

ANTI TANK GUNS.

Position No. 1   B.22.a.2.2.
Position No. 2   B.13.d.55.35.

TRENCH MORTAR BATTERIES.

FORWARD ZONE.   Y/36th Trench Mortar Battery.

BATTLE ZONE.   Z/36th Trench Mortar Battery.

Advanced Wagon Lines were established for all Batteries of the Right and Left Groups in the Valley in G.14.b. and G.8.d.

The 36th Divisional Ammunition Column was at ST. SIMON.

March 20th.

Counter Preparation had been carried out continuously during the previous few days, suspected Trench Mortar Emplacements being specially dealt with.

A bombardment was carried out at 10 p.m., on the night of March 20th, for 30 minutes during a raid by 61st Division. The result of this raid confirmed previous information of an impending attack, and a further bombardment took place from 2.30 a.m. to 3 a.m. on March 21st.

The normal Bombardment Programme was being carried out when the attack started.

March 21st.

4.35 a.m. The enemy barrage opened.
XVIII Corps, R.A., were immediately informed and Groups were ordered to open fire on Counter Preparation Schemes.

A very thick mist prevented any observation and visibility rarely exceeded 50 yards.

As far as can be ascertained, the enemy barrage appeared to consist of :

1. A barrage by Trench Mortars of all calibres on the forward system.

2. A mixed Phosgene and H.E. bombardment by 105, 150 and 210 m.m. shell directed against -
   (a) The Line of Strong Points and the Valley immediately in rear.
   (b) The Battle Zone.
   (c) Battery Valley from G.3. to ESSIGNY STATION.

This barrage was especially heavy on battery positions.

The proportion of lethal shell to H.E. gradually decreased until the barrage was entirely comprised of H.E. There was a remarkable absence of 77 m.m. shell and of instantaneous fuzes.

3. A bombardment of selected points by H.V. Guns of all calibres. These points included almost all villages within range, the canal crossings and the R.E. Dump near GRAND SERAUCOURT.

4.55 a.m. The order 'Man Battle Stations' was sent from 36th Division 'G' and was communicated to Groups.

The 'B' Brigade was still kept under XVIII Corps orders.

Telephonic communications between Right Group Headquarters and the batteries were all destroyed in the first five minutes, and it was found impossible to lay and maintain air lines.

5.35 a.m. All Right Group communications forward had been cut except to JEANNE D'ARC O.P. which reported a heavy gas shell bombardment there. This wire was cut soon afterwards.

LEFT GROUP. Communications only lasted a little longer; communication with RAPHANEL O.P. being maintained till 5.45 a.m. but by 7.45 a.m. all forward wires had gone except to the 463rd Battery R.F.A. and to ARARAT O.P. which latter wire remained working till 7.10 p.m. when the enemy apparently captured the O.P.

Right Group Batteries opened fire on their S.O.S. Lines soon after communication with the rear was interrupted.

Instructions were sent out by the Group by runners ordering Counter-Preparation. Targets to be engaged until news was received that an attack had been launched.

Left Group Batteries opened on their S.O.S. Lines immediately the bombardment opened, but at once changed to Counter-Preparation bombardments on receipt of the order from H.Q., 36th Divisional Artillery.

XVIII Corps R.A., ordered a Gas Shell bombardment from 5.45 a.m for 30 minutes. D/232nd Brigade R.F.A., was ordered to fire on its target No. 7.

6.40 a.m.   XVIII Corps, R.A., ordered the telephone exchange at B.9.c.9.7. to be engaged. D/232nd Brigade R.F.A., was turned on to this Target.

9.10 a.m.   XVIII Corps, R.A., ordered - Commence 2nd Counter-Preparation 3rd Period - Unobserved Fire. Targets given by deserters to have priority.

10.0 a.m.   Orders were issued to commence filling up to 400 rounds a gun Battle Zone positions which were detailed to be occupied.

Ammunition was sent up to batteries in the Forward Zone, and it was found possible to replenish all batteries at the expense of some casualties.

10.40 a.m. XVIII Corps, R.A., reported that the S.O.S. Signal had been sent up on the 30th and 61st Divisional Fronts at 10.24 a.m.

No communication at this time existed to any of the Redoubts on 36th Divisional Front.

11.10 a.m. 35th H.A.G., was handed over to 36th Divisional control.

12.10 p.m. The barrage for the Line of Strong Points was ordered by 36th Division, 'G' (after previously ordering that for the Left Redoubt only).

Orders were issued to Groups accordingly.

The 35th H.A.G., were still in communication with most of their batteries.   The Right and Left Groups only by runner.

12.15 p.m. Groups were warned to be prepared to withdraw batteries to Battle Zone positions, one section per battery at first and then the remainder, and at 12.40 p.m. this was ordered to be carried out.

At about this time information was received on the right, that the enemy were advancing in the neighbourhood of LA MANUFACTURE FARM, and he appears to have progressed very rapidly towards ESSIGNY STATION, being reported on the Railway in G.6.a. at 12.45 p.m. and in G.12.b. at 1.10 p.m.

The advance was apparently in two parties, one making South along the Railway and the other West from the direction of ESSIGNY.

Gun Limbers sent up by the Right Group were turned back in G.10.a. by retiring Infantry. (A further attempt was made at 2.45 p.m but found impossible).

The enemy's barrage had ceased on the right, though there was still a good deal of intermittent shelling in G.8. and 9.

The mist had cleared by this time.

At 1.15 p.m. C/173rd and A/173rd Brigade R.F.A., in action in G.6.c. and G.5.d. respectively, withdrew their personnel from their positions as they were then under machine gun fire from front, flank and rear, and the enemy appeared to be advancing rapidly from ESSIGNY.

At 12.15 p.m. on the left the SWAN O.P. at CONTESCOURT reported that the enemy were coming over the BOADICEA Ridge.

12.40 p.m.   Information was received that the enemy were in the CASTRES VALLEY.

1.0 p.m.   Left Group reported that information had been received from 108th Infantry Brigade that the enemy were in CONTESCOURT.

All communications from 35th H.A.G. to batteries were cut.

1.10 p.m.   The advanced sections of 170th)
                                    232nd) Siege
                                    214th) Batteries
                                    267th)
were ordered to withdraw at once by XVIII Corps, R.A.,
Orders were then issued for advanced sections of 153rd Brigade R.F.A. to join their batteries in the main positions.

Information filtered through very slowly and appeared unreliable. The situation, as known, was very vague. At 2 p.m. a reconnaissance was ordered by the Right Group Commander to ascertain the situation on the Right flank, and the enemy was reported to be holding ESSIGNY Station, and was in B.11.b. and infantry were holding a line in A.27.d. in some strength, also that our batteries were still in action in G.4.b. and G.5.c. though exposed to machine gun fire.

The situation remained more or less unchanged during the afternoon. The enemy appeared to be advancing slowly and the situation was obscure.

Left Group batteries engaged troops massing along the Canal Bank between DALLON AND FONTAINE LES CLERCS, and also on the open ground to the South of DALLON.
The fire was observed and controlled from ARARAT O.P. A.26.b.95.40. and numerous casualties appear to have been inflicted.
The enemy ran a forward gun into FONTAINE LES CLERCS, but all attempts to serve it were prevented by the 463rd Battery R.F.A.

In retirement through the Battle Zone, batteries were gradually regrouped, The H.Q., 173rd Brigade, R.F.A., ceasing to exist as Right Group and the H.Q., 153rd Brigade R.F.A. taking its place. B, and D/91st Brigade R.F.A. arrived at 3 p.m. and went into Battle Zone positions.
The guns of A, B, & C/173rd Brigade R.F.A., and 462nd Battery R.F.A. had to be abandoned in the Forward Zone.

Positions in the Battle Zone were as follows :

464th Battery R.F.A., withdrew to Position 15, L.11.c.32.67.
                                    and joined the Left Group.
383rd Battery R.F.A., withdrew to Position 6, G.20.a.96.42.
                                    and joined the Right Group.
463rd Battery R.F.A., withdrew to Position 12, L.11.c.85.49.
                                    remaining in the Left Group.
A/153rd Bde. R.F.A., remained in Position 7, G.8.d.78.55.
                                    and joined the Right Group.
B/153rd Bde. R.F.A., remained in Position 8, G.14.a.49.69.
                                    and joined the Right Group.
C/153rd Bde. R.F.A., remained in Position 19, L.4.a.29.28.
                                    and joined the Left Group.
D/153rd Bde. R.F.A., remained in Position 29, G.7.d.15.00.
                                    and joined the Left Group.
D/232nd Bde. R.F.A., withdrew to Position 20, L.12.c.70.28.
                                    and joined the Left Group.

B/91st Bde. R.F.A., went to Position 24, L.11.c.12.37.
                                    and joined the Left Group.
D/91st Bde. R.F.A., went to 6" how. Position at L.23.a.6.0.
                                    and joined the Right Group.
D/173rd Bde. R.F.A., withdrew to Position 31, G.14.b.33.50.
                                    and joined the Right Group.

This last battery sent forward an F.O.O. to the Copse at A.28.d.0.2. and succeeded in maintaining communications. Observed fire was brought to bear on the advancing enemy at ranges down to 800 yards.

The guns were finally withdrawn from their forward position at 6.30 p.m. after all the ammunition had been expended.

<u>5 p.m. to 6.30 p.m.</u> All available batteries prepared for and barraged in support of a counter-attack to be made on CONTESCOURT by the 1st R.I.R. starting from the QUARRIES in A.27.c. At 7 p.m. ARARAT O.P. reported this attack had failed and the enemy were advancing towards the O.P.

At 7.15 p.m. the enemy were reported to be advancing in G.4.b. and G.5.a.

By 7.45 p.m. he was in G.4.c. and G.3.d.

Groups were ordered to withdraw all batteries in action East of the SOMME to positions near ARTEMPS, and to be prepared to take up positions on the West side of the SOMME.

The attached order was issued at 9.15 p.m. in accordance with 36th Division Order No. 178.

The Right Group Commander on arriving at ARTEMPS was informed by telephone.

The Left Group Commander reported personally at H.Q., 36th Divisional Artillery.

H.Q., 173rd Brigade R.F.A. and personnel of A, B & C/173rd Brigade R.F.A., and 462nd Battery R.F.A., were placed under the O.C. 36th D.A.C.,

Communication with the 35th H.A.G., failed about 2 p.m.

The Group retired to fresh H.Q., somewhere near TUGNY and no touch could be obtained for several hours, till eventually an Officer reported during the evening to H.Q., 36th Divisional Artillery.

The batteries of the Group, which were able to, retired through ARTEMPS and were regrouped under orders of XVIII Corps, R.A.

Touch was maintained with the 35th Heavy Battery in L.17.d. through the 93rd H.A.G., and objectives given to the battery till it was ordered to retire.

The 35th H.A.G., were kept under the 36th Division, and were allotted the following batteries by XVIII Corps, R.A.,
        35th Heavy Battery,
        145th Heavy Battery.
        232nd Siege Battery.

The two Heavy batteries were ordered to proceed to positions just South of HAM with H.Q., at LES VERTS GALANTS.

Communication to be established via XVIII Corps H.A., in HAM.

The 232nd Siege Battery was attached to Lt. Col. ERSKINE'S Group.

These batteries were then on the move, but were in action by dawn on the 22nd March.

H.Q. 91st Brigade R.F.A., arrived at H.Q., 36th Divisional Artillery during the evening, and A and C/91st Brigade R.F.A., on arrival at midnight were formed into the Right Group, as shown on the attached order.

TRENCH MORTARS.

March 21st.

The only Medium Trench Mortar operations known on this date are as follows :

FORWARD ZONE. There were two 6" Newton Mortars in each of the Strong Points, manned by detachments from Y/36th Trench Mortar Battery. Scarcely any information as to what happened to these detachments can be obtained. Owing to the thick mist the enemy were practically into the Right Strong Point 'JEANNE D'ARC' before being discovered. As the Officer in charge of the Mortars was last seen running into the emplacement it is probable that a number of rounds were fired before the Strong Point was taken.

The Centre Strong Point at GRUGIES was attacked in the rear and an Infantryman reports that the enemy were bombing the Trench Mortar dugouts as he escaped. As to whether the Mortars were fired he could not say.

Regarding the Left Strong Point nothing is known.

BATTLE ZONE. The Mortars in the Battle Zone were manned by X/36th Trench Mortar Battery. One Mortar was situated on the Railway embankment at A.30.c.7.3. Sheet 66 C N.W. The Officer in charge here was killed early in the bombardment in his O.P. The enemy were close to the emplacement before being seen and the Sergeant in charge was killed immediately afterwards. Two rounds were fired. One of the detachment escaped.

Two Mortars were in an emplacement in the bank of the roadway at A.29.c.7.4. The enemy first appeared here in front of the wire about 300 yards away at 11.45 a.m. Fire was immediately opened on the Valleys in A.23.c. and d. in accordance with the barrage table. After 40 rounds were expended, one Mortar went out of action. By this time parties of the enemy were visible from the emplacement so fire was directed on these until ammunition was expended. Altogether 113 rounds were fired from this position. The Mortars were taken back to a trench held by our Infantry and buried in the parados A.29.c.62.41.

Two Mortars were in the Sunken Road at A.28.c.6.2. These were fired until hard pressed by the enemy, when the detachments retired at the order of the Officer in Command of V/18th Heavy Trench Mortars, their own Officer by this time having been severely wounded. Seventy five rounds were fired and the Mortars were partially destroyed before the position was abandoned.

One Mortar was in the Keep in A.20.a. This gun first came into action about 3.0 p.m. on the 21st March. The enemy by this time were advancing on this part of the Battle Line from the HAM.- ST. QUENTIN Road in A.2. and A.3. and beginning to occupy the Sunken Roads in A. 14. also FONTAINE. On this occasion 30 rounds were fired in the barrage line (Valley in A.14) and as far right as the bed would allow. From then and during the night the enemy made no further advance except down the bank of the Canal, but about 6.30 a.m. on the 22nd an intense and accurate machine gun fire was directed on the whole position from much closer than on the previous evening, and also from the Canal Bank as far down as A.20.c.50.50. Three S.O.S. Rockets were sent up by the Infantry, but the thick mist rendered then invisible from any distance. The remaining rounds (50) were then fired from this Mortar on the barrage line and up to 20° more Left at a rate of two a minute. The gun was finally dismounted and taken back to Battalion Headquarters and the clinometer removed.

March 22nd

There was again a thick mist during the first part of the morning.

H.Q., 36th Divisional Artillery reached ESTOUILLY at 4 a.m. and joined H.Q., 36th Division, already established there.
At 6 p.m. the whole Headquarters moved back to FRENICHES.

RIGHT GROUP. (ERSKINE). Communication was kept with the Right Group via HAM throughout the day, but pressure of work on the lines prevented much conversation.

The Group was in close touch with 61st Infantry Brigade the whole time.

Batteries were in action shortly after midnight, as follows:

    A/91st Brigade R.F.A.,   Q.6.c.3.0.
    C/91st Brigade R.F.A.,   K.36.c.1.5.
    232nd Siege Battery.   Q.5.b.2.5.

H.Q., were at OLLEZY alongside H.Q., 61st Infantry Brigade.

6.0 a.m. O.Ps. were established in L.26.d. and R.2.d.
Bursts of Fire were concentrated on the Eastern bank of the Canal all the morning, and 232nd Siege Battery engaged ST. SIMON.

In the afternoon the O.Ps. reported our Infantry were falling back from the Canal on DURY.

By nightfall the Infantry line was along the Canal- HAM-ST. SIMON-AVESNE.

The front held by 61st Infantry Brigade extended from SOMMETTE EAUCOURT to AVESNE.

8.0 p.m. Fresh Battery positions were taken up to cover this line,

    A/91st Brigade R.F.A.,   R.13.d.4.0.
    C/91st Brigade R.F.A.,   Q.17.a.1.4.
    D/173rd Brigade R.F.A.,   Q.12.c.0.0. (ordered to join Right Group during the afternoon).

    232nd Siege Battery.   Q.15.b.9.3.

11.0 p.m. H.Q., Right Group (91st Brigade, R.F.A.,) were established at EAUCOURT.

CENTRE GROUP. (POTTER). The Group was collected with difficulty, and marching all night via TUGNY Bridge came into action just South of BRAY ST. CHRISTOPHE. After a short time in action they were ordered to positions further back, (on information received that the trenches East of ST. SIMON Bridgehead were not to be held).

    Headquarters   L.13.b.2.5.
    B/153rd Brigade R.F.A.,   in AUBIGNY.
    383rd Battery R.F.A.,   S.E. of AUBIGNY.
    A/153rd Brigade R.F.A.,   K.18.c.
    D/173rd Brigade R.F.A.,   K.24.a.
    D/91st Brigade R.F.A.,   K.18.c.

Group H.Q., remained at BRAY ST. CHRISTOPHE with 108th Infantry Brigade.

Not much shooting was done, the range being very great, and there being little attempt on the part of the enemy to advance on this front, (probably due to the opposition met with on the Left Flank).

The situation was obscure, and an emergency route was laid down by H.Q., 36th Divisional Artillery for batteries to retire by, in case of necessity, via SANCOURT and OFFOY, with a rendezvous at the Cross-roads in J.33.b.

<u>2.0 p.m.</u> 108th Infantry Brigade H.Q., and Centre Group H.Q., were ordered to move to PITHON and arrived at 4 p.m.

The 36th and 61st Divisions were ordered to retire to the line of the SOMME DEFENCES, the retirement being covered by the remaining Infantry Brigades of the 20th Division.

The Centre Group was placed at the disposal of the 20th Division for this purpose.

The Centre Group H.Q., had lost touch with its batteries, having no telephonic communication. The 3 18-pr. batteries had moved back to the rendezvous at J.33.b. and the Group was not collected till after 9 p.m. when it received orders from the 20th Divisional Artillery to march via the HAM - NESLE Road to BACQUENCOURT, and to take up positions in and about that village, covering the line of the SOMME from CANIZY to VOYENNES.

<u>LEFT GROUP (ELEY)</u>. Batteries of this Group were in action by 6.0 a.m. on the 22nd March, as follows:

Headquarters,	L.7.d.5.5.
463rd Battery R.F.A.,	L.2.b.3.7.
464th "	L.2.b.3.4.
C/153rd Brigade R.F.A.,	L.8.a.3.2.
D/153rd "	L.2.c.2.7.
B/91st "	L.8.a.5.6.
D/232nd A. " (2 Hows.only)	L.2.a.5.7.

Batteries continued in action in these positions until noon, when the Group was ordered to withdraw South of the SOMME and to come into action near BROUCHY. The Group Commander reconnoitred positions and batteries proceeded into action, the move being complete by 9.30 p.m.

<u>35th H.A.G.</u> Communication with this Group was obtained through XVIII Corps, H.A., and orders were issued for the 2 60-pdr. batteries to shell all the Roads and Tracks leading to the Bridge-heads of AVESNE, ST. SIMON and TUGNY.

During the night the 35th H.A.G., moved to positions round ERCHEU, and touch was lost with H.Q., 36th Divisional Artillery.

<u>36th D.A.C.</u>, Headquarters and Nos. 1 and 2 Sections marched from VERLAINES to FRETOY LE CHATEAU.

S.A.A. Section marched from VERLAINES to FLAVY LE MELDEUX and came under the orders of 36th Division, 'Q'.

Two ammunition dumps were established; one on the road between FRENICHES and FLAVY, and one at GUISCARD, for the use of all batteries.

March 23rd.

Very thick mist in the early morning, after which the day became fine and clear.

H.Q., 36th Divisional Artillery. Information was received early in the morning from XVIII Corps, R.A., regarding Rear Zone positions as reconnoitred before the Battle.
The whole 36th Divisional Headquarters moved to BEAULIEU during the evening.

RIGHT GROUP. (ERSKINE). Telephonic communication with this Group was difficult all day.

8.0 a.m. The Group received a report that the enemy had crossed the Canal at HAM, and were also advancing South towards CUGNY on the right flank.
All Batteries barraged the line of the Canal.

9.0 a.m. O.C. A/91st Brigade R.F.A., reported our Infantry had retired on to the line of his guns.
A/91st Brigade R.F.A., was ordered to move by the Group to Q.23.d.5.0. to cover our Infantry in CUGNY. After completion of this move C/91st Brigade R.F.A., was ordered to take up position at Q.33.a.8.8.
232nd Siege Battery was ordered to move to BERLANCOURT by H.Q., 36th Divisional Artillery, and came under their direct orders.

10.0 a.m. D/173rd Brigade R.F.A., position was heavily shelled causing casualties. The battery was moved to Q.29.c.8.4.
Group Headquarters were moved to VILLESELVE with 61st Infantry Brigade.

The Infantry Line was then believed to run as follows :
On the Left the 36th Division MUILLEVILETTE - BROUCHY, 61st Infantry Brigade EAUCOURT - Posts on Railway in R.7. and 8. - CUGNY, then 14th Division continued towards Q.36.

6.0 p.m. The enemy occupied BROUCHY, 36th Division Infantry fell back on A/91st Brigade, R.F.A., position.

8.0 p.m. 61st Infantry Brigade fell back on C/91st Brigade R.F.A., position.

These Batteries rallied the Infantry, and helped them to entrench in front of the guns.

The POTTER GROUP came into action round BACQUENCOURT about 5 a.m. under the 20th Divisional Artillery. During the early morning, fire was maintained on the roads leading down to the SOMME from the North on the Group Zone, and on to the villages of OFFOY, VOYENNES, CANIZY, etc.,

At 9.0 a.m. orders issued by H.Q., 36th Divisional Artillery, were received detailing the Group to rejoin 36th Division, and to move via BREUIL - MOYENCOURT - ERCHEU - LIBERMONT to a rendezvous near the Canal Crossing West of FRETOY LE CHATEAU (U.23.b.).
The Group arrived at 2 p.m. and horses which were very done up were exchanged with complete teams loaned from the 173rd Brigade, R.F.A.,

The Group was ordered to take up positions in or about FLAVY LE MELDEUX, covering the Zone SOMMETTE EAUCOURT - EPPEVILLE, with special reference to the HAM - GOLANCOURT Road.
Batteries were in action by dusk.
Fire was maintained throughout the night on the Roads leading South from the SOMME.

March 23rd.

LEFT GROUP (ELEY).   Officers patrols sent out early in the morning to reconnoitre, reported that the Bridge at DURY was still intact, (having been repaired to enable some of our troops to retire), that the enemy was in HAM and our line followed the line of the Canal from HAM to ST. SIMON.

Roads and approaches to DURY were engaged, also ST. SIMON.

10.30 a.m. The infantry reported that the enemy were in MUILLE VILETTE and were advancing.

All batteries retired by sections, and came into action in the vicinity of COLLEZY, as follows:

        Headquarters, BERLANCOURT,   W.13.b.1.9.
        463rd Battery R.F.A.,   W.3.a.6.2.
        464th   "   Q.32.d.6.6.
        C/153rd Brigade R.F.A.,   W.3.b.3.5.
        D/153rd   "   W.3.a.5.5.
        B/91st   "   W.3.c.4.4.
        D/232nd A. Bde. R.F.A.,   W.2.b.9.9.

where they remained all that day and night.

35th H.A.G.,   Orders to this Group could only be given through the 20th Divisional Artillery, and batteries were ordered to shell all the approaches to HAM during the day.
20th Divisional Artillery were asked to give them further orders, as the range would not allow the guns to cover the front held by the 36th Division.
The 232nd Siege Battery was ordered to move back to a position in U.21.a., which it occupied during the afternoon, but no ammunition could be obtained for it.

At noon the 148th Brigade R.F.A., being out of touch with its Division, reported for orders, and was sent into action by L'HOPITAL FARM in P.25.b. and 26.a. with orders to cover the area between the HAM-GOLANCOURT and HAM-ESMERY HALLON Roads.
The Group left the control of the 36th Divisional Artillery soon after dark.

36th D.A.C.,   No. 1 Section, 20th D.A.C., were attached to Column, also A/173rd, B/173rd, C/173rd, D/232nd Brigades and 462nd Battery R.F.A., less guns, B.A.C., 179th Army Brigade R.F.A., and 36th T.M. personnel came under its orders.
The Column, with attached units, marched to AVRICOURT where S.A.A. Section rejoined, but marched out same evening with Infantry.
Ammunition supply was maintained.
A.R.P. was established at Cross-roads between AVRICOURT and BEAULIEU LES FONTAINE with Forward Dumps at BEAULIEU LES FONTAINE and MUIRANCOURT.

March 24th.

Thick mist again in the early morning.

H.Q., 36th Divisional Artillery remained at BEAULIEU.

Groups were concentrated as far as possible in retirement. Telephonic communication was satisfactory with the POTTER Group, but was very intermittent with the ERSKINE and ELEY Groups throughout the day.

3.0 p.m. The ERSKINE Group was put at the disposal of the 9th French Division.
The ELEY and POTTER Groups were put under the 62nd French Division, under the control of the 36th Divisional Artillery.

The 36th Division was ordered to withdraw through the French Troops then holding a line behind them.

The two Groups were to withdraw as follows :

The ELEY Group to positions in U.18.d.
When the move was completed-
The POTTER Group was to move to positions in U.15.

A Liaison Officer from each Group was to be sent to the Infantry Regimental Commander at LIBERMONT forthwith.
Communication between them and the Groups would be by the line through BEAULIEU and the French Divisional Headquarters.
These orders were carried out as stated in Group narratives.

Groups were constituted as follows on this day :

ERSKINE GROUP.
    A, B, & C/91st Brigade, R.F.A.,
    D/173rd Brigade, R.F.A.,

ELEY GROUP.
    463rd & 464th Batteries, R.F.A.,
    C/153rd Brigade, R.F.A.,
    D/232nd Brigade, R.F.A.,
    D/153rd Brigade, R.F.A.,

POTTER GROUP.
    A & B/153rd Brigade, R.F.A.,
    383rd Battery, R.F.A.,
    D/91st Brigade, R.F.A.,

35th H. A. G.
    35th Heavy Battery, R.G.A.,
    145th Heavy Battery, R.G.A.,
    232nd Siege Battery R.G.A.,(directly under orders
                of H.Q., 36th Division-
                 al Artillery).

ERSKINE GROUP.

1.0 a.m. Batteries were withdrawn one at a time to positions in W.4.

6.0 a.m. B/91st Brigade, R.F.A., came under the control of the Group by orders of 36th Divisional Artillery.

8.0 a.m. Our Infantry began to fall back on VILLESELVE.
The Group was out of touch with 36th Divisional Artillery Headquarters, and was ordered by H.Q., 61st Infantry Brigade to take up positions in W.15. to barrage the further side of VILLESELVE and to shell CUGNY and BROUCHY, which was done.

1.0 p.m. The Infantry commenced to retire through the guns,

including the French who had been sent up to reinforce the
Infantry in VILLESELVE.

3.0 p.m.   All the Infantry had apparently retired through the guns.
Cavalry made a successful local attack on BROUCHY
capturing prisoners.

5.0 P.m.   French Infantry retired through BEINES from woods on the
right of bank in W.12. and 18.

5.30 p.m.   As there appeared to be no Infantry left in front and
the enemy were getting round the right flank, the Group
Commander ordered all batteries except C/91st Brigade, R.F.A., to
retire and take up positions in V.28. and 29.
    C/91st Brigade, R.F.A., remained in position until dark and
was able to support the retirement both of the French on their
right rear and the Cavalry to the West of the GUISCARD – VILLESELVE
Road. This battery retired by the only available road after the
enemy had captured BERLANCOURT and BOUCHOIRE, and took up positions
with the rest of the Brigade in V.28.

7.0 p.m.   On orders received from H.Q., 30th Divisional Artillery,
the Group Commander reported to the G.O.C., 9th French
Infantry Division at QUESNY for orders and was instructed to move
the Group back to CRISOLLES and report there for further instructions.

11.0 p.m.   Batteries retired successfully, although the enemy were
close up to GUISCARD at the time.

POTTER GROUP.   At 3.30 a.m. a report was received by the Group
Headquarters from an Infantry Officer, that
GOLANCOURT had been captured and the enemy was advancing. there
was considerable machine gun fire at close range about this time;
the mist was also very thick.
    Batteries were withdrawn from their positions at FLAVY and
formed up in a position of readiness in a field 800 yards west of
FLAVY.
    Officers Patrols and further information having established
the fact that though the enemy were in GOLANCOURT no further advance was
being made, batteries were ordered back into action in their former
positions at 7 a.m.
    In the course of the morning as the mist cleared and
information began to be obtained, it was apparent that the enemy
was in GOLANCOURT, BROUCHY, AUBIGNY, VILETTE and BONNEUIL CHATEAU
in considerable strength and appeared to be massing for an attack.
Fire was therefore maintained on these places and on the HAM-
GOLANCOURT Road. The shooting on GOLANCOURT and on BONNEUIL CHATEAU
was seen to be very effective, and caused the enemy, who were in the
open in large numbers, considerable casualties.
    Beyond possibly one 4.2" battery, which fired a few shell into
the village of FLAVY during the morning, the enemy did not appear
to have any guns S. of the river until late in the day.
    During the morning, probably about 10 a.m. the enemy
commenced to attack all along the front, but made little if any
progress on the front opposite the Group, the shell fire and
effective fire of the French M.Gs. prevented him from debouching
from GOLANCOURT. He appeared, however, to have gained considerable
success on the left about ESMERY HALLON and on the front of the
14th Division on the right, necessitating a retirement on the part
of the troops we were covering. About midday, therefore, orders
were issued for the Group to retire to positions between FLAVY and
FRENICHES. This was done by batteries, (sections in succession),
without hindrance from the enemy, 383rd battery going to ROUVREL,
(V.9.b.) B/153 to a position about 1000 yards E. of it (V.10.d.)
and A/153 and D/91 to positions about half a mile N.E. of
FRENICHES and just N. of the FRENICHES-FLAVY Road (V.9.a. and c.)
Group H.Q., were established at ROUVREL FARM. The enemy's
positions and his lines of approach were kept under continuous
bursts of fire throughout the day, and he showed no inclination to
push on on our immediate front. Except for a few 5.9's which fell
near D/91, the enemy did not fire on the batteries throughout the
day.

About 6 p.m. the enemy having gained considerable success opposite the Division on our right in the direction of BERLANCOURT and VILLESELVE, a further withdrawal was ordered, and by dusk the four batteries were in action about 1000 yards E. of FRENICHES and just S. of the FRENICHES-FLAVY Road (square V.9.d.) Group H.Q., in FRENICHES.

At 8 p.m. the orders were received to reconnoitre new positions in U.15. and occupy them when ordered by H.Q., 36th Divisional Artillery.

At 12 midnight these orders were received, and all batteries were in action in the new positions by 4 a.m. 25th March.

Group H.Q., were established in the FME. DES FONDS GAMETS.

ELEY GROUP. Batteries engaged AUBIGNY, BROUCHY, GOLANCOURT and LAMOY WOOD, where the enemy was in strength.

At 11.40 a.m. the batteries were ordered to retire to the vicinity of BERLANCOURT and supported the French Infantry in position at COLLEZY, in addition to our own Infantry.

At 2.30 p.m. a further retirement was carried out by Sections to BUCHOIRE and barrage fire was opened at the request of the French to the North and West of COLLEZY.

While in action here the 463rd and 464th Batteries were heavily shelled.

At 6 p.m. the Group received orders from H.Q., 36th Divisional Artillery to retire to positions just East of FRETOY LE CHATEAU, and all batteries were in action in their new positions by 10 p.m.

35th H.A.G., The 60-pdr. batteries continued to shell the approaches from HAM to ESMERY HALLON during the day supporting the Division on our left.

The 232nd Siege Battery remained in action in U.21.a. No ammunition was available as yet.

36th D.A.C., The supply of ammunition was continued to the Forward Dumps.

25th March.

Brig: Gen. H.J. BROCK, C.M.G., D.S.O., assumed Command of the 36th Divisional Artillery on return from Leave.
Lieut. Col. H.C. SIMPSON, D.S.O., R.F.A., hitherto Acting C.R.A., became Artillery Liaison Officer with the 62nd French Division, (H.Q., in BEAULIEU).
During the afternoon the Headquarters moved to CANDOR, (B.17.b. Sheet 70 E).

POTTER GROUP. 12 midnight 24/25.The Group was ordered to move back to the new positions in U.15. (Sheet 66 D) which was carried out successfully, without hindrance from the enemy, who were by that time fairly close up to batteries.

4.0 a.m. All batteries were again in action. Group H.Q., were in the FME. DES FONDS GAMETS (U.15.a.)

About 7 a.m. on a misty morning heavy firing was heard in front indicating an enemy attack. Throughout the morning barrages were fired on the BOIS DE L'HOPITAL, FRENICHES-FRETOY LE CHATEAU Road-WOOD in squares U.6., U.12., and U.18. etc., in support of the French 62nd Division who were now holding the front from LIBERMONT to the FRETOY LE CHATEAU-BEAULIEU Road. The enemy attacked repeatedly during the morning in great strength especially in front of LIBERMONT and in the BOIS DE L'HOPITAL where he at first gained no success, and suffered very heavy casualties. At about 12 noon, however, he appears to have succeeded in crossing the Canal N. of LEBERMONT near MOYENCOURT and to have advanced on ERCHEU. At the same time the French were slowly pressed back through LIBERMONT and the BOIS DE L'HOPITAL. About 1 p.m., the situation on the left making a general retirement necessary, batteries of the Group were ordered to be prepared to withdraw to positions in square U.19.c. immediately W. of BEAULIEU. These were reconnoitred, and after covering the withdrawal of the ELEY Group, the POTTER Group withdrew to these positions, being all in action again by 3 p.m. Group H.Q., at BOUVRESSE Farm, T.23.a.

Fire was carried out to protect the Canal gap, and also enfilade barrages in U.18., and V.13. to defend FRETOY LE CHATEAU from the North.
Positions further in rear were reconnoitred near AVRICOURT, and batteries commenced withdrawing about 7 p.m. (the last battery leaving when the enemy's Infantry were a few hundred yards away), and came into action in the vicinity of the ammunition dump at the Cross-roads in T.29.a. All batteries were in action by 10.30 p.m. Group H.Q., were established in AVRICOURT.
The Zone given by the French 62nd Division to the 36th Divisional Artillery for barrage purposes extended
from CATIGNY C.9.a. (Sheet 70 E).
to U.16.a. (Sheet 66 D).

ELEY GROUP. At 3 a.m. batteries were ordered to move at once to positions in U.9. N.E. of BEAULIEU. All batteries were in their new positions by 5 a.m. H.Q., were established with the H.Q., POTTER GROUP at the FME. DES FONDS GAMETS.
Continuous barrage fire was carried out all morning against the enemy attacking from the BOIS DE L'HOPITAL against LIBERMONT and the Canal gap in U.10.
At 1 p.m. the Group was ordered, by 62nd French Division H.Q., to retire to positions in U.13.c., H.Q., to proceed to BOUVRESSE FARM, F.23.a.
All batteries were in action by 2 p.m. and fire was carried out to protect LIBERMONT and the Canal gap.
By 4 p.m. LIBERMONT was known to have fallen, and the barrage was dropped to protect the line of the Canal, as far south as U.4.d.8.6. (Sheet 66 D).
The advance of the enemy was retarded, but eventually he succeeded in gaining ground W. of the Canal at LIBERMONT, and in U.10.a. and c. (Sheet 66 D). This necessitated a further withdrawal

to positions in T.23. (Sheet 66 D) close to AVRICOURT.

C/153rd Brigade, R.F.A., and 383rd Battery R.F.A., changed Groups during the day by order of H.Q., 36th Divisional Artillery.

35th H.A.G.,   The two 60-pdr. batteries were in action W. of ERCHEU.
Group H.Q., were at SOLENTE.
Fire was carried out all day in defence of LIBERMONT, and the Salient in the Canal in O.18., which was heavily attacked.
In the afternoon batteries retired to MARGNY to take up positions W. of the BOIS DE CHAMPIEN.
The 232nd Siege Battery, under direct orders of H.Q., 36th Divisional Artillery, bombarded the BOIS DE L'HOPITAL and objectives in the vicinity all morning, and at midday withdrew by Sections to a position in T.22.c. (Sheet 66 D), where it continued firing to protect the gap in the Canal in U.11. and also bombarded FRENICHES.

36th D.A.C.,   The Column, with attached units, marched at 6 p.m. to FRESNIERS and established a Dump.

March 26th.

The 62nd French Division issued orders for the withdrawal of all artillery during the night March 25th/26th, the new positions to be occupied by dawn and allotted an area for the 36th Divisional Artillery.

Orders were issued to Groups to occupy positions, as follows:
POTTER GROUP.   Round BALNY in B.14.d. and B.20.b.
ELEY GROUP.   In B.14.a. and b. (Sheet 70 E).
35th H.A.G.   All batteries in the vicinity of the Sugar Factory, B.18.d.
36th Divisional Artillery H.Q., were to be in CANNY SUR MATZ.

36th Divisional Artillery H.Q., moved back rather hurriedly at 4 a.m.

In consequence of a premature retirement by the French Infantry on our right flank Groups had to be withdrawn rapidly at 9 a.m. from what had become dangerously exposed positions.

Groups moved to a rendezvous at GURY, G.28.a. and the 36th Divisional Artillery came under the orders of the 77th French Division, and proceeded into action -
POTTER GROUP in N.21.a. (Sheet 70 E)
ELEY GROUP   in G.35.c.
covering the front CANNECTANCOURT-THIESCOURT-LASSIGNY-CANNY SUR MATZ.

D/91st and D/153rd Brigades R.F.A. changed Groups by orders of H.Q., 36th Divisional Artillery.

36th Divisional Artillery H.Q., were at MOREUIL LAMOTTE, and worked as a Group under the 77th French Divisional Artillery Commander.

Lieut. Col. SIMPSON, D.S.O.,R.F.A., acted as Liaison Officer with the French Division.

POTTER GROUP.   Batteries moved off at 2.30 a.m. and were in action by 5.30 a.m. in the area ordered. Group H.Q., were in BALNY FARM.
9 a.m.   Batteries retired via LASSIGNY to the rendezvous at GURY, and thence into action in N.21.a. to cover the right regimental sector CANNECTANCOURT-THIESCOURT. H.Q., at LA CENSE FARM.
Batteries were not in action until very late on in the night.

ELEY GROUP.   Batteries moved off at 2 a.m. and came into action in the area ordered by 6 a.m. Group H.Q., were in BALNY FARM.
9 a.m.   On receipt of orders from H.Q., 36th Divisional Artillery, batteries moved back independently through CANNY (reporting there for orders) to the rendezvous at GURY, and thence into action in positions in G.35.c. Group H.Q., at M.3.d.6.3.

Lieut. Col. ELEY, C.M.G.,D.S.O.,R.F.A., having lost touch with his Group during the retirement, proceeded to H.Q., XVIII Corps, R.A., and the Group was commanded by Major G. EARLE, D.S.O.,R.F.A., D/91st Brigade, R.F.A.,

35th H.A.G.,   never came into action as ordered but continued to retire.
The two 60-pdr. batteries moved to the rendezvous at GURY and thence into action close to MAREUIL LAMOTTE in M.9.c.

The 232nd Siege Battery lost touch with the Group during the retirement, and could not be recovered. It eventually regained its original Group, the 93rd H.A.G.

36th D.A.C.,   The Column and attached units marched to ORVILLERS SOREL; here 462nd Battery and 179th B.A.C., were detached, and were marched under separate orders to ST. JUST by O.C. 179th Army Brigade R.F.A.,

An A.R.F. was established at RESSONS from which ammunition was supplied to Forward Dumps at MARGNY SUR MATZ and MAREUIL LAMOTTE.

March 27th.

The front of the 77th Division was readjusted so as to cover a front from PLEMONT to CANNY SUR MATZ.

The POTTER GROUP, which was out of touch with H.Q., 36th Divisional Artillery in N.21. was moved round to positions in M.5. with H.Q., at M.5.central, batteries getting into action by 2.45 p.m.

The ELEY GROUP remained in the same positions.

Determined enemy attacks took place during the afternoon and were beaten off, in all cases suffering heavily from our barrage fire.

The 35th H.A.G., returned to the control of the XVIII Corps R.A., moving at 6 a.m.

36th D.A.C. Orders were received to supply 36th Divisional Artillery and all attached units with forage and rations. These were drawn from a Reserve Dump at RESSONS and delivered daily to units.

On the same date the Column, with attached units, marched to MERY and kept up supply of ammunition to MAREUIL LAMOTTE Dump. MARGNY SUR MATZ Dump was cleared of ammunition and ceased to be used.

March 28th.

The enemy made continual attacks throughout the day, principally against the valley in square 19, W. of PLEMONT HILL and against CANNY.

Effective barrages were put down, and the enemy obtained no success except at CANNY, which he eventually succeeded in capturing.

Heavy rain fell during the night.

Extensive Harassing fire was carried out during the night, and concentrations at various times were fired on LASSIGNY with great effect.

The 56th H.A.G., (220th and 306th 6" How. batteries arrived,
                 (and came under the orders of H.Q., 36th
                 (Divisional Artillery.

Batteries went into action just S.W. of MAREUIL LAMOTTE. Group H.Q., in the village.

36th D.A.C., The Column and attached units marched to GOURNAY. Supply of ammunition, forage and rations was maintained.

March 29th.

A very quiet day.

Harassing Fire and Concentrations were carried out throughout the 24 hours.

36th D.A.C., Ammunition was drawn by Motor Lorry from REMY and dumped at GOURNAY, where the Column and attached units refilled and continued to supply MAREUIL LAMOTTE Dump.
Supply of ammunition, forage and rations maintained.

March 30th.

The enemy started a very strong attack about 8 a.m. supported by fairly strong artillery fire against the fronts held by the 53rd and 77th French Divisions.

At one time the enemy succeeded in capturing PLEMONT HILL, held by the 53rd French Division, but it was recaptured almost at once by a counter-attack.

He also succeeded in capturing PLESSIER LE ROYE and the Chateau Park in G.23., 24., and 30, and by 10.30 a.m. a number had reached the CARRIERE MADAME in square G.29.d. only a few hundred yards from the position of C and D/153rd Brigade R.F.A., These batteries were withdrawn at midday to positions near ST. CLAUDE FARM in M.5.c. and a section from each of A and B/153rd Brigade R.F.A., were also withdrawn to this vicinity. All batteries were subjected to a certain amount of shelling, which caused casualties to the gun detachments and in the advanced wagon lines.

The left of the 77th Division in front of GURY stood firm and a counter-attack was prepared for to restore the situation in the centre. A continuous bombardment was maintained on PLESSIER LE ROYE, the Chateau Park and LASSIGNY till 5.30 p.m. when the French counter-attacked from the East and West and were completely successful, restoring the whole line and capturing 700 prisoners.

Throughout the day the artillery barrage proved extremely effective, and observed fire was brought to bear on large enemy bodies inflicting considerable casualties.

4 p.m. A warning order was issued in accordance with instructions sent by H.Q., III Corps, R.A., for Groups to be prepared to withdraw from action and proceed to the ARSY Area to billet.

8.30 p.m. Final orders were issued and batteries commenced to withdraw at 9.0 p.m.

The 36th D.A.C., and all details not in action had already withdrawn during the afternoon, after clearing the RESSONS ammunition dump.

After a trying march all units reached GRAND FRESNOY by 5.0 a.m. on 31st March.

The 56th H.A.G., were ordered to remain in action under the 77th French Division.

March 31st.

Units of the 36th Divisional Artillery marched via CLERMONT to billets at ETOUY, LA RUE ST. PIERRE, and WARREVILLE (BEAUVAIS 1/100,000) en route for the Artillery Concentration Area, POIX.

NARRATIVE OF THE OPERATIONS CARRIED OUT BY THE
36TH DIVISIONAL ARTILLERY FOR THE PERIOD
MARCH 21st – MARCH 31st INCLUSIVE.   APPENDIX 'A'

Reference Maps :
   66 C N.W. 1/20,000)
   66 D N.E. 1/20,000)
   66 D   1/40,000)
   70 E   1/40,000)

All details as to the organisation of the Artillery covering the 36th Divisional Front, and arrangements for Defence prior to the enemy's attack on March 21st, are contained in the 36th Divisional Artillery Defence Scheme. The following modifications to the above are given herewith :

(a) On the 28th February the 'A' Reinforcing Brigade (153rd Brigade, R.F.A.,) had occupied its allotted positions for the defence of the Battle Zone on receipt of the order from XVIII Corps, R.A., "Prepare for attack".

(b) Owing to the intense Gas Shell bombardment by the enemy on the V Corps Front between 11th and 14th March, certain Batteries which had been carrying out most of the firing up to date were moved back to positions less likely to be located, and remained 'silent' in their new positions except for registration and concentrated bombardments.

On the night 17th/18th, 3 guns from each of –

C/173rd Brigade R.F.A., to F 9 G.6.c.60.00.
D/173rd Brigade R.F.A., to F 2 G.4.b.30.50.
D/232nd Brigade R.F.A., to F 24 A.28.c.85.11.

On the night 19th/20th –

B/173rd Bde.R.F.A., 1 gun to F 10 A.27.a.58.55.
403rd Bty. R.F.A., 2 guns to F 27 A.20.b.12.14.

On the night 20th/21st at 10.30 p.m. –

B/173rd Brigade R.F.A.,)
C/173rd Brigade R.F.A.,)
D/173rd Brigade R.F.A.,) completed their moves
403rd Battery R.F.A.,   )

all ammunition having been fired or removed.

The positions thus vacated by B, C & D/173rd Brigade, R.F.A., and 403rd Battery R.F.A., were reported to have been subjected to extremely heavy destructive fire, and Batteries would have been entirely neutralised if they had remained there.

The Location List of Units at the commencement of the Battle was as follows :

36th Divisional Artillery Headquarters,   OLLEZY, E.1.b.

RIGHT GROUP.

Headquarters, 173rd Brigade R.F.A.,   G.8.a.0.4.
A/173rd Brigade R.F.A.,   F 5   G.5.d.69.34
B/173rd   "   F 10 A.27.a.58.55.
C/173rd   "   F 9   G.6.c.60.00.
D/173rd   "   F 2   G.4.b.30.50.
402nd Battery R.F.A.,   F 7   A.29.a.95.43.
404th   "   F 3   G.5.c.62.73.

LEFT GROUP.

Headquarters, 179th Army Brigade, R.F.A., L.12.a.9.8.
383rd Battery, R.F.A.,   F 6   G.4.b.93.30.
463rd   F 27   A.20.b.12.14.
D/232nd Brigade, R.F.A., { F 28   A.21.d.82.27. 3 guns.
                          { F 24   A.28.c.85.11. 3 guns.

BATTLE ZONE GROUP.

Headquarters, 153rd Brigade, R.F.A., ("A" Brigade R.F.A.,)

A/153rd Brigade R.F.A.,   7   G.8.d.78.55.   4 guns.
                           7A   G.17.a.24.15.   2 guns.

B/153rd   "   { 8   G.14.a.49.69.   2 guns.
                          { 8   G.13.b.92.03.   2 guns.
                           8A   G.10.c.81.19.   2 guns.

C/153rd   "   19   L.4.a.29.28.   4 guns.
                          19A   G.4.a.88.61.   2 guns.

D/153rd   "   29   G.7.d.15.00.   4 guns.
                          29A   G.9.b.49.48.   2 guns.

ANTI TANK GUNS.

Position No. 1   B.22.a.2.2.
Position No. 2   B.13.d.55.35.

TRENCH MORTAR BATTERIES.

FORWARD ZONE.   V/36th Trench Mortar Battery.

BATTLE ZONE.   Z/36th Trench Mortar Battery.

Advanced Wagon Lines were established for all Batteries of the Right and Left Groups in the Valley in G.14.b. and G.8.d.

The 36th Divisional Ammunition Column was at ST. AMON.

March 20th.

Counter Preparation had been carried out continuously during the previous few days, suspected Trench Mortar Emplacements being specially dealt with.

A bombardment was carried out at 10 p.m., on the night of March 20th, for 30 minutes during a raid by 61st Division. The result of this raid confirmed previous information of an impending attack, and a further bombardment took place from 2.30 a.m. to 3 a.m. on March 21st.

The normal Bombardment Programme was being carried out when the attack started.

March 21st.

4.35 a.m. The enemy barrage opened.
XVIII Corps, R.A., were immediately informed and Groups were ordered to open fire on Counter Preparation Schemes.

A very thick mist prevented any observation and visibility rarely exceeded 50 yards.

As far as can be ascertained, the enemy barrage appeared to consist of :

1. A barrage by Trench Mortars of all calibres on the forward system.

2. A mixed Phosgene and H.E. bombardment by 105, 150 and 210 m.m. shell directed against -
    (a) The Line of Strong Points and the Valley immediately in rear.
    (b) The Battle Zone.
    (c) Battery Valley from G.3. to ESSIGNY STATION.

This barrage was especially heavy on battery positions.

The proportion of lethal shell to H.E. gradually decreased until the barrage was entirely comprised of H.E. There was a remarkable absence of 77 m.m. shell and of instantaneous fuzes.

3. A bombardment of selected points by H.V. Guns of all calibres. These points included almost all villages within range, the canal crossings and the R.E. Dump near GRAND SERAUCOURT.

4.55 a.m. The order 'Man Battle Stations' was sent from 36th Division 'G' and was communicated to Groups.

The 'B' Brigade was still kept under XVIII Corps orders.

Telephonic communications between Right Group Headquarters and the batteries were all destroyed in the first five minutes, and it was found impossible to lay and maintain air lines.

5.35 a.m. All Right Group communications forward had been cut except to JEANNE D'ARC O.P. which reported a heavy gas shell bombardment there, this wire was cut soon afterwards.

LEFT GROUP. Communications only lasted a little longer; communication with RAPHAEL O.P. being maintained till 5.45 a.m. but by 7.45 a.m. all forward wires had gone except to the 463rd Battery R.F.A. and to ARARAT O.P. which latter wire remained working till 7.10 p.m. when the enemy apparently captured the O.P.

Right Group Batteries opened fire on their S.O.S. Lines soon after communication with the rear was interrupted.

Instructions were sent out by the Group by runners ordering Counter-Preparation. Targets to be engaged until news was received that an attack had been launched.

Left Group Batteries opened on their S.O.S. Lines immediately the bombardment opened, and at once changed to Counter-Preparation bombardments on receipt of the order from H.Q., 36th Divisional Artillery.

XVIII Corps R.A., ordered a Gas Shell bombardment from 8.45 a.m for 30 minutes. D/232nd Brigade R.F.A., was ordered to fire on its target No. 7.

8.40 a.m. XVIII Corps, R.A., ordered the telephone exchange at R.9.c.9.7. to be engaged. D/232nd Brigade R.F.A., was turned on to this Target.

9.10 a.m. XVIII Corps, R.A., ordered - Commence 2nd Counter-Preparation 3rd Period - Unobserved Fire. Targets given by deserters to have priority.

10.0 a.m. Orders were issued to commence filling up to 400 rounds a gun Battle Zone positions which were detailed to be occupied.

Ammunition was sent up to batteries in the Forward Zone, and it was found possible to replenish all batteries at the expense of some casualties.

10.40 a.m. XVIII Corps, R.A., reported that the S.O.S. Signal had been sent up on the 30th and 61st Divisional Fronts at 10.24 a.m.

No communication at this time existed to any of the Redoubts on 36th Divisional Front.

11.10 a.m. 35th H.A.G., was handed over to 36th Divisional control.

12.10 p.m. The barrage for the Line of Strong Points was ordered by 36th Division, 'G' (after previously ordering that for the Left Redoubt only).

Orders were issued to Groups accordingly.

The 35th H.A.G., were still in communication with most of their batteries. The Right and Left Groups only by runner.

12.15 p.m. Groups were warned to be prepared to withdraw batteries to Battle Zone positions, one section per battery at first and then the remainder, and at 12.40 p.m. this was ordered to be carried out.

At about this time information was received on the right, that the enemy were advancing in the neighbourhood of LA MANUFACTURE FARM, and he appears to have progressed very rapidly towards ESSIGNY STATION, being reported on the Railway in G.6.a. at 12.45 p.m. and in G.12.b. at 1.10 p.m.

The advance was apparently in two parties, one making South along the Railway and the other West from the direction of ESSIGNY.

Gun Limbers sent up by the Right Group were turned back in G.10.a. by retiring Infantry. (A further attempt was made at 2.45 p.m but found impossible).

The enemy's barrage had ceased on the right, though there was still a good deal of intermittent shelling in G.6. and 9.

The mist had cleared by this time.

At 1.15 p.m. C/173rd and A/173rd Brigade R.F.A., in action in G.6.c. and C.5.d. respectively, withdrew their personnel from their positions as they were then under machine gun fire from front, flank and rear, and the enemy appeared to be advancing rapidly from ESSIGNY.

At 1.15 p.m. on the left the Area O.P. at CONTESCOURT reported that the enemy were coming over the ROUPICH Ridge.

12.40 p.m.   Information was received that the enemy were in the CASTRES VALLEY.

1.0 p.m.   Left Group reported that information had been received from 108th Infantry Brigade that the enemy were in CONTESCOURT.

All communications from 36th H.A.G. to batteries were cut.

1.10 p.m. The advanced sections of 170th)
            232nd) Siege
            214th) Batteries
            267th)
were ordered to withdraw at once by XVIII Corps, R.A.,
  Orders were then issued for advanced sections of 153rd Brigade R.F.A. to join their batteries in the main positions.

Information filtered through very slowly and appeared unreliable. The situation, as known, was very vague. At 2 p.m. a reconnaissance was ordered by the Right Group Commander to ascertain the situation on the Right flank, and the enemy was reported to be holding ESSIGNY Station, and was in B.11.b. and Infantry were holding a line in A.27.d. in some strength, also that our batteries were still in action in G.4.b. and G.5.c. though exposed to machine gun fire.

The situation remained more or less unchanged during the afternoon. The enemy appeared to be advancing slowly and the situation was obscure.

Left Group batteries engaged troops massing along the Canal Bank between DALLON AND FONTAINE LES CLERCS, and also on the open ground to the South of DALLON.
 The fire was observed and controlled from ARARAT O.P. A.26.b. 95.40. and numerous casualties appear to have been inflicted.
 The enemy ran a forward gun into FONTAINE LES CLERCS, but all attempts to serve it were prevented by the 463rd Battery R.F.A.

In retirement through the Battle Zone, batteries were gradually regrouped, The H.Q., 173rd Brigade, R.F.A., ceasing to exist as Right Group and the H.Q., 153rd Brigade R.F.A., taking its place.   B, and D/91st Brigade R.F.A., arrived at 3 p.m. and went into Battle Zone positions.
 The guns of A, B, & C/173rd Brigade R.F.A., and 462nd Battery R.F.A. had to be abandoned in the Forward Zone.

Positions in the Battle Zone were as follows :

464th Battery R.F.A., withdrew to Position 15, L.11.c.32.67.
         and joined the Left Group.
383rd Battery R.F.A., withdrew to Position 6, G.20.a.96.42.
         and joined the Right Group.
463rd Battery R.F.A., withdrew to Position 12, L.11.c.85.49.
         remaining in the Left Group.
A/153rd Bde. R.F.A., remained in Position 7, G.8.c.78.55.
         and joined the Right Group.
B/153rd Bde. R.F.A., remained in Position 8, G.14.a.49.69.
         and joined the Right Group.
C/153rd Bde. R.F.A., remained in Position 19, L.4.a.29.28.
         and joined the Left Group.
D/153rd Bde. R.F.A., remained in Position 29, G.7.d.15.00.
         and joined the Left Group.
D/232nd Bde. R.F.A., withdrew to Position 20, L.12.c.70.28.
         and joined the Left Group.
B/91st Bde. R.F.A., went to Position 24, L.11.c.12.37.
         and joined the Left Group.
D/91st Bde. R.F.A., went to 6" How. Position at L.23.a.6.0.
         and joined the Right Group.
D/173rd Bde. R.F.A., withdrew to Position 31, G.14.b.33.50.
         and joined the Right Group.

-6-

This last battery sent forward an F.O.O. to the Copse at A.28.d.0.2. and succeeded in maintaining communications. Observed fire was brought to bear on the advancing enemy at ranges down to 800 yards.

The Guns were finally withdrawn, *from their forward position* at 6.30 p.m. after all the ammunition had been expended.

<u>5 p.m. to 6.30 p.m.</u> All available batteries prepared for and barraged in support of a counter-attack to be made on CONTESCOURT by the 1st R.I.R. starting from the QUARRIES in A.27.c. At 7 p.m. ARARAT O.P. reported this attack had failed and the enemy were advancing towards the O.P.

At 7.15 p.m. the enemy were reported to be advancing in G.4.b. and G.5.a.

By 7.45 p.m. he was in G.4.c. and G.3.d.

Groups were ordered to withdraw all batteries in action East of the SOMME to positions near ARTEMPS, and to be prepared to take up positions on the West side of the SOMME.

The attached order was issued at 9.15 p.m. In accordance with 36th Division Order No. 178.

The Right Group Commander on arriving at ARTEMPS was informed by telephone.

The Left Group Commander reported personally at H.Q., 36th Divisional Artillery.

H.Q., 173rd Brigade R.F.A. and personnel of A, B & C/173rd Brigade R.F.A., and 452nd Battery R.F.A., were placed under the C.O. 36th D.A.C.,

Communication with the 35th H.A.G., failed about 2 p.m.

The Group retired to fresh H.Q., somewhere near TUGNY and no touch could be obtained for several hours, till eventually an Officer reported during the evening to H.Q., 36th Divisional Artillery.

The batteries of the Group, which were able to, retired through ARTEMPS and were regrouped under orders of XVIII Corps, R.A.,

Touch was maintained with the 35th Heavy Battery in L.17.d. through the 93rd H.A.G., and objectives given to the battery till it was ordered to retire.

The 36th H.A.G., were kept under the 36th Division, and were allotted the following batteries by XVIII Corps, R.A.,
  35th Heavy Battery,
  110th Heavy Battery.
  232nd Siege Battery.

The two Heavy batteries were ordered to proceed to positions just South of HAM with H.Q., at LES VERTS GALETS.

Communication to be established via XVIII Corps H.A., in H.M.

The 232nd Siege Battery was attached to Lt. Col. ERSKINE'S Group.

These batteries were then on the move, but were in action by dawn on the 22nd March.

H.Q. 91st Brigade R.F.A., arrived at H.Q., 36th Divisional Artillery during the evening, and A and C/91st Brigade R.F.A., on arrival at midnight were formed into the Right Group, as shown on the attached order.

TRENCH MORTARS.

March 21st.

The only Medium Trench Mortar operations known on this date are as follows :-

FORWARD ZONE. There were two 6" Newton Mortars in each of the Strong Points, manned by detachments from X/36th Trench Mortar Battery. Scarcely any information as to what happened to these detachments can be obtained. Owing to the thick mist the enemy were practically into the Right Strong Point 'JEANNE D'ARC' before being discovered. As the Officer in charge of the Mortars was last seen running into the emplacement it is probable that a number of rounds were fired before the Strong Point was taken.

The Centre Strong Point at GRUGIES was attacked in the rear and an Infantryman reports that the enemy were bombing the Trench Mortar dugouts as he escaped. As to whether the Mortars were fired he could not say.

Regarding the Left Strong Point nothing is known.

BATTLE ZONE. The Mortars in the Battle Zone were manned by Y/36th Trench Mortar Battery. One Mortar was situated on the Railway embankment at A.30.c.7.3. Sheet 66 C.N.W. The Officer in charge here was killed early in the bombardment in his O.P. The enemy were close to the emplacement before being seen and the Sergeant in charge was killed immediately afterwards. Two rounds were fired. One of the detachment escaped.

Two Mortars were in an emplacement in the bank of the roadway at A.29.c.7.4. The enemy first appeared here in front of the wire about 500 yards away at 11.45 a.m. Fire was immediately opened on the Valleys in A.23.c. and d. in accordance with the barrage table. After 40 rounds were expended, one Mortar went out of action. By this time parties of the enemy were visible from the emplacement so fire was directed on these until ammunition was expended. Altogether 115 rounds were fired from this position. The Mortars were taken back to a trench held by our Infantry and buried in the parados A.29.c.68.41.

Two Mortars were in the Sunken Road at A.28.c.6.2. These were fired until hard pressed by the enemy, when the detachments retired at the order of the Officer in Command of V/16th Heavy Trench Mortars, their own Officer by this time having been severely wounded. Seventy five rounds were fired and the Mortars were partially destroyed before the position was abandoned.

One Mortar was in the Keep in A.20.a. This gun first came into action about 3.0 p.m. on the 21st March. The enemy by this time were advancing on this part of the Battle Line from the HAM - ST. QUENTIN Road in A.2. and A.3. and beginning to occupy the Sunken Roads in A. 14. also FONTAINE. On this occasion 30 rounds were fired in the barrage line (Valley in A.14) and as far right as the bed would allow. From then and during the night the enemy made no further advance except down the bank of the Canal, but about 6.30 a.m. on the 22nd an intense and accurate machine gun fire was directed on the whole position from much closer than on the previous evening, and also from the Canal Bank as far down as A.20.c.50.50. Three S.O.S. Rockets were sent up by the Infantry, but the thick mist rendered them invisible from any distance. The remaining rounds (50) were then fired from this Mortar on the barrage line and up to 20° more Left at a rate of two a minute. The gun was finally dismounted and taken back to Battalion Headquarters and the clinometer removed.

March 22nd

There was again a thick mist during the first part of the morning.

H.Q., 36th Divisional Artillery reached ROTOUILLY at 4 a.m. and joined H.Q., 36th Division, already established there.
At 6 p.m. the whole Headquarters moved back to FRENICHES.

RIGHT GROUP. (ERSKINE). Communication was kept with the Right Group via BAM throughout the day, but pressure of work on the lines prevented much conversation.

The Group was in close touch with 61st Infantry Brigade the whole time.

Batteries were in action shortly after midnight, as follows:

A/91st Brigade R.F.A.,   Q.6.c.3.0.
C/91st Brigade R.F.A.,   K.36.c.1.5.
232nd Siege Battery.   Q.5.b.2.5.

H.Q., were at OLLEZY alongside H.Q., 61st Infantry Brigade.

9.0 a.m. O.Ps. were established in L.36.d. and R.2.d.

Bursts of Fire were concentrated on the Eastern bank of the Canal all the morning, and 232nd Siege Battery engaged ST. SIMON.

In the afternoon the O.Ps. reported our Infantry were falling back from the Canal on DURY.

By nightfall the Infantry line was along the Canal - HAM - ST. SIMON - AVESNE.

The front held by 61st Infantry Brigade extended from SOMMETTE EAUCOURT to AVESNE.

8.0 p.m. Fresh Battery positions were taken up to cover this line,

A/91st Brigade R.F.A.,   R.13.d.4.0.
C/91st Brigade R.F.A.,   Q.17.a.1.4.
D/173rd Brigade R.F.A., Q.12.c.0.0. (ordered to join Right Group during the afternoon).

232nd Siege Battery.   Q.15.b.9.3.

11.0 p.m. H.Q., Right Group (91st Brigade, R.F.A.,) were established at EAUCOURT.

CENTRE GROUP. (POTTER). The Group was collected with difficulty, and marching all night via TUGNY Bridge came into action just South of BRAY ST. CHRISTOPHE. After a short time in action they were ordered to positions further back, (on information received that the trenches East of ST. SIMON Bridgehead were not to be held).

Headquarters   L.13.h.2.5.
B/153rd Brigade R.F.A., in AUBIGNY.
363rd Battery R.F.A.,   S.E. of AUBIGNY.
A/153rd Brigade R.F.A.,   K.18.c.
D/173rd Brigade R.F.A.,   K.24.a.
D/91st Brigade R.F.A.,   K.18.c.

Group H.Q., remained at BRAY ST. CHRISTOPHE with 106th Infantry Brigade.

Not much shooting was done, the range being very great, and there being little attempt on the part of the enemy to advance on this front, (probably due to the opposition met with on the Left Flank).

The situation was obscure, and an emergency route was laid down by H.Q., 36th Divisional Artillery for batteries to retire by, in case of necessity, via SANCOURT and OFFOY, with a rendezvous at the Cross-roads in J.33.b.

2.0 p.m. 106th Infantry Brigade H.Q., and Centre Group H.Q., were ordered to move to PITHON and arrived at 4 p.m.

The 36th and 61st Divisions were ordered to retire to the line of the SOMME DEFENCES, the retirement being covered by the remaining Infantry Brigades of the 20th Division.

The Centre Group was placed at the disposal of the 20th Division for this purpose.

The Centre Group H.Q., had lost touch with its batteries, having no telephonic communication. The 3 18-pr. batteries had moved back to the rendezvous at J.33.b. and the Group was not collected till after 9 p.m. when it received orders from the 20th Divisional Artillery to march via the HAM - NESLE Road to BACQUENCOURT, and to take up positions in and about that village, covering the line of the SOMME from CANIZY to VOYENNES.

LEFT GROUP (FLAY). Batteries of this Group were in action by 6.0 a.m. on the 22nd March, as follows:

Headquarters,	L.7.d.5.5.
463rd Battery R.F.A.,	L.2.b.3.7.
464th "	L.2.b.3.4.
C/153rd Brigade R.F.A.,	L.8.a.3.1.
D/153rd "	L.2.c.2.7.
B/91st "	L.8.a.5.6.
D/232nd A. " (2 Hows.only)	L.2.a.5.7.

Batteries continued in action in these positions until noon, when the Group was ordered to withdraw South of the SOMME and to come into action near EROUCHY. The Group Commander reconnoitred positions and batteries proceeded into action, the move being complete by 9.30 p.m.

35th H.A.G. Communication with this Group was obtained through XVIII Corps, R.A., and orders were issued for the 2 60-pdr. batteries to shell all the Roads and Tracks leading to the Bridge-heads of AVESNE, ST. SIMON and TUGNY.

During the night the 35th H.A.G., moved to positions round ERCHEU, and touch was lost with H.Q., 36th Divisional Artillery.

36th D.A.C., Headquarters and Nos. 1 and 2 Sections marched from VERLAINES to FRETOY LE CHATEAU.

B.A.A. Section marched from VERLAINES to FLAVY LE MELDEUX and came under the orders of 36th Division, 'G.'

Two ammunition dumps were established; one on the road between FRENICHES and FLAVY, and one at GUISCARD, for the use of all batteries.

March 23rd.

Very thick mist in the early morning, after which the day became fine and clear.

H.Q., 36th Divisional Artillery. Information was received early in the morning from XVIII Corps, R.A., regarding Rear Zone positions as reconnoitred before the Battle.

The whole 36th Divisional Headquarters moved to BEAULIEU during the evening.

RIGHT GROUP. (ERSKINE). Telephonic communication with this Group was difficult all day.

8.0 a.m. The Group received a report that the enemy had crossed the Canal at HAM, and were also advancing South towards CUGNY on the right flank.
All Batteries barraged the line of the Canal.

9.0 a.m. O.C. A/91st Brigade R.F.A., reported our Infantry had retired on to the line of his guns.
A/91st Brigade R.F.A., was ordered to move by the Group to Q.23.d.5.0. to cover our Infantry in CUGNY. After completion of this move C/91st Brigade R.F.A., was ordered to take up position at Q.36.a.8.8.
232nd Siege Battery was ordered to move to BERLANCOURT by H.Q., 36th Divisional Artillery, and came under their direct orders.

10.0 a.m. D/173rd Brigade R.F.A., position was heavily shelled causing casualties. The battery was moved to Q.29.c.8.4.
Group Headquarters were moved to VILLESELVE with 61st Infantry Brigade.

The Infantry Line was then believed to run as follows:
On the Left the 36th Division NUILLEVILLETTE - BROUCHY, 61st Infantry Brigade EAUCOURT - Posts on Railway in R.7. and 8. - CUGNY, then 14th Division continued towards Q.36.

2.0 p.m. The enemy occupied BROUCHY, 36th Division Infantry fell back on A/91st Brigade, R.F.A., position.

8.0 p.m. 61st Infantry Brigade fell back on C/91st Brigade R.F.A., position.

These Batteries rallied the Infantry, and helped them to entrench in front of the guns.

The POTTER GROUP came into action round BACQUENCOURT about 5 a.m. under the 20th Divisional Artillery. During the early morning, fire was maintained on the roads leading down to the SOMME from the North on the Group Zone, and on to the villages of OFFOY, VOYENNES, CANIZY, etc.,

At 9.0 a.m. orders issued by H.Q., 36th Divisional Artillery, were received detailing the Group to rejoin 36th Division, and to move via BREUIL - MOYENCOURT - ERCHEU - LIBERMONT to a rendezvous near the Canal Crossing West of FRETOY LE CHATEAU (U.23.b.).
The Group arrived at 2 p.m. and horses which were very done up were exchanged with complete teams loaned from the 173rd Brigade, R.F.A.,

The Group was ordered to take up positions in or about FLAVY LE MELDEUX, covering the Zone SOMMETTE EAUCOURT - EPPEVILLE, with special reference to the HAM - GOLANCOURT Road.
Batteries were in action by dusk.
Fire was maintained throughout the night on the Roads leading South from the SOMME.

March 23rd.

LEFT GROUP (ELEY).   Officers Patrols sent out early in the morning to reconnoitre, reported that the Bridge at DURY was still intact, (having been repaired to enable some of our troops to retire), that the enemy was in HAM and our line followed the line of the Canal from HAM to ST. SIMON.

Roads and approaches to DURY were engaged, also ST. SIMON.

10.30 a.m.   The Infantry reported that the enemy were in MUILLE VILETTE and were advancing.

All batteries retired by sections, and came into action in the vicinity of COLLEZY, as follows:-

Headquarters, BERLANCOURT,	W.13.b.1.9.
463rd Battery R.F.A.,	W.3.a.0.2.
464th "	Q.32.d.6.6.
C/153rd Brigade R.F.A.,	W.3.b.3.5.
D/153rd "	W.3.a.5.5.
B/91st "	W.3.c.4.4.
D/232nd A. Bde. R.F.A.,	W.2.b.9.9.

where they remained all that day and night.

35th H.A.G.,   Orders to this Group could only be given through the 20th Divisional Artillery, and batteries were ordered to shell all the approaches to HAM during the day.
20th Divisional Artillery were asked to give them further orders, as the range would not allow the guns to cover the front held by the 36th Division.
The 232nd Siege Battery was ordered to move back to a position in U.21.a., which it occupied during the afternoon, but no ammunition could be obtained for it.

At noon the 148th Brigade R.F.A., being out of touch with its Division, reported for orders, and was sent into action by L'HOPITAL FARM in P.25.b. and 26.a. with orders to cover the area between the HAM-GOLANCOURT and HAM-NESLE BALLON Roads.
The Group left the control of the 36th Divisional Artillery soon after dark.

36th D.A.C.,   No. 1 Section, 20th D.A.C., ~~and part of B/91st Battery~~ were attached to Column, also A/173rd, B/173rd C/173rd, D/232nd Brigades and 462nd Battery R.F.A., less guns. D.A.C., 179th Army Brigade R.F.A., and 36th T.M. personnel came under its orders.
The Column, with attached units, marched to AVRICOURT where D.A.C. Section rejoined, but marched out same evening with Infantry.
Ammunition supply was maintained.
A.S.D. was established at Cross-roads between AVRICOURT and BEAULIEU LES FONTAINE with Forward Dumps at BEAULIEU LES FONTAINE and MUIRANCOURT.

March 24th.

Thick mist again in the early morning.

H.Q., 36th Divisional Artillery remained at BEAULIEU.

Groups were concentrated as far as possible in retirement. Telephonic communication was satisfactory with the POTTER Group, but was very intermittent with the ERSKINE and ELEY Groups throughout the day.

3.0 p.m.   The ERSKINE Group was put at the disposal of the 9th French Division.
The ELEY and POTTER Groups were put under the 62nd French Division, under the control of 36th Divisional Artillery.

The 36th Division was ordered to withdraw through the French Troops then holding a line behind them.

The two Groups were to withdraw as follows :

The ELEY Group to positions in U.18.d.
When the move was completed-
The POTTER Group was to move to positions in U.15.

A Liaison Officer from each Group was to be sent to the Infantry Regimental Commander at LIBERMONT forthwith.
Communication between them and the Groups would be by the line through BEAULIEU and the French Divisional Headquarters.
These orders were carried out as stated in Group narratives.

Groups were constituted as follows on this day :

ERSKINE GROUP.

　　　　A, B, & C/91st Brigade, R.F.A.,
　　　　D/173rd Brigade, R.F.A.,

ELEY GROUP.

　　　　463rd & 464th Batteries, R.F.A.,
　　　　C/153rd Brigade, R.F.A.,
　　　　D/232nd Brigade, R.F.A.,
　　　　D/153rd Brigade, R.F.A.,

POTTER GROUP.

　　　　A & B/153rd Brigade, R.F.A.,
　　　　383rd Battery, R.F.A.,
　　　　D/91st Brigade, R.F.A.,

35th H. A. G.

　　　　35th Heavy Battery, R.G.A.,
　　　　145th Heavy Battery, R.G.A.,
　　　　232nd Siege Battery R.G.A.,(directly under orders
　　　　　　　　　　　　　　　　　　　　of H.Q., 36th Division-
　　　　　　　　　　　　　　　　　　　　al Artillery).

ERSKINE GROUP.

1.0 a.m.   Batteries were withdrawn one at a time to positions in W.4.

6.0 a.m.   B/91st Brigade, R.F.A., came under the control of the Group by orders of 36th Divisional Artillery.

8.0 a.m.   Our Infantry began to fall back on VILLESELVE.
The Group was out of touch with 36th Divisional Artillery Headquarters, and was ordered by H.Q., 61st Infantry Brigade to take up positions in W.15. to barrage the further side of VILLESELVE and to shell CUGNY and BROUCHY, which was done.

1.0 p.m.   The Infantry commenced to retire through the guns, including the French who had been sent up to reinforce the Infantry in VILLESELVE.

3.0 p.m. All the Infantry had apparently retired through the guns. Cavalry made a successful local attack on BROUCHY capturing prisoners.

5.0 P.M. French Infantry retired through BEINES from woods on the right of bank in W.12. and 18.

5.30 p.m. As there appeared to be no Infantry left in front and the enemy were getting round the right flank, the Group Commander ordered all batteries except C/91st Brigade, R.F.A., to retire and take up positions in V.28. and 29.
C/91st Brigade, R.F.A., remained in position until dark and was able to support the retirement both of the French on their right rear and the Cavalry to the West of the GUISCARD - VILLESELVE Road. This battery retired by the only available road after the enemy had captured BERLANCOURT and BOUCHOIRE, and took up positions with the rest of the Brigade in V.28.

7.0 p.m. On orders received from H.Q., 36th Divisional Artillery, the Group Commander reported to the G.O.C., 9th French Infantry Division at QUESNY for orders and was instructed to move the Group back to CRISOLLES and report there for further instructions.

11.0 p.m. Batteries retired successfully, although the enemy were close up to GUISCARD at the time.

POTTER GROUP. At 5.30 a.m. a report was received by the Group Headquarters from an Infantry Officer, that GOLANCOURT had been captured and the enemy was advancing, and there was considerable machine gun fire at close range about this time; the mist was also very thick.
Batteries were withdrawn from their positions at FLAVY and formed up in a position of readiness in a field 800 yards west of FLAVY.
Officers Patrols and further information having established the fact that though were in GOLANCOURT no further advance was being made, batteries were ordered back into action in their former positions at 7 a.m.
In the course of the morning as the mist cleared and information began to be obtained, it was apparent that the enemy was in GOLANCOURT, BROUCHY, AUBIGNY, VILLATTE and BOUVUIL CHATEAU in considerable strength and appeared to be massing for an attack. Fire was therefore maintained on these places and on the HAM-GOLANCOURT Road. The shooting on GOLANCOURT and on BOUVUIL CHATEAU was seen to be very effective, and caused the enemy, who were in the open in large numbers, considerable casualties.
Beyond possibly one 4.2" battery, which fired a few shell into the village of FLAVY during the morning, the enemy did not appear to have any guns S. of the river until late in the day.
During the morning, probably about 10 a.m. the enemy commenced to attack all along the front, but made little if any progress on the front opposite the Group, the shell fire and effective fire of the French M.Gs. prevented him from debouching from GOLANCOURT. He appeared, however, to have gained considerable success on the left about ESMERY HALLON and on the front of the 14th Division on the right, necessitating a retirement on the part of the troops we were covering. About midday, therefore, orders were issued for the Group to retire to positions between FLAVY and FRENICHES. This was done by batteries, (sections in succession), without hindrance from the enemy, 363rd battery going to ROUVREL (V.9.b.) B/153 to a position about 1000 yards E. of it (V.10.d.) and A/153 and D/91 to positions about half a mile S.E. of FRENICHES and just N. of the FRENICHES-FLAVY Road (V.9.a. and c.) Group H.Q. were established at ROUVREL FARM. The enemy's positions and his lines of approach were kept under continuous bursts of fire throughout the day, and he showed no inclination to push on on our immediate front. Except for a few 5.9's which fell near D/91, the enemy did not fire on the batteries throughout the day.

About 6 p.m. the enemy having gained considerable success opposite the Division on our right in the direction of BERLANCOURT and VILLESELVE, a further withdrawal was ordered, and by dusk the four batteries were in action about 1000 yards W. of FRENICHES and just S. of the FRENICHES-FLAVY Road (square V.9.d.) Group H.Q., in FRENICHES.

At 8 p.m. the orders were received to reconnoitre new positions in U.15. and occupy them when ordered by H.Q., 36th Divisional Artillery.

At 12 midnight these orders were received, and all batteries were in action in the new positions by 4 a.m. 25th March.

Group H.Q., were established in the FME. DES FONDS CARETS.

BLEW GROUP. Batteries engaged AUBIGNY, BROUCHY, GOLANCOURT and LAMOY WOOD, where the enemy was in strength.

At 11.40 a.m. the batteries were ordered to retire to the vicinity of BERLANCOURT and supported the French Infantry in position at COLLEZY, in addition to our own infantry.

At 2.30 p.m. a further retirement was carried out by Sections to BUCHOIRE and barrage fire was opened at the request of the French to the North and West of COLLEZY.

While in action here the 463rd and 464th Batteries were heavily shelled.

At 6 p.m. the Group received orders from H.Q., 36th Divisional Artillery to retire to positions just East of FRETOY LE CHATEAU, and all batteries were in action in their new positions by 10 p.m.

35th H.A.G., The 60-pdr. batteries continued to shell the approaches from HAM to ESMERY HALLON during the day supporting the Division on our left.

The 232nd Siege Battery remained in action in U.21.a. No ammunition was available as yet.

36th D.A.C., The supply of ammunition was continued to the Forward Dumps.

25th March.

Brig: Gen. H.J. BROCK, C.M.G., D.S.O., assumed Command of the 36th Divisional Artillery on return from Leave,
Lieut. Col. H.C. SIMPSON, D.S.O., R.F.A., hitherto Acting C.R.A., became Artillery Liaison Officer with the 62nd French Division, (H.Q., in BEAULIEU).
During the afternoon the Headquarters moved to CANDOR. (T.17.b. Sheet 70 B).

POTTER GROUP.   12 midnight 24/25 The Group was ordered to move back to the new positions in U.15. (Sheet 66 D) which was carried out successfully, without hindrance from the enemy, who were by that time fairly close up to batteries.

4.0 a.m.   All batteries were again in action. Group H.Q., were in the FME. DES FONDS GAMETS (U.15.a.)

About 7 a.m. on a misty morning heavy firing was heard in front indicating an enemy attack. Throughout the morning barrages were fired on the BOIS DE L'HOPITAL, FRENICHES-FRETOY LE CHATEAU Road-WOOD in squares U.6., U.12., and U.18. etc., in support of the French 62nd Division who were now holding the front from LIBERMONT to the FRETOY LE CHATEAU-BEAULIEU Road. The enemy attacked repeatedly during the morning in great strength especially in front of LIBERMONT and in the BOIS DE L'HOPITAL where he at first gained no success, and suffered very heavy casualties. At about 12 noon, however, he appears to have succeeded in crossing the Canal S. of LIBERMONT near MOYENCOURT and to have advanced on ERCHEU. At the same time the French were slowly pressed back through LIBERMONT and the BOIS DE L'HOPITAL. About 1 p.m., the situation on the left making a general retirement necessary, batteries of the Group were ordered to be prepared to withdraw to positions in square U.19.c. immediately W. of BEAULIEU. These were reconnoitred, and after covering the withdrawal of the ELEY Group, the POTTER Group withdrew to these positions, being all in action again by 3 p.m.   Group H.Q., at BOUVRESSE Farm, T.23.a.

Fire was carried out to protect the Canal gap, and also enfilade barrages in U.18., and V.13. to defend FRETOY LE CHATEAU from the North.
Positions further in rear were reconnoitred near AVRICOURT, and batteries commenced withdrawing about 7 p.m. (the last battery leaving when the enemy's Infantry were a few hundred yards away), and came into action in the vicinity of the ammunition dump at the Cross-roads in T.29.a. All batteries were in action by 10.30 p.m.   Group H.Q., were established in AVRICOURT.
The Zone given by the French 62nd Division to the 36th Divisional Artillery for barrage purposes extended
from CATIGNY C.9.c. (Sheet 70 B).
to U.16.a. (Sheet 66 D).

ELEY GROUP.   At 3 a.m. batteries were ordered to move at once to positions in U.9. N.E. of BEAULIEU. All batteries were in their new positions by 5 a.m.   H.Q., were established with the H.Q., POTTER GROUP at the FME. DES FONDS GAMETS.
Continuous barrage fire was carried out all morning against the enemy attacking from the BOIS DE L'HOPITAL against LIBERMONT and the Canal gap in U.10.
At 1 p.m. the Group was ordered, by 62nd French Division H.Q., to retire to positions in U.13.c., H.Q., to proceed to BOUVRESSE FARM, T.23.a.
All batteries were in action by 2 p.m. and fire was carried out to protect LIBERMONT and the Canal gap.
By 4 p.m. LIBERMONT was known to have fallen, and the barrage was dropped to protect the line of the Canal, as far south as U.4.d.8.6. (Sheet 66 D).
The advance of the enemy was retarded, but eventually he succeeded in gaining ground W. of the Canal at LIBERMONT, and in U.10.a. and c. (Sheet 66 D). This necessitated a further withdrawal

to positions in T.23. (Sheet 66 D) close to AVRICOURT.

C/153rd Brigade, R.F.A., and 383rd Battery R.F.A., changed Groups during the day by order of H.Q., 36th Divisional Artillery.

35th H.A.G.,   The two 60-pdr. batteries were in action W. of ERCHEU.
Group H.Q., were at SOLENTE.

Fire was carried out all day in defence of LIBERMONT, and the Salient in the Canal in O.18., which was heavily attacked.

In the afternoon batteries retired to MARGNY to take up positions W. of the BOIS DE CHAMPIEN.

The 232nd Siege Battery, under direct orders of H.Q., 36th Divisional Artillery, bombarded the BOIS DE L'HOPITAL and objectives in the vicinity all morning, and at midday withdrew by Sections to a position in T.22.c. (Sheet 66 D), where it continued firing to protect the gap in the Canal in U.11. and also bombarded FRENICHES.

36th D.A.C.,   The Column, with attached units, marched at 6 p.m. to FRESNIERS and established a Dump.

March 26th.

The 62nd French Division issued orders for the withdrawal of all artillery during the night March 25th/26th, the new positions to be occupied by dawn and allotted an area for the 36th Divisional Artillery.

Orders were issued to Groups to occupy positions, as follows:-

POTTER GROUP.   Round BALNY in R.14.d. and R.20.b.
ELEY GROUP.   In R.14.a. and b. (Sheet 70 E).
36th H.A.G.   All batteries in the vicinity of the Sugar Factory, R.16.d.

36th Divisional Artillery H.Q., were to be in CANNY SUR MATZ.

36th Divisional Artillery H.Q., moved back rather hurriedly at 4 a.m.

In consequence of a premature retirement by the French Infantry on our right flank Groups had to be withdrawn rapidly at 9 a.m. from what had become dangerously exposed positions.

Groups moved to a rendezvous at GURY, O.28.a. and the 36th Divisional Artillery came under the orders of the 77th French Division, and proceeded into action -

POTTER GROUP in N.21.a. (Sheet 70 E)
ELEY GROUP   in O.35.c.

covering the front CANNECTANCOURT–THIESCOURT–LASSIGNY–CANNY SUR MATZ.

D/91st and D/152nd Brigades R.F.A. changed Groups by orders of H.Q., 36th Divisional Artillery.

36th Divisional Artillery H.Q., were at MONCHY LAMOTTE, and worked as a Group under the 77th French Divisional Artillery Commander.

Lieut. Col. SIMPSON, D.S.O., R.F.A., acted as Liaison Officer with the French Division.

POTTER GROUP.   Batteries moved off at 2.30 a.m. and were in action by 5.30 a.m. in the area ordered. Group H.Q., were in BALNY FARM.

9 a.m.   Batteries retired via LASSIGNY to the rendezvous at GURY, and thence into action in N.21.a. to cover the right regimental sector CANNECTANCOURT–THIESCOURT. H.Q., at LA COMBE FARM.

Batteries were not in action until very late on in the night.

ELEY GROUP.   Batteries moved off at 2 a.m. and came into action in the area ordered by 6 a.m. Group H.Q., were in BALNY FARM.

9 a.m.   On receipt of orders from H.Q., 36th Divisional Artillery, batteries moved back independently through CANNY (reporting there for orders) to the rendezvous at GURY, and thence into action in positions in O.35.c. Group H.Q., at N.3.d.6.3.

Lieut. Col. ELEY, C.M.G., D.S.O., R.F.A., having lost touch with his Group during the retirement, proceeded to H.Q., XVIII Corps, R.A. and the Group was commanded by Major G. EAGLE, D.S.O., R.F.A., D/91st Brigade, R.F.A.,

36th H.A.G.,   never came into action as ordered but continued to retire.

The two 60-pdr. batteries moved to the rendezvous at GURY and thence into action close to MONCHUIL LAMOTTE in N.9.c.

The 232nd Siege Battery lost touch with the Group during the retirement, and could not be recovered. It eventually rejoined its original Group, the 95th H.A.G.

36th D.A.C.,   The Column and attached units marched to ORVILLERS SOREL; here 42nd Battery and 179th B.A.C., were detached, and were marched under separate orders to ST. JUST by O.C., 179th Army Brigade R.F.A.,

An A.R.P. was established at RESSONS from which ammunition was supplied to Forward Dumps at MARGNY SUR MATZ and MONCHUIL LAMOTTE.

March 27th.

The front of the 77th Division was readjusted so as to cover a front from PLEMONT to CANNY SUR MATZ.

The POTTER GROUP, which was out of touch with H.Q., 36th Divisional Artillery in N.21. was moved round to positions in M.5. with H.Q., at M.5.central, batteries getting into action by 2.45 p.m.

The ELEY GROUP remained in the same positions.

Determined enemy attacks took place during the afternoon and were beaten off, in all cases suffering heavily from our barrage fire.

The 35th H.A.G., returned to the control of the XVIII Corps R.A., moving at 6 a.m.

36th D.A.C. Orders were received to supply 36th Divisional Artillery and all attached units with forage and rations. These were drawn from a Reserve Dump at RESSONS and delivered daily to units.

On the same date the Column, with attached units, marched to MERY and kept up supply of ammunition to MAREUIL LAMOTTE Dump. MARGNY SUR MATZ Dump was cleared of ammunition and ceased to be used.

March 28th.

The enemy made continual attacks throughout the day, principally against the Valley in square 19, W. of PLEMONT HILL and against CANNY.

Effective barrages were put down, and the enemy obtained no success except at CANNY, which he eventually succeeded in capturing.

Heavy rain fell during the night.

Extensive Harassing fire was carried out during the night, and Concentrations at various times were fired on LASSIGNY with great effect.

The 56th H.A.G., (220th and 306th 6" How. batteries arrived, (and came under the orders of H.Q., 36th (Divisional Artillery.

Batteries went into action just S.W. of MAREUIL LAMOTTE, Group H.Q., in the village.

36th D.A.C., The Column and attached units marched to GOURNAY. Supply of ammunition, forage and rations was maintained.

March 29th.

A very quiet day.

Harassing Fire and Concentrations were carried out throughout the 24 hours.

36th D.A.C., Ammunition was drawn by Motor Lorry from REMY and dumped at GOURNAY, where the Column and attached units refilled and continued to supply MAREUIL LAMOTTE Dump.
Supply of ammunition, forage and rations maintained.

March 30th.

The enemy started a very strong attack about 8 a.m. supported by fairly strong artillery fire against the fronts held by the 53rd and 77th French Divisions.

At one time the enemy succeeded in capturing PLEMONT HILL, held by the 53rd French Division, but it was recaptured almost at once by a counter-attack.

He also succeeded in capturing PLESSIER LE ROYE and the Chateau Park in G.23., 24., and 30, and by 10.30 a.m. a number had reached the CARRIERE MADAME in square G.29.d. only a few hundred yards from the position of C and D/153rd Brigade R.F.A., These batteries were withdrawn at midday to positions near ST. CLAUDE FARM in H.5.c. and a section from each of A and B/153rd Brigade R.F.A., were also withdrawn to this vicinity. All batteries were subjected to a certain amount of shelling, which caused casualties to the gun detachments and in the advanced wagon lines.

The left of the 77th Division in front of GURY stood firm and a counter-attack was prepared for to restore the situation in the centre. A continuous bombardment was maintained on PLESSIER LE ROYE, the Chateau Park and LASSIGNY till 5.30 p.m. when the French counter-attacked from the East and West and were completely successful, restoring the whole line and capturing 700 prisoners.

Throughout the day the artillery barrage proved extremely effective, and observed fire was brought to bear on large enemy bodies inflicting considerable casualties.

4 p.m. A warning order was issued in accordance with instructions sent by H.Q., III Corps, R.A., for Groups to be prepared to withdraw from action and proceed to the ARSY area to billet.

8.30 p.m. Final orders were issued and batteries commenced to withdraw at 9.0 p.m.

The 36th D.A.C., and all details not in action had already withdrawn during the afternoon, after clearing the RESSONS ammunition dump.

After a trying march all units reached GRAND FRESNOY by 5.0 a.m. on 31st March.

The 36th H.A.G., were ordered to remain in action under the 77th French Division.

March 31st.

Units of the 36th Divisional Artillery marched via CLERMONT to billets at ETOUY, LA RUE ST. PIERRE, and WARREVILLE (BEAUVAIS 1/100,000) en route for the Artillery Concentration Area, POIX.

Colonel POTTER, D.S.O., R.F.A.,
Colonel ELEY, C.M.G., D.S.O., R.F.A.,
Colonel ERSKINE, D.S.O., R.F.A.,

The 36th Divisional Artillery will be divided into Groups as under :
CENTRE GROUP, under Colonel POTTER, D.S.O., R.F.A.,
                363rd Battery R.F.A.,
                D/91st Brigade R.F.A.,
                B/153rd   "
                A/153rd   "
                D/173rd   "

LEFT GROUP, under Colonel ELEY, C.M.G., D.S.O., R.F.A.,
                463rd Battery R.F.A.,
                C/153rd Brigade R.F.A.,
                D/232nd Brigade R.F.A.,
                D/153rd   "
                464th Battery R.F.A.,
                B/91st Brigade R.F.A.,

These Groups will take up positions forthwith to cover the Divisional Front, which will extend to FONTAINE LES CLERCS in the North to RIVER at L.16.c. in the South.
The CENTRE Group will take up positions at L.14.a. and c. and
The LEFT Group will take up positions at L.8.a., L.2.c. and a.

These positions will be reconnoitred at once under orders of the Group Commanders.
Batteries on the East of the River will cross by TUGNY BRIDGE at once.
The D.A.C., will move to the Railway Crossing at K.10.c.6.2. and Battery Wagon Lines will refill at this position. Battery Echelons can fill up when crossing the river at TUGNY with 18-pr. ammunition or at ST. SIMON Dump with S.X.

The CENTRE Group will cover 108th Infantry Brigade Front, and the LEFT Group the 107th and 109th fronts.
The fronts of the Infantry Brigades will be as follows :
108th Infantry Brigade : from L.16.a. to Cemetery in L.3.d.
107th Infantry Brigade : from LOCK in L.12.a. to the ROUPY -
                                    SERAUCOURT Road, inclusive.
109th Infantry Brigade : from the ROUPY - SERAUCOURT Road, exclusive
                                    to the right of the Battalion in the Battle
                                    Zone of R. South.

RIGHT GROUP, Lt. Col. ERSKINE, D.S.O., R.F.A., H.Q., OLLEZY.
                A/91st and C/91st Brigade R.F.A.,
                232nd Siege Battery.
will cover the front of the 61st Infantry Brigade, 30th Division, extending from L.22. to L.30.

       ACKNOWLEDGE.

                                  (sd)   G.T. RUGER, Major, R.F.A.,
                                              for Major, B.A.,
21.3.1918.   Brigade Major, 36th Divisional Artillery.

NOTE on above Order.
The 36th D.A.C., moved at 4 p.m. 21st March from ST. SIMON to SOMMETTE EAUCOURT and established a Dump there.
The Instructions detailed in the above order for 36th D.A.C., were cancelled, and at 11 p.m. they were ordered to march to VERLAINES.

Copy of 36th Divisional Artillery Order, issued on 24th March.

1. The Artillery covering the 36th Divisional Front will be reorganised into Groups as follows, from 6 a.m. today 24th instant. The necessary communications will be arranged by that time.

ERSKINE GROUP: A/91st Bde.R.F.A.   B/91st Bde.R.F.A.(now at W.3.c.4.4.
                C/91st   "   in the ELEY Group.
                D/173rd   "

ELEY GROUP.   463rd Bty.R.F.A.,   464th Bty. R.F.A.
     C/153? C/163rd Bde.R.F.A.   D/153rd Bde.R.F.A.
                D/232nd Bde.R.F.A.

POTTER GROUP.   A/153rd Bde.R.F.A.   B/153rd Bde.R.F.A.
                383rd Bty. R.F.A.   D/91st Bde.R.F.A.

2. Normal S.O.S. ZONES will now be as follows :
       ERSKINE GROUP   L.34.c.0.0.   -   L.32.c.0.0.
       ELEY GROUP   L.32.c.0.0.   -   K.36.c.0.0.
       POTTER GROUP   K.36.c.0.0.   -   K.34.c.0.0.

3. XVIII Corps H.A. are now attached to 36th Division as follows :
      35th H.A.G. (35th Heavy Battery & 145th Heavy Battery.)
      232nd Siege Battery.

S.O.S. Lines will be given as required from this office.

In case of advance batteries will support their Infantry as closely as possible.
The 232nd Siege Battery R.G.A. will advance under orders from H.Q., 36th Divisional Artillery to a position about FLAVY LE MELDEUX (V.5).
The 35th and 145th Heavy Batteries will advance under orders from this office.
The ERSKINE & ELEY Groups will advance as arranged by G.Os.C. Infantry Brigades with whom these Groups are respectively working.
The POTTER Group will advance to a line about GOLANCOURT-BONNEUIL CHATEAU.

In case of a retirement, batteries will retire by sections.
The 232nd Siege battery will take up a position about V.21.a.5.7.
The 35th and 145th Heavy Batteries will remain in present positions until further orders.
The ERSKINE & ELEY Groups will retire to a line W.16.centl, V.12.centl.
The POTTER Group will cover the retirement of the above Groups and after these Groups are in action will retire to a line V.16.d.0.0., V.8. central, with H.Q., at FRENICHES.
The H.Q., of the ERSKINE & ELEY Groups will in all cases remain with the H.Q., of the Infantry Brigades they cover.
Further advanced or retired positions will be arranged for later as necessity arises.
In all cases advanced Mobile Wagon Lines will be established in the vicinity of gun positions to facilitate rapidity of movement.
The policy for todays operations are not yet definitely settled. The line held by the British troops as far as is known runs from S. of CUGNY-BROUCHY-MUILLEY VILETTE (?) -VERLANES-EPPEVILLE and thence along S. bank of River. The line held by the French Army runs through R.32.-Q.32.-V.5.
Some elements of our troops, including Cavalry, hold an intermediate line about Q.20.centl.-GOLANCOURT-Fme de BONNEUIL-P.23.c.0.0.
The information concerning dispositions contained in this order will not be distributed beyond Group H.Q.,

AMMUNITION SUPPLY. 36th D.A.C.,   )
                179th B.A.C.   ) are at AVRICOURT T.21.
                462nd Battery   )

A.R.P. is at Cross-roads T.29.a.1.5.
O.C. D.A.C., (using 179th B.A.C.etc.,) will forthwith create FORWARD DUMPS.
   (a) At Cross-roads V.23.b.8.1. and
   (b) Between road junctions V.9.c.0.5. & V.8.c.8.6.
with an Officer in charge of each and an adequate dump party.
These dumps will be maintained at -
4000 rounds 18-pr. 1000 rounds 4.5"How. in each.

RATIONS.

If the situation permits rations for consumption 25th for all batteries and H.Qs. of 153rd, D/173rd, 179th and 91st Brigades R.F.A., will be at the road junction V.14.a.6.7. any time after 2 p.m. today (24th).

Batteries will send guides (or supply wagons if these are with units) there at that time prepared to await the arrival of the convoy. Rations for 173rd, D.A.C., 462nd and 36th T.Ms. will be delivered to AVRICOURT as today.

36th Divisional Train is at AMRICOURT.

(sd) H.F. GRANT-SUTTIE.

Major, R.A.,
24.3.1918. Brigade Major, 36th Divisional Artillery.

DISTRIBUTION.

Col. ERSKINE, D.S.O.,R.F.A.,
Col. ELEY, C.M.G.,D.S.O.,R.F.A.,
Col. POTTER, D.S.O.,R.F.A.,
O.C. 232nd Siege Battery R.G.A.,
O.C. 35th H.A.G.,
H.Q., R.A., XVIII Corps.
H.Q., 36th Division, 'G'.
O.C. 36th D.A.C.,

Copy of 36th Divisional Artillery Order No. 33.

Ref: Map 70 E 1/40,000.

The 36th Divisional Artillery has come under the orders of the 77th French Division.

The Line held by the Infantry is as follows :

(a) An Outpost line running from N.12.c.8.9. - N.12.a.0.4. - N.35.c. 0.0. - N.34.a.0.6. - N.27.central. - N.21.c.0.0. - N.20.central. N.20.a.0.4. - N.13.a.0.0. - G.13.a.0.7. - G.4.central.

(b) A Line of Resistance in rear running from N.12.c.4.0. - N.11.central. - N.5.central. - N.33.d.6.0. - N.33.central - N.26.central - N.19.central - Cross roads G.13.c. - G.9. central - G.8.b.35.20.

The Line is held by three regiments of Infantry in the Front System, each regiment having two battalions in the Front Line and one in support.

The Field Artillery covering the front will be organised in two Groups as follows :

The POTTER GROUP.   Headquarters, LA SENSE FARM.
                  Consisting of A)
                              B)
                              C) 153rd Brigade R.F.A.
                              D)

The ELMY GROUP.   Headquarters, N.3.d.6.3.
                  Consisting of
                        383rd Battery R.F.A.
                        463rd Battery R.F.A.
                        464th Battery R.F.A.
                        D/91st Brigade R.F.A.
                        D/232nd Brigade R.F.A.

The dividing line between Groups for S.O.S. purposes will be a line drawn through N.26.central.
                N.21.central.

Normal S.O.S. Lines in case of a general attack.
The barrage will be as follows :
RIGHT GROUP:
Southern and Western exits from CANNECTANCOURT & THIESCOURT.

LEFT GROUP:
The Southern and Western exits of LASSIGNY.
The Northern half of CANNY SUR MATZ.

In case of an enemy attack coming from the direction of one of these villages only, all available guns and howitzers will be turned on to the exits of the one which the attack is developing from.

In no case is a barrage to be put down without orders from the Divisional Infantry Commander.

The Right and Left Infantry regiments will send up Red S.O.S. Rockets till the barrage is put down. On the Right the signal will be sent up from the direction of the line: on the Left - from GURY.

For the present the Centre Regiment will not fire Rockets, but send S.O.S. by telephone only.

Colonel SIMPSON, D.S.O.,R.F.A., will act as Liaison Officer with the Divisional Infantry Commander at G.5.c.0.7.
The POTTER GROUP is furnishing a Liaison Officer with the Right Infantry Regiment.
The ELMY GROUP is furnishing a Liaison Officer with the Centre Infantry ~~Brigade~~ Regiment

- 2 -

Each Group will establish an O.P. to cover the Sector allotted to it to be manned continuously.

Batteries must also establish an O.P. each, if possible, and a system of Visual Communication must be arranged.

The 35th H.A.G.   Headquarters, F.3.d.8.2.
covers the front of the 77th French Division and consists of the
    35th Heavy Battery
    145th Heavy Battery
    232nd Siege Battery

with S.O.S. Lines as under :

One 60-pr. battery THIESCOURT and its Northern approaches.
One 60-pr. battery LASSIGNY and its Northern approaches.
One 6" How. Battery - 2 guns on the villages -
    CANNECTANCOURT.
    THIESCOURT.
    LASSIGNY.

AMMUNITION.

Sheet AMIENS 17.   D.A.C., is at ORVILLERS-SOREL (4 miles W.of GURY).

  - do -   A.R.P. is at RESSONS Railway Station where there is

                  18-pr.   4.5" How.   60-pr.   6" How.

                  10,000   4,000   2,000   1,000 rounds.

                  (The 60-pr. and 6" How. had not reached the Dump
                                at 6 p.m. tonight).

Sheet 70 K   Two Forward Dumps are being established at
                               For   Capacity
                                          18-pr.   4.5" How.
        (a) N.8.b.8.3.   Left Group   1800   300

        (b) N.29.d.9.2. Right Group   1800   300

RATIONS.

    Arrangements will be notified later.

                        (sd)   H.F. GRANT-SUTTIE.

                                    Major, R.A.,
26.3.1918.   Brigade Major, 36th Divisional Artillery.

36th Divisional Artillery.

C. R. A.

36th DIVISION.

APRIL 1918.

Army Form C. 2118.

WAR DIARY
or
INTELLIGENCE SUMMARY.
(Erase heading not required.)

HQ 36 Div Arty
Vol 31

Place	Date	Hour	Summary of Events and Information	Remarks and references to Appendices
ETOUY	1st April		36th Divisional artillery, remained today at ETOUY, LA RUE ST PIERRE, WARAIVILLE area	Reference Maps BEAUVAIS 01/EPPE 1/100000
	2nd "		all units marched 2nd April to FRANCASTEL billeting area	36 Div Arty war No 37
	3rd "		all units marched to the POIX area for refitment 1/Q + 179th Army brigade before the movement of the 1st Bgde 36 DA into billets as follows	36 Div Arty war No 35
MORVILLERS			H/Q & DA and 173rd Bgde RFA — MORVILLERS St Selve Veeur 173rd Brigade RFA — OFFIGNIES 36 DAC & TR Reserve — CHEPOY D/232	
	4th April		2nd DTC reported yesterday & DTC reported today 173rd Brigade R.F.A. at Le Chapelle sous Poix No 26	36 Div Arty war No 26

Army Form C. 2118.

WAR DIARY
or
INTELLIGENCE SUMMARY.
(Erase heading not required.)

Instructions regarding War Diaries and Intelligence Summaries are contained in F. S. Regs., Part II. and the Staff Manual respectively. Title pages will be prepared in manuscript.

Place	Date	Hour	Summary of Events and Information	Remarks and references to Appendices
MOYENCOURT SOUS POIX	April 8th		36th Divisional artillery marched to fresh billets in the POIX Area, preparatory to entraining to rejoin the division. H.Q. R.A. billeted at MOYENCOURT SOUS POIX in chateau	36 D.A. order No 37.
PONT de METZ	April 11th		36th Divisional artillery marched to billets at PONT de METZ and RENANCOURT. R.A.H.Q. being in chateau in latter village.	36 D.A. order No 38.
	April 14th		36th Divisional artillery marched to the place of entrainment at ROUEN station AMIENS and entrained for POPERINGHE and HOPOUTRE to rejoin the 36th Division (2nd Corps) in front of YPRES. Route via ABBEVILLE BOULOGNE CAZANDS HAZEBROUCK	36 D.A. order No 39. and Entrainment order No 1 and Detrainment order No 1
Monday April 15th			Just train with H.Q. 36 D.A. arrives HOPOUTRE and entrains to the 1X corps, to come under the orders of C.R.A. 58th Division covering the 34th Inf Division (in process of being relieved by the 59th Inf Division)	

A 5834   Wt W4973/M687   750,000   8/16   D. D. & L., Ltd.   Forms/C.2118/13.

Army Form C. 2118.

WAR DIARY
or
INTELLIGENCE SUMMARY.
(Erase heading not required.)

Instructions regarding War Diaries and Intelligence Summaries are contained in F. S. Regs., Part II. and the Staff Manual respectively. Title pages will be prepared in manuscript.

Place	Date	Hour	Summary of Events and Information	Remarks and references to Appendices
HOMPSTEY	16th April		Entrainment complete by 2.00 training 15th Month. Units in upper lines 152nd Bde R.F.A. and 91st Bde R.F.A. went into action in positions near BERTHEN besides the 38th DA during the morning.	Reference Map HAZEBROUCK 1/100,000 Sheets 77,28 1/40,000
	17th April		Heavy shelling in forward & back areas by the enemy, all troops coming out of the 28th Brigade R.A. engaged after into action about 6 BERTHEN during the night. Being the nearer of H.Q. 36th D.A. H.Q. 36 D.A. had to frequently remove in CAESTRE-CASSEL road (P.2.1.6.9.8.) and remained there till the 24th April	
	23rd April		The night 22nd/23rd April The 152nd Bde R.F.A. being again out of action came under the orders of H.Q. 36 D.A. and marched to HAHHOEK STANDING	36 D.A. orders No. 40
	24th April		The 170 to Bde R.F.A. & 36th D.A.C. marched to fields in Eecke area 152nd Bde R.F.A. to HAHHOEK Standing. 75 D.A.C. to OUDEZEELE H.Q. 36 D.A. moved to Ten ELMS CAMP (1995) 36 D.A. 2 miles W. Caps	36 D.A. orders No. 41

A 5834 Wt.W4923/M987 750,000 816 D.D.& L.Ltd. Forms/C.2118/13.

Army Form C. 2118.

WAR DIARY
or
INTELLIGENCE SUMMARY.
(Erase heading not required.)

Instructions regarding War Diaries and Intelligence Summaries are contained in F. S. Regs., Part II. and the Staff Manual respectively. Title pages will be prepared in manuscript.

Place	Date	Hour	Summary of Events and Information	Remarks and references to Appendices
TEN ELMS CAMP	25th April		The 36 Div Artillery Brigades & D.A.C. move then back to further forward. H.Q. 36 D.A. remained at TEN ELMS CAMP	36 D.A. Orders No 42
BORDAS CAMP.			The Brigades 25/26 and 26/27 April relieved the H.Q. 65 The D.A. and 230 The Brigades R.F.A., in the line covering the 36th Division. 26th April the 153rd Bde R.F.A. moved their wagon lines to the East near Vlamertinghe R.F.A.	36 D.A. orders No 44
	26th April		On the night 26th/27th April the 36th Division withdrew to the line of the Ypres HAZEBROUCK canal and the Reserve line of YPRES defences (with an outpost line to form in the line POPERINGHE OBLONG FORT (or lines opposite the line PICKEM-YPRES). The following day a section of each of the two Front batteries 37/15 & the Brigade R.F.A. were withdrawn further back in consequence.	36 D.A. orders No 43. 36 D.A. Orders 45
	27th April		H.Q. 36 Div broke back to Poperinghe Camp P.A.10.C.3.4 The 173rd Bde R.F.A. went in to action in position for defence of the canal E/7/2 H/1/B5 Heavy shelling in trying both (against roads & rivers) causing casualties in horses & men.	36 D.A. Orders 46

(A7092) Wt. W12859/M1293 750,000 4/17 D. D. & L., Ltd. Forms/C.2118-14.

Army Form C. 2118.

WAR DIARY
or
INTELLIGENCE SUMMARY.
(Erase heading not required.)

Instructions regarding War Diaries and Intelligence Summaries are contained in F. S. Regs., Part II. and the Staff Manual respectively. Title pages will be prepared in manuscript.

Place	Date	Hour	Summary of Events and Information	Remarks and references to Appendices
JEATON CAMP	April 27th		17.32d Brigade received instructions to be able to move the At outpost line. The higher 28/h/g to give positions were reallysated and two batteries per group were withdrawn from their forward positions and the Canal bank to positions approximately 3000 yards from the existing positions PICKET HOUSE FARM & OBLONG FARM.	
	April 3/12		Rechange in front; no infantry relation to 32nd Div. Front traveling line - Group Commanders and C.O.'s Caual reserve turns were carried out continuously.	

4.5.18.

H. J. Brock.
Lieut. Col. R.A.
Comdg. 36. Div. Art.

36TH DIVISIONAL ARTILLERY ORDER No. 34.

The 36th Divisional Artillery will march from their present billets to the FRANCASTEL Billeting Area on the 2nd April 1918, according to March Table on reverse.

Units must send forward small advanced parties to report to the Staff Captain, R.A., at the Mairie, FRANCASTEL, to obtain information as to the location of their billets and to guide their Units there.

Columns are not to exceed 200 yards in length on the march, and 150 yards interval must be maintained between columns.

The usual Military Precautions will be observed.

A C K N O W L E D G E.

[signature]

Major, R.A.,

1.4.1918.   Brigade Major, 36th Divisional Artillery.

DISTRIBUTION.

O.C. 153rd Brigade, R.F.A., (5).
O.C. 173rd Brigade, R.F.A., (5).
O.C. 179th A. Brigade, R.F.A., (7).
O.C. 36th D.A.C., (4).
H.Q., R.A., XVIII Corps.
Staff Captain, R.A.,
War Diary (2).
File (2).

MARCH TABLE.

UNIT	FROM	TO	ROUTE	REMARKS.
179th A. Brigade R.F.A., D/91st Brigade R.F.A.; D/232nd Brigade R.F.A.,	BPGUY	FRANCASTEL Billeting Area	BULLES-MONTREUIL SUR FRECHE-NOYERS ST. MARTIN	To be clear of LORTIET by 9.0 a.m.
153rd Brigade R.F.A.,	WARVILLE LORTIET & LA NEUVILLE	-do-	-do-	WAR I. Not to leave VILL: &LORTIET before 9.30 a.m. The Battery in LA NEUVILLE to join the Brigade LITZ - WARIVILLE. by the Road
173rd Brigade R.F.A.,	La Rue ST. PIERRE.	-do-	REMERANGLES-HOUDIVILLERS LAFRAYE- LE BOIS ST. MARTIN AUCHY LE MONTAGNE.	To be clear of La Rue St. PIERRE by 9.0 am.
38th D.A.C., No.1 Sect.20th D.A.C., 36th T.M. Personnel.		-do-	-do-	Not to leave La Rue St. PIERRE before 9.30 am.

36TH DIVISIONAL ARTILLERY ORDER NO. 35.

Ref:
AMIENS Sheet) 1/100,000
DIEPPE Sheet)

The 36th Divisional Artillery will march from their present billets to the POIX Billeting Area on the 3rd April, 1918, according to the March Table on reverse.

Units must send forward small advanced parties to be at the Church at FREMONTIERES by 12 noon tomorrow, where guides will meet them with information as to the definite location of their billets. Arrangements are being made for guides to meet remaining Units on the GRANDVILLIERS-POIX Road to direct them to their billets. of the 179th A. Bde. R.F.A.,

Columns are not to exceed 200 yards in length on the march, and 150 yards interval must be maintained between columns.

The usual Military Precautions will be observed.

A C K N O W L E D G E.

Major, R.A.,

3.4.1918.   Brigade Major, 36th Divisional Artillery.

DISTRIBUTION.
O.C. 153rd Brigade, R.F.A.,
O.C. 173rd Brigade, R.F.A.,
O.C. 179th Army Brigade, R.F.A.,
O.C. 36th D.A.C.,
H.Q., R.A., XVIII Corps.
STAFF CAPTAIN, R.A.,
War Diary.
File.

MARCH TABLE.

UNIT	FROM	TO	ROUTE	REMARKS.
179th A. Bde. R.F.A.,	FRANCASTEL & OURSEL MAISON	POIX Billeting Area	LE CROCQ/sur CROISSY CELIF MOJSURES- CONTY-FLEURY- FREMONTIER'S	To be clear of LE CROCQ by 10 a.m.
D/91st Bde.R.F.A.,				
153rd Bde. R.F.A.,	FRANCASTEL	"	CREVEGOEUR LE GRAND-METDEESNIL- GRANDVILLIERS	To be clear of FRANCASTEL by 8.30 a.m.
173rd Bde. R.F.A.,	"	"	"	To follow 153rd Bde. R.F.A.,
D/232nd Bde.R.F.A.,	"	"	"	To follow 173rd Bde. R.F.A.,
36th D.A.C., 1 Sect. 20th D.A.C., 36th T.M. Personnel	"	"	"	Not to enter CREVECOEUR LE GRAND before 11.30 a.m.

As soon as Brigade Headquarters and Battery Locations are determined send a mounted Orderly or cyclist Orderly to O.C. No. 1 Coy Divisional Train at NAMCS-AU-VAL, instructing him where to send rations for consumption 4.4.1918.

Urgent

36TH DIVISIONAL ARTILLERY ORDER No. 36.

The following moves will take place tomorrow 4.4.1918.

1. D/173rd Brigade, R.F.A., will join 173rd Brigade, R.F.A., at OFFIGNIES.

2. No. 1 Section, 20th D.A.C., will join 91st Brigade, R.F.A., at LA CHAPELLE-sous-POIX (Marching by CHARNY-MORVILLERS-LIGNIERES and MEIGNEUX). To be clear of CHARNY by 10 a.m.

Publ'd
159p.m. 3.4.1918

H. Martin.
Captain, R.A., for

Brigade Major, 36th Divisional Artillery.

DISTRIBUTION
1. O.C. 173rd Brigade R.F.A.,
2.& 3 O.C. 36th D.A.C., (one for No. 1 Sect. 20th D.A.C.,)
4. Billeting Officer, POIX.
5. O.C. No. 1 Coy. 36th Divisional Train.
6.& 7 War Diary.
8 & 9 File.

36TH DIVISIONAL ARTILLERY ORDER NO. 37.

Refce: Sheets- AMIENS) 1/100,000
DIEPPE)

The 36th Divisional Artillery will march tomorrow April 8th to Billets in the POIX Area, according to the attached Table.

Columns will not exceed 200 yards in length; an interval of 150 yards will be kept between columns.

The completion of moves and exact locations will be reported immediately to this Office.

The 36th Divisional Artillery is being transferred to II Army (2nd Corps) and will proceed by rail. Entrainment will take place at ST. ROCH GROUP (AMIENS) commencing 12.0 midnight April 9th/10th under orders to be issued later.

Billeting parties will be sent forward to take over Billets as shown in remarks column of March Table attached. O.C. 173rd Brigade, R.F.A., will be responsible for all billeting arrangements in COURCELLES SOUS MOYENCOURT.

Major, R.A.,
7.4.1918. Brigade Major, 36th Divisional Artillery.

DISTRIBUTION.

```
1  -  5   O.C. 153rd Brigade, R.F.A.,
6  - 10   O.C. 173rd Brigade, R.F.A.,
11 - 13   O.C. 36th D.A.C.,
14        O.C. D/232nd Brigade, R.F.A.,
15        O.C. No. 1 Coy. 36th Divisional Train.
16        Billeting Officer, POIX.
17 - 18   War Diary.
19        Staff Captain, R.A.,
20 - 21   File.
```

MARCH TABLE.

UNIT.	FROM	TO	ROUTE	REMARKS.
173rd Brigade, R.F.A.,	OFFIGNIES (D/175rd Bde.RFA from BL~NGIEL).	COURCELLES SOUS MOYENCOURT	HORNOY - FRICAMPS	Starting Point LA FRESNOYE - HORNOY Road-Junction in ORIVAL. All Units to be clear of Starting Point by 9.0 a.m.
53rd Brigade, R.F.A.,	MORVILLERS	MOYENCOURT SOUS POIX	HORNOY THIEULLOY L'ABBAYE CROIXRAULT	Take over billets from 83rd Bde.R.F.A., Head of column not to pass Starting Point before 9.15 a.m. Rear of column to be clear of this point by 10.30 a.m.
36th D.A.C., 36th Divl. T.Hq. (less V/18th H.T.M.B.)	CHARNY	COURCELLES SOUS MOYENCOURT	ORIVAL HORNOY FRICAMPS	Head of column not to pass the starting point before 11.0 a.m.
No. 1 Coy. 36th Dvl. Train.	CHARNY	BUSSY LES POIX	ORIVAL HORNOY FRICAMP.	To march in rear of 36th D.A.C.,
B/232nd A. Brigade R.F.A.,	CHARNY	SEN RPONT	MONTMARQUET LEUVILLE-COPPEQUELE	To join 232nd A. Brigade. To move before 12 noon (not to interfere with the march of 36th DAC. & No.1 Coy.36th Dvl.Train.
V/18th H.T.M.Battery.				To remain at CHARNY and be attached to 18th Divl Arty.

SECRET.

36TH DIVISIONAL ARTILLERY

ENTRAINMENT ORDER NO.1.

----

1. The 36th Divisional Artillery (less S.A.A.Section D.A.C.) and No.1 Coy 36th Divisional Train will entrain on 12th and 13th April, in accordance with attached Entraining Tables.

2. Entrainment will take place at two Stations ('A' & 'B') ST ROCH (AMIENS) and detrainment at HOPOUTRE (for Units entraining at 'A' Station) and PESSELHOEK (for Units entraining at 'B' Station).

3. The duration of the journey will be from eight to ten hours.

4. (a) Rations for consumption 12th will be delivered tonight 10.4.18.
   (b) Rations for consumption 13th will be delivered tomorrow 11.4.18.
   (c) Rations for consumption 14th will be loaded on supply wagons which will report to battery wagon lines tomorrow 11.4.18. These wagons will entrain with batteries &c.

5. All Units will thus entrain rationed for consumption up to and including 14th, which will be carried as follows :-

   Unexpended portion of rations for 12th) On the man and
   and complete rations for 13th.   ) on the horse.

   Rations for 14th.   In supply wagons.

6. Orders as to forward entraining parties &c., will be issued later.

7. Zero time on attached entraining table is the time of departure of 1st train from Station "B" which will be notified later and will probably be 10.47 a.m. April 12th.

8. Acknowledge.

10.4.18.   H. Martin   Captain, R.A.
                       Staff Captain, 36th Divisional Artillery.

DISTRIBUTION :-

O.C.153rd Brigade,R.F.A.   (5).
    173rd Brigade,R.F.A.   (5).
    D.A.C.   (5).
    No.1 Coy.36th Div.Train.(2)   (To include 'X' & 'Y' T.M.Bs.)
S.O.
Brigade Major, R.A.
Lieut. R.B.SOLOMON.R.A.
R.A.Signal Officer.

ENTRAINING TABLE NO.(1).

ENTRAINING STATION ST ROCH (STATION 'A')
DETRAINING STATION HOPOUTRE.

Train No.	Departs at.	Detail.	Officers Coach.	Officers All.	REMARKS.
2	1.00 Hrs.	A/153rd Battery plus 1 G.S. and 4 ammunition wagons and teams of No.1 Sec. D.A.C.	A/153rd Bty. No.1 Sec.DAC.	All. 1.	
4	4.00 Hrs.	B/153rd Battery plus 1 G.S. and 4 Ammunition J.F. wagons and teams of No.1 Sec.DAC.	B/153rd Bty. No.1 Sec.DAC. H.Q. DAC.(V.O).	All. 1. 1.	
6	7.00 Hrs.	153rd Bde.H.Q. and No.1 Sec.D.A.C. (less 4 G.S. Wagons 16 Ammunition Wagons and teams (- see trains No.2, 4, 8 and10). plus one wagon R.H.R.A. and 4 horses and drivers. Y/36th T.M.Battery, cable cart and team 36th Div.Sigs and unmotorised transport of 153rd Bde.	HQ.153rd Bde. No.1 D.A.C. Y/36th T.M.B.	4 1 1	
8	10.00 Hrs.	C/153rd Battery plus 1 G.S. and 4 ammunition J.F. wagons and teams of No.1 Sec. D.A.C.	C/153rd Bty. No.1 D.A.C. H.Q. DAC (M.O)	All. 1. 1.	
10	13.00 Hrs.	D/153rd Battery plus 1 G.S. and 4 ammunition J.F. wagons and No.1 Sec. D.A.C.	D/153rd Bty.	All.	

ENTRAINING TABLE NO.(II)

ENTRAINING STATION ST ROCH (STATION 'B').
DETRAINING STATION. PESELHOEK.

Train No.	Departs at.	Detail.	Officers Coach.	Compartments.	Officers.	Remarks.
1	0.00 Hrs. (probably 10.47 am 124.18).	H.Q.R.A. H.Q. D.A.C. No.1 Coy 36th Divisional Train.	H.Q.R.A. H.Q. D.A.C. No.1 Coy.36th Div.Train.	1½. 1. 1½.		
3	3.00 Hrs.	A/173rd Battery plus G.S. and 4 ammunition Q.F. wagons and teams of No.2 Section, D.A.C.	A/173rd Bty. No.2 Sec.DAC.		Officers. 1	
5	6.00 Hrs.	173rd Bde. H.Q. and No.2 Sec. D.A.C. (Less 4 G.S. 16 ammunition Q.F. wagons and teams.(- See trains No. 3, 7, 9 and 11) plus 1 G.S. and team H.Q.R.A. and X/36th T.M.Battery and unauthorised transport of 173rd Bde, R.F.A.	173rd BdeH.Q. No.2 Sec. DAC. X/36th T.M.Bty.		4 2 8	
7	9.00 Hrs.	B/173rd Battery plus 1 GS. and 4 ammunition Q.F.wagons and teams of No.2 Section, 36th DAC.	B/173rd Bty. H.Q.173rd (V.O) No.2 Sec.DAC.	All 1 1		
9	12.00 Hrs.	C/173rd Battery, plus 1 G.S. and 4 ammunition Q.F. wagons and teams No.2 Section, D.A.C.	C/173rd Bty. H.Q.173rd (M.O) No.2 Sec. DAC.	All 1 1		
11	14.00 or 15.00 Hrs.	D/173rd Battery, plus 1 G.S. and 4 ammunition Q.F. wagons and teams No.2 Sec. DAC.	D/173rd Bty. No.2.Soc.DAC. Entraining Officer. (Capt.H.J.WELLINGHAM-MC)	All 1 1		This train may go from Station "A" and arrive at HOPOUTRE.

36TH DIVISIONAL ARTILLERY ORDER NO. 38.

Ref:
AMIENS Sheet 1/100,000

The 36th Divisional Artillery will march to-day the 11th April to billets at PONT de METZ and RENANCOURT.

Further instructions as to billeting will be issued later.

The starting point will be on the Main POIX-AMIENS Road at the cross-roads 1 kilometre due East of COURCELLES.

No Column will exceed 200 yards in length. 150 yards interval will be kept between columns.

ACKNOWLEDGE.

[signature]
Major, R.A.,
11.4.1918.   Brigade Major, 36th Divisional Artillery.

MARCH TABLE.

UNIT.	From.	To	Route	Remarks.
153rd Bde. R.F.A.	MOYENCOURT SOUS POIX	PONT de METZ or RENANCOURT	QUEVAUVILLERS and SALOUEL	To clear the starting point by 9.30 am.
173rd Bde. R.F.A.	COURCELLES SOUS MOYENCOURT	-do-	-do-	Head not to pass starting point before 9.45 am. To be clear by 10.30 am.
36th D.A.C., 36th T.M. Personnel	-do-	-do-	-do-	Head not to pass the starting point before 10.45 am.
No.1 Co. 36th Divl. Train	BUSSY LES POIX	-do-	-do-	To march in rear of D.A.C.,

DISTRIBUTION.

```
1  -  5   O.C. 153rd Brigade, R.F.A.,
6  - 10   O.C. 173rd Brigade, R.F.A.,
11 - 14   O.C. 36th D.A.C.,
15        O.C. No.1 Co. 36th Divl. Train.
16        Staff Captain, R.F.,
17 - 18   War Diary.
19 - 20   File.
```

SECRET.   Copy No. 22

36TH DIVISIONAL ARTILLERY ORDER NO. 39.

The 36th Divisional Artillery (less S.A.A., Section, D.A.C.,) and No. 1 Company, 36th Divisional Train, will march tomorrow 14th instant to the place of entrainment in accordance with attached Table.

Battery Commanders concerned will be responsible for getting in touch with and marching the Details of 36th D.A.C., preceeding by their train.

The Route for Units entraining at Station 'A' will be from PONT DE METZ, South of LACELLE River - PONT ST. JEAN, direct to Station.

The Route for Units entraining at Station 'B' will be North of LACELLE River via RENANCOURT as far as main ABBEVILLE - AMIENS Railway and thence direct to ST. ROCH Station.

Units must arrive three hours prior to scheduled time of departure of train.

Columns will not exceed 200 yards in length, with 100 yards interval between columns.

A C K N O W L E D G E.

                                              Major, R.A.,
13.4.1918.   Brigade Major, 36th Divisional Artillery.

DISTRIBUTION.
---

1 - 5 O.C. 153rd Brigade, R.F.A.,
6 - 10 O.C. 173rd Brigade, R.F.A.,
11 - 15 O.C. 36th D.A.C., (to include 'X' & 'Y' T.M.Bys).
16 - 17 O.C. No. 1 Coy. 36th Divl. Train.
18   S.O.,
19   S.C., R.A.,
20   R.O., R.A.,
21   O. i/c R.A., Signals.
22 - 23 War Diary.
24 - 25 File.

MARCH TABLE.

Serial No.	UNIT.	From	To	Time of arrival at Station.
1.	H.Q., 36th D.A.C., No. 1 Coy. 36th Divl. Train.	PONT DE METZ. RENANCOURT	Station A "	4.42 hours.
2.	A/153rd Brigade R.F.A., plus Details of No. 1 Section D.A.C.	RENANCOURT PONT DE METZ	Station B	5.42 hours.
3.	A/173rd Brigade R.F.A., plus Details of No. 2 Section D.A.C.	PONT DE METZ "	Station A	7.42 hours.
4.	E/153rd Brigade R.F.A., plus Details of No. 1 Section D.A.C.,	RENANCOURT PONT DE METZ	Station B	8.42 hours.
5.	173rd Brigade H.Q., plus Details as shown in Entraining Table No. 1.	PONT DE METZ	Station A	10.42 hours.
6.	153rd Brigade H.Q., plus Details as shown in Entraining Table No. II.	RENANCOURT	Station B	11.42 hours.
7.	B/173rd Brigade R.F.A., plus Details of No. 2 Section D.A.C.,	PONT DE METZ	Station A	13.42 hours.

Page 2.

Serial No.	UNIT.	From	To	Time of arrival at Station.
8.	C/153rd Brigade R.F.A., plus Details of No. 1 Section D.A.C.,	RENANCOURT	PONT DE METZ Station B	14.42 hours.
9.	C/173rd Brigade R.F.A., plus Details of No. 2 Section D.A.C.,	PONT DE METZ.	Station A	15.42 hours.
10.	D/153rd Brigade R.F.A. plus Details of No. 1 Section D.A.C.,	RENANCOURT	PONT DE METZ Station B	17.42 hours.
11.	D/173rd Brigade R.F.A. plus Details of No. 2 Section D.A.C.,	PONT DE METZ	Station A	19.42 hours.

S E C R E T.

36TH DIVISIONAL ARTILLERY ORDER No. 40.

The 183rd Brigade, R.F.A., will march tomorrow 23rd instant to HAMROSE Standings in F.24. and F.18. (Sheet 27). These Standings are clearly labelled, and are close to Road.

The route, unless otherwise ordered by superior authority, will be by BUSSCHEPE - ABEELE - POPERINGHE, avoiding town by Switch Road.

Head of Column will not arrive before 11 a.m.

Forward Billeting parties will take over billets vacated by 330th Brigade, R.F.A., 66th Division, and should report at HAMROSE Standings by 9.0 a.m.

25 yards interval will be maintained between Sections - 200 yards between Batteries.

R.A.H.Q., will remain at P.21.b.0.0.

A C K N O W L E D G E.

Major, R.A.,
22.4.1918.   Brigade Major, 36th Divisional Artillery.

DISTRIBUTION.

O.C. 183rd Brigade, R.F.A., c/o H.Q., 38th Divl. Arty.
H.Q., 36th Divisional Artillery.
O.C. 173rd Brigade, R.F.A.,
O.C. 36th D.A.C.,
O.C. No. 1 Coy. 36th Divisional Train.
H.Q., 36th Division, 'Q'.
Staff Captain, R.A.,

SECRET.

36TH DIVISIONAL ARTILLERY ORDER No. 41.

Reference : Sheet 27 - 1/40,000.

173rd Brigade, R.F.A., and 36th D.A.C., will march tomorrow 24th instant to billets in HAMHOEK Standings (F.18. and 24.).

    Route :   ABEELE - POPERINGHE, avoiding latter town by SWITCH ROAD.

Order of March :

<u>36th D.A.C.</u>,   The column to be clear of Cross-Roads L.26.c.7.8. by 10 a.m.

<u>173rd Brigade R.F.A.</u>,   Head of column not to reach Cross-Roads L.26.c.7.8. before 10.30 a.m.

Intervals between batteries and sections of D.A.C., 200 yards, between sections of batteries 25 yards.

Advanced billeting parties will report to Staff Captain, 36th Divisional Artillery at TEN ELMS CAMP, A.25. at 9.0 a.m. 24th inst.

Headquarters, 36th Divisional Artillery will move to TEN ELMS CAMP, A.25.

No. 1 Company, 36th Divisional Train will march to-day, 23rd instant, to F.14.d.5.3. via ABEELE and SWITCH ROAD, POPERINGHE.

                                              Major, R.A.,
23.4.1918.   Brigade Major, 36th Divisional Artillery.

<u>DISTRIBUTION</u>.

O.C. 173rd Brigade, R.F.A.,
O.C. 36th D. A. C.
O.C. No. 1 Coy. 36th Divisional Train.
H.Q., 36th Division, 'G'.
H.Q., 38th Divisional Artillery.

SECRET.

36TH DIVISIONAL ARTILLERY ORDER No. 42.

1. The 36th Divisional Artillery will march to billets, as follows, tomorrow 25th instant.

2. An interval of 200 yards will be maintained between Batteries and Sections D.A.C., and 25 yards between sections of Batteries.

UNIT.	FROM.	TO	ROUTE	REMARKS.
153rd Bde.R.F.A.	HAMHOEK ARTY. STANDINGS.	BRIELEN ARTY. STANDINGS. (B.29.centl. to B.22.d.)	POPERINGHE SWITCH Rd.- VLAMERTINGHE	To be clear of Cross-roads in A.25.d.2.2. by 10.0 a.m.
173rd Bde.R.F.A.) B/173rd ")	- do - F.19.d.5.5. (Sheet 27)	HOSPITAL FARM STGS. B.19.d.	POPERINGHE SWITCH RD.- Cross-roads G.5.d.0.2.- DIRTY BUCKET CORNER.	Forward party will report to Area Commandant No.1 Siege C-., B.20.b.2.7.when exact location of billets will be given b
				To march in rear of 153rd Bde.RFA. rear of column to be clear of Cross- roads A.25.d.2.2. by 10.45 a.m.
36th D.A.C.,) 36th T.M.) Personnel.)	Camp A.14.b.	RESELHOEK STGS A.21.a.	Road-Junct. A.20.d.3.1.	Move to be com- plete by 11 a.m.

3. H.Q., 36th Divisional Artillery will remain at TEN ELMS CAMP.

4. Completion of moves will be reported to this Office by cycle orderly, who will be prepared to remain at R.A.H.Q.,

5. Officer i/c R.A., Signals, 36th Division, will arrange the necessary telephonic communications.

6. ACKNOWLEDGE.

Major, R.A.,
Brigade Major, 36th Divisional Artillery.

24.4.1918.

DISTRIBUTION.
```
1  -  5  O.C. 153rd Brigade R.F.A.,     6 - 10 O.C. 173rd Brigade R.F.A.,
11 - 14  O.C. 36th D.A.C.,             15      O.i/c R.A. Signals.
16       O.C. No.1 Coy. 36th Div.Train. 17     H.Q., R.A., II Corps.
18       H.Q., 36th Division, 'G'       19     H.Q., 36th Division, 'Q'.
20       A.P.M. 36th Division.          21     A.D.M.S. 36th Division.
22       D.A.D.O.S.    "                23     D.A.D.V.S.       "
24       C.R.E.        "                25 - 26 War Diary.
27       Staff Captain, R.A.,           28 - 29 File.
```

SECRET.   Copy No. 26

36TH DIVISIONAL ARTILLERY ORDER NO: 43.

1. 173rd Brigade, R.F.A., will move on 26.4.1918, as follows :

FROM	TO	ROUTE	REMARKS.
BRIELEN.	(a) Standings in B.20.b. (H.Q. and 2 Batteries)	Road Junction B.22.c.70.99 - Road Junction B.20.d.5.8.	(a) Accommodation will be shown by Captain WILLIAMSON, No. 3 Section, 36th D.A.C., who is at B.20.b.5.1.
	(b) Standings in B.20.a.8.7. and B.20.a.8.4. (2 Batteries)		(b) Labelled : 'A Brigade Transport Lines.' Move to be completed by 11.0 a.m.

2. O.C. 153rd Brigade, R.F.A., will reconnoitre Wagon Lines as follows, and will take over and occupy them when vacated, which will be probably on the evening of 26.4.1918.

UNIT OCCUPYING.	LOCATION.
H.Q., 330 Brigade R.F.A.) C/330 Brigade R.F.A.,)	B.22.c.4.9.
A/330 Brigade R.F.A.,	B.15.c.8.2.
C/331 Brigade R.F.A.,	B.21.d.2.8.
D/331 Brigade R.F.A.,	B.21.c.3.7.

3. O.C. 36th D.A.C., will reconnoitre a Wagon Line, as under, and will detail one Section to take over and occupy it when vacated (probably on the evening of 26.4.1918.).

UNIT OCCUPYING	LOCATION.
66th D.A.C.,	B.13.a.c.

4. ACKNOWLEDGE.

                                              Major, R.A.,
25.4.1918.   Brigade Major, 36th Divisional Artillery.

DISTRIBUTION.

1 - 5	O.C. 153rd Brigade R.F.A.,	6 -10	O.C. 173rd Brigade R.F.A.,
11-14	O.C. 36th D.A.C.,	15	O. i/c R.A. Signals.
16	O.C. No. 1 Coy. 36th Dvl. Train.	17	H.Q., R.A., II Corps.
18	H.Q., 36th Division, 'G'	19	H.Q., 36th Division, 'Q'.
20	A.P.M. 36th Division.	21	A.D.M.S. 36th Division.
22	D.A.D.O.S. "	23	D.A.D.V.S. "
24	C.R.E. "	25	Staff Captain, R.A.,
26-27	War Diary.	28-29	File.

S E C R E T.　　　　　　　　　　　　　　　Copy No. 28....

36TH DIVISIONAL ARTILLERY ORDER NO. 44.

Reference : 1/20,000 Sheet 28 N.W.

RELIEF.

1.　　Headquarters, 36th Divisional Artillery and 153rd Brigade, R.F.A., will relieve the Headquarters 66th Divisional Artillery and 330th (Composite) Brigade, R.F.A., in the line on the 25th/26th April, and 26th/27th April, 1918.

2.　　The relief will be carried out as under :-

On the night 25th/26th April -

1 Section A/153rd Bde will relieve 1 Sect. A/330th at C.26.a.9.3.
1　"　　B/153rd　　"　　"　　"　C/331st at C.20.d.9.2.
1　"　　C/153rd　　"　　"　　"　C/330th at C.26.a.35.05.
1　"　　D/153rd　　"　　"　　"　D/331st at C.20.c.7.3.
　　　　　　　　　　　　　　　　　　　　　(vacant position).

(The Sections relieved are remaining in position for the night).

On the night 26th/27th April -

　　H.Q., and 1 Sect. A/153rd to C.26.a.9.3.
　　　　　　　1 Sect. A/153rd to B.30.b.2.0.
　　H.Q., and 1 Sect. B/153rd to C.20.a.9.1.
　　　　　　　1 Sect. B/153rd to B.30.b.05.65.
　　H.Q., and 1 Sect. C/153rd to C.26.a.35.05.
　　　　　　　1 Sect. C/153rd to C.25.c.8.2.
　　H.Q., and 1 Sect. D/153rd to C.20.c.7.3.
　　　　　　　1 Sect. D/153rd to C.25.c.8.0.

3.　　Headquarters, 153rd Brigade, R.F.A., will relieve Headquarters 330th (Composite) Brigade, R.F.A., on completion of Battery reliefs.

4.　　Command of the Artillery covering the Front of the 36th Division will pass to the C.R.A., 36th Division on completion of relief.

5.　　The relief will be completed by 8.0 p.m. on 26th April.

6.　　At 8.0 p.m. on 26th April the two batteries of 49th Army Brigade, R.F.A., (A/49th and B/49th) will come under the orders of O.C. 153rd Brigade, R.F.A.,
　　　The Artillery covering the 36th Division will then be organised as one Group, and will be known as the POTTER GROUP.

7.　　All Maps, Artillery Boards and Photographs and other information concerning the Front will be taken over on relief.

8.　　Ammunition at the Guns will be taken over by relieving batteries as at 12.0 noon, 26th April, amounts taken over being reported to this Office by the usual noon wire.

9.　　FRONTAGE & BOUNDARIES.

　　The Front held by the 36th Division extends from
　　　　C.24.b.05.45.　to　C.11.b.2.3.

- 2 -

Southern Boundary - C.24.b.05.45 - C.23.d.0.0 - C.28.a.0.0 -
I.2.a.40.75 - I.2.a.25.92 - I.1.a.45.60.

Northern Boundary - C.11.b.2.8.- C.11.c.3.0 - C.16.d.8.3 -
C.16.c.0.0 - C.21.a.0.1 - C.20.centl -
B.24.a.0.0.

Inter-Bde Boundary - C.18.c.1.8.-C.17.d.00.45 - C.23.a.0.8 -
C.22.c.6.8 - BUFFS ROAD and track to
ZOUAVE VILLA and along road to
C.25.a.70.95.

Boundaries E. of the STEENBEEK for Harassing Fire, etc.,
will be as follows -
Southern Boundary C.14.b.05.45 - D.13.c.0.8.
Northern Boundary C.11.b.2.8. - V.25.c.0.0.

Dividing line between Heavy Artillery and Field
Artillery is a line through U.30.d.4.0.-D.1.c.0.0 - D.13.c.0.8.

10.   FLANKS.

36th Division is the Left Division of the II Corps.
41st Divn. covered by 29th D.A. is on the Right.
4th Belgian Divn. covered by 4th Belgian D.A. is on the
Left.

11.   INFANTRY.

The front is held by -
109th Infantry Brigade on the Right.
107th Infantry Brigade on the Left.

The Main Line of Resistance runs from the left-hand
boundary along the STEENBEEK as far as C.18.c.0.7., and from
thence to C.23.d.7.5.

There is an Outpost Line in front of this with Posts at -
C.18.d.2.3.
C.18.c.7.9.
C.12.c.9.6.
C.12.a.65.55.

12.   LIAISON.

Liaison arrangements will be as follows :
O.C. 153rd Brigade, R.F.A., will act as Liaison Officer
with both Infantry Brigades holding the Line.
There will be a Liaison Officer with each Battalion in
the front line.

13.   O.Ps.

Each Battery will man an O.P. from dawn till dusk.
One or more Rocket Picquet O.Ps. will be manned
continuously by day and night, so as to ensure the S.O.S.
Signal being seen along the whole Divisional front.
The S.O.S. Signal will be repeated from Rocket Picquet
O.Ps.

14.   S.O.S.

From 12 noon 26th April the S.O.S. Signal will be a
rifle grenade signal bursting into three coloured stars -
Red - over Red - over Red.
Rates of fire for S.O.S. will be as follows :

First five minutes - 3 rounds per gun per minute.
Next ten minutes - 2 rounds per gun per minute.
Fire will then cease unless the S.O.S. Signal is repeated, when the above procedure will be repeated.

By 6 p.m. 26th The O.C. POTTER GROUP will take over the present S.O.S. Lines, consulting G.Os.C. Infantry Brigades for any alteration required, the same to be reported to this office immediately.

15. **AMMUNITION.**

Dumps at guns will be maintained as follows :

18-pdr.   400 rounds per gun.

4.5" How. (300 rounds per gun.
         (50 rounds (Gas) per gun.

The A.R.P. is at ORILLA Dump, H.2.c.

Ammunition can be expended as required; there is no limit of expenditure laid down.

16. **ACKNOWLEDGE.**

[signature]

Major, R.A.,
25.4.1918.   Brigade Major, 36th Divisional Artillery.

DISTRIBUTION.

1 - 5	O.C. 153rd Brigade R.F.A.,	6 -10	O.C. 173rd Brigade R.F.A.
11-14	O.C. 36th D.A.C.,	15	O. i/c R.A. Signals.
16	O.C. No.1 Coy. 36th D.Tn.	17	H.Q.,R.A., II Corps.
18	H.Q., 36th Division, 'G'.	19	H.Q., 36th Division, 'Q'.
20	A.P.M. 36th Division.	21	Signals, 36th Division.
22	D.A.D.O.S. "	23	A.D.M.S. "
24	D.A.D.V.S. "	25	C.R.E. "
26	H.Q., 66th Div.Arty.	27	Staff Captain, R.A.,
28-29	War Diary.	30-31	File.
32	H.Q., 29th DIV. Arty.	33	4th Belgian D.A., (through 66th D.A.)

SECRET.

To all recipients of –

    36th Divisional Artillery Order No. 44.

Reference 36th Divisional Artillery Order No. 44.

1. Para. 6. The two Batteries of the 49th Army Brigade, R.F.A. will be withdrawn from the Line by 8.0 p.m. 26th inst and will not come under the orders of the POTTER Group.

2. All Batteries of the 153rd Brigade, R.F.A. will be concentrated in Positions West of the Canal. Locations will be as follows :

H.Q., 153rd Brigade, R.F.A.	C.25.d.2.7.
A/153rd Brigade, R.F.A.	B.30.b.2.0.
B/153rd Brigade, R.F.A.	B.30.b.03.66.
C/153rd Brigade, R.F.A.	C.25.c.8.2.
D/153rd Brigade, R.F.A.	C.25.c.8.8.

26.4.1918.

                                  Major, R.A.,
                Brigade Major, 36th Divisional Artillery.

S E C R E T.

Copy No............

36TH DIVISIONAL ARTILLERY ORDER NO: 45.

1. The 36th Division is withdrawing to the Line of the YPRES - HET SAS Canal tonight 26th/27th inst. April, (to be held as the Line of Resistance, with Outposts on the Line WHITE CHATEAU, PICKELHAUBE, OBLONG FARM.)

2. The standing patrols East of the STEENBEEK are being withdrawn after dark.

3. The withdrawal of Troops and Machine Guns to the Line PICKELHAUBE - OBLONG FARM is to be completed by 4.0 a.m. 27th inst.

C/153rd and D/153rd Brigade R.F.A. will each move back, two sections as soon as possible after dawn tomorrow 27th inst., to positions in rear, as follows :

C/153rd Brigade R.F.A. to B.29.c.0.7.
D/153rd Brigade R.F.A. to B.29.d.7.6. or some suitable position between B.28.central and B.29.central.

Batteries will move one at a time.

4. Till 4.0 a.m. 27th inst. the S.O.S. Barrage if called for will be put down on the line of the STEENBEEK, paying particular attention to all the crossings. After 4.0 a.m. the S.O.S. Barrage will be put down on our actual Outpost Line running through -
C.16.b.3.0 - C.16.d.4.4.- C.16.d.7.0 - C.22.b.6.7.- C.23.c.20.75 - and C.23.a.45.15 - C.23.c.8.6 -,C.23.c.8.4.- C.23.c.5.0.

5. Should the POTTER Group H.Q., be ordered to retire, they will move with Infantry Brigade H.Q., to HOSPITAL FARM, B.19.d.0.0.

6. H.Q., 36th Divisional Artillery will close at BORDER CAMP at 11.0 a.m. 27th April and open at DRAGON CAMP, A.15.b.2.6. at the same hour.

7. 153rd Brigade Wagon Lines will move to B.26.a. and c. at 6.0 a.m. tomorrow 27th April. Forward party will report to Area Commandant, No. 1 Siege Camp, B.20.b.2.7. at 6.0 a.m for exact location of billets.

8. A C K N O W L E D G E.

26.4.1918.

Major, R.A.,
Brigade Major, 36th Divisional Artillery.

To all recipients of 36th Divisional Artillery Order No. 44.

SECRET.   Copy No.........

36TH DIVISIONAL ARTILLERY ORDER NO; 46.

The 173rd Brigade, R.F.A., will advance to positions as under, tomorrow 28th April.
Batteries will be in action by 6.30 a.m.

H.Q., 173rd Brigade, R.F.A.,	
A/173rd Brigade, R.F.A.,	C.25.d.1.7.
B/173rd Brigade, R.F.A.,	B.24.a.4.3.
C/173rd Brigade, R.F.A.,	B.24.d.3.8.
D/173rd Brigade, R.F.A.,	B.24.c.7.2.
	C.24.b.1.9.

As soon as these Batteries are in position they will be given S.O.S. Lines to cover the whole Divisional Front, superimposed on the S.O.S. Lines of the POTTER Group.

As soon as these Batteries are registered, two Groups will be formed -
    The POTTER Group (153rd Brigade, R.F.A.,)
        covering the 109th Infantry Brigade.
    The SIMPSON Group (173rd Brigade, R.F.A.,)
        covering the 107th Infantry Brigade.

Group Commanders will arrange S.O.S. Lines in consultation with G.Os.C. Infantry Brigades, and will report the same to this office as soon as possible.

A Tracing showing the Machine Gun Barrage will be forwarded when received.

A very active policy of Harassing Fire will be maintained:
Each Group will fire 75 rounds 18-pr. ammunition per hour.
                      25 rounds 4.5" How. ammunition per hour.
by day and night in bursts of fire at varying times.

The dividing line between Groups for Harassing Fire will be the WIELTJE - ST. JULIAN - WINNIPEG Road inclusive to the SIMPSON Group.

The Zone for Field Artillery Harassing Fire will extend as far as -
    The Line of the STEENBEEK River from the Northern Boundary as far as ST. JULIAN, and thence along the road to SPREE FARM to the Southern boundary inclusive to the Field Artillery

The proportion of 18-pr. ammunition to be expended will be 75% H.E. and 25% Shrapnel.
This percentage must be rigidly adhered to.

A C K N O W L E D G E.

27.4.1918.   Brigade Major, 36th Divisional Artillery.
                                              Major, R.A.,

To all recipients of 36th Divisional Artillery Order No. 45.

WAR DIARY or INTELLIGENCE SUMMARY

Army Form C. 2118

HQ 36th Div Artillery

WD 37

Place	Date	Hour	Summary of Events and Information	Remarks and references to Appendices
Bn & SOS CAMP A15d 24	May 1st		The location of H.Q. and Batteries covers a+b of Maps 107th Infantry Brigade.	22ND 17 NE MAPS
			RIGHT GROUP	
			153 H.Q. B&C R 34	
			H.Q. c 25 d 17.	
			A 153 B 23 b 6 20	
			B 153 B 24 c 25	
			C 153 B 22 b 12 (advanced section)	
			D 153 B 29 c 8 2	
			B 29 c 6·6	
			LEFT GROUP Group 16 F.A. Defenly Bnjns	
			173 H.Q. R16 d A R	
			H.Q. c 25 c 17.	
			A 173 B 24 a 24	
			B 173 B 23 c 42	
			C 173 B 23 c 77	
			D 173 B 23 c 82	

Army Form C. 2118.

WAR DIARY
or
INTELLIGENCE SUMMARY.
(Erase heading not required.)

Instructions regarding War Diaries and Intelligence Summaries are contained in F. S. Regs., Part II. and the Staff Manual respectively. Title pages will be prepared in manuscript.

Place	Date	Hour	Summary of Events and Information	Remarks and references to Appendices
DRAGON CAMP	May 2nd to May 8		No action of any importance took place during this period. There was no infantry action of any kind. Counter preparation was fired on certain walks to deter 17, 2nd Corps R.A. The reconnaissance for positions and O.Ps. for harassing fire, defence was carried out and was continued in Zones for the Fire Two Rivers – namely The CANAL LINE and the BRIELEN LINE. The enemy artillery activity was not great. Certain counter battery shots were carried out by the enemy against positions in B30 Posts. was under observation from the High Ground West of the P.B. Guns fired from Eben to Dag 8 of the Canal and J30 from FORTRAY to FOCHTRAM. Decided with Div. Section to be a 6.6. Corps and 9 counter battery shoots required.	

(A7092). Wt. W12839/M1293. 75,000. 1/17. D. D. & L., Ltd. Forms/C.2118-14.

Army Form C. 2118.

Instructions regarding War Diaries and Intelligence
Summaries are contained in F. S. Regs., Part II.
and the Staff Manual respectively. Title pages
will be prepared in manuscript.

WAR DIARY
or
INTELLIGENCE SUMMARY.
(Erase heading not required.)

Place	Date	Hour	Summary of Events and Information	Remarks and references to Appendices
DRAGON RYNE CAMP	Aug 11th		As the weather so th the 36th Division [illegible] the schedule [illegible] southwards to include a portion of the 41st Divisional Sector. The artillery programme commenced as usual, but A/172 & A/163 Batteries, which had been withdrawn from action for 6 days, came into the line again as per [illegible]. A programme of two Creeping barrages was drawn up and suitable targets selected on the Divisional front. The main Barrage commenced at 11/12 & barrage 16/17 a bay . 18/19 a bay . 20/21 a bay & 22/23 a bay.	36th Division Diary Appx No 47
	June 25th		During this period no important action took place. The weather remained fine with sunny periods throughout. The enemy artillery retaliation was but spasmodic and only one defensive counter battery shoot took place opposite 11/17 Battery & on to B.30 & which [illegible] enemy barrage was reported. Front of the Canal.	36th Divl Arty War Diary see No 48

Army Form C. 2118.

WAR DIARY
or
INTELLIGENCE SUMMARY.
(Erase heading not required.)

Instructions regarding War Diaries and Intelligence Summaries are contained in F. S. Regs., Part II. and the Staff Manual respectively. Title pages will be prepared in manuscript.

Place	Date	Hour	Summary of Events and Information	Remarks and references to Appendices
DRAGON CAMP	May 1		In CALIFORNIA DRIVE. A raid was carried out by 108 Inf Bde with Artillery support on night 27/28. No identification was secured	SOS Div Arty Order No 49
	May 28-31		No infantry action. The raid mentioned above was repeated on night 31st May 1st June without previous bombardment. Divisional Artillery stood by last put a bose barrage round the post, but was not called upon to do so. No identification was secured. Harassing Fire and Group Concentrations were carried out through out this period and a gun concentration was fired on night 28/29th.	

H.J. Huck
Brig Gen RA
Comdg 36 Div Arty

3.6.18

Army Form C. 2118.

WAR DIARY
or
INTELLIGENCE SUMMARY.
(Erase heading not required.)

HQ
36 Div. Arty

J61 33

Instructions regarding War Diaries and Intelligence Summaries are contained in F. S. Regs., Part II. and the Staff Manual respectively. Title pages will be prepared in manuscript.

Place	Date	Hour	Summary of Events and Information	Remarks and references to Appendices
DRAGON CAMP	June 1st 1918	1st–4th	The Commanding Officer and Staff of 12th CADI (Belgian Artillery) called to discuss plans of relief. Reconnaissance of Btty. positions by Belgian Artillery Officers. On night 2/3 June a Gas Concentration was fired on Pill Boxes in C 12 c and SPREE FARM. On night 3/4 June One Group of Belgian Horse Artillery reinforced this Artillery on the Right Group Sector. 36th Division was relieved by 12th Belgian Division of Infantry (2nd Division d'Armée). Artillery relief to shown on Appendix A. Gas Concentration was fired on night 4/5 June on hostile forward batteries and sensitive points. An enemy relief was suspected opposite Right Group Front.	28 NW 27 NE 1/20000 36 Div'n's War No 50 36 Div'n's War No 51 36 Div'n's War No 52 36th Div'n's War No. 53 & 54.
	June 5th 6th 7th		The 12th Belgian Divl Artillery relieved the 36th Divisional artillery in the line Command passing at 12 midnight 6/7 of June. X + Y 7th Batteries remained in the line under the orders of the 12th Belgian Division.	

Army Form C. 2118.

WAR DIARY
or
INTELLIGENCE SUMMARY.
(Erase heading not required.)

Place	Date	Hour	Summary of Events and Information	Remarks and references to Appendices
COUTHOVE CHATEAU	June 8th		Units of 36th Divisional Artillery withdrew to Longue lines in relief and marched to the hut area west of Cafe Remeve.	36th Div Art instructions No 20 + Lochin appendices
	June 9th		The G army Commander inspected the 36th Divisional artillery 1.5 DB RA & No 173 Battery in the morning - the 1.5 DB RA & No 173 Battery in the afternoon. Divisional forward Dice meet, followed by a lunch party.	
	June 10		The return for battery going into action in rear- positions for the defence of the approach to Cafes Point in the East POPERINGHE lines. (BLUELINE)	36 Div Arty inst No 55 + Lochin statement.
	June 11th		Units remained in rest. A training programme was carried out. The two weeks being alloted to section training, the remainder of the time to Battery training.	
	June 12th		The BLUE LINE positions were completed to B for positions instead of 5 of RDA. BLUELINE positions for the 2 Brigades R.F.A. telling the line should they be forced to retire, were also constructed in accordance with instructions issued by 2nd Corps Arty.

Army Form C. 2118.

Instructions regarding War Diaries and Intelligence Summaries are contained in F. S. Regs., Part II. and the Staff Manual respectively. Title pages will be prepared in manuscript.

WAR DIARY
or
INTELLIGENCE SUMMARY.
(Erase heading not required.)

Place	Date	Hour	Summary of Events and Information	Remarks and references to Appendices
COUTHOVE CHATEAU	From June 12th to June 30th		See June reports were carried out by the Brown batteries in the 2nd army artillery range at TIRQUES. June 28th XXY TM Batteries course over of action, rejoined the Division in rest.	

7. 6. 18

H. J. Brock
Maj. for R.A.
Cmdt 36th Div. Art.

Army Form C. 2118.

WAR DIARY
or
INTELLIGENCE SUMMARY.
(Erase heading not required.)

Headquarters 36" Div. Arty.

Vol 34

Place	Date	Hour	Summary of Events and Information	Remarks and references to Appendices
COUTHOVE	July 1st to July 3rd		The 36th Divisional Artillery continued in rest, with the right of July 2nd/3rd. The sections in action for the defence of the RUE LINE were withdrawn to rejoin brigades.	Ref nos for 27/40000 27524 28530 1/20000 Gtaffords nos No 52
	2nd 4th		The 36th Divas marched to the WEMARS CAPPEL - HARDIFORT area. H.Q. R.A. moved to CAPPEL.	26 Divas nos No 57
	July 1st to July 8th		The 36th Divas relieved the 41st French Div arty in the St Jans CAPPEL sector & took over command of the 9th Army Group R.T.A. Along in action under command of the artillery. HQ R.A. moved to MONT DES CATS & command passed at 3 am on July 8th.	36th Divas nos No 58

Army Form C. 2118.

WAR DIARY
or
INTELLIGENCE SUMMARY.
(Erase heading not required.)

Instructions regarding War Diaries and Intelligence Summaries are contained in F. S. Regs., Part II. and the Staff Manual respectively. Title pages will be prepared in manuscript.

Place	Date	Hour	Summary of Events and Information	Remarks and references to Appendices
MONT DES CATS	July 9th to July 13th		Registration continues. Harassing fire carried out during this period. The enemy artillery showed increasing activity to counter.	
TERDEGHEM	July 14th		H.Q. R.A. moved back into the remainder of W. Hdqp. to TERDEGHEM.	
	July 14th		The POTTYZE group fired in support of a raid carried out by the 10th Infantry Brigade. No authentic observations were secured.	
	July 5th		The 416th Battery (96th wing Brigade) from POTTYZE group. Mth batteries' stations withdrew to rear positions, 8" Howr. were withdrawn to positions from Rear Hd. BLUE ZONE could be effectively covered, & counter preparation schemes were fired throughout the night, in anticipation of a large hostile attack, which did not however develop.	

A5834 Wt. W4973/M687 730,000 8/16 D. D. & L. Ltd. Forms/C.2118/13.

Army Form C. 2118.

WAR DIARY
or
INTELLIGENCE SUMMARY.
(Erase heading not required.)

Instructions regarding War Diaries and Intelligence Summaries are contained in F. S. Regs., Part II. and the Staff Manual respectively. Title pages will be prepared in manuscript.

Place	Date	Hour	Summary of Events and Information	Remarks and references to Appendices
TRAGETTEN	July 5 1918		The 2 6-in D.R. out supported the 9th Division offensive which resulted in the capture of METEREN. Groups were reorganised for their operation.	35 Appy/a/5 also No. 59480
	July 7th		The POTTERSDORP supplied a trail carried m.m.g. the 10 R. Brigade consisting of 1 personnel & 1 machine guns being left hand.	
	July 21 to Aug 2nd		Harassing fire was carried out. An average at the rate of 200 rounds from 110th battery & 150 rounds heat & S. Rrot battery. Fire was carried out by selected detached gunners, remainder of battery personnel being kept in reserve as possible. Gas concentrations were fired on the nights 28/29, 29/30 & 30/31 July by enemy billets & battery. Enemy artillery activity culminated action, principally on areas roads. There was considerable counter battery work.	

A5834 Wt W4973/M687 750,000 8/16 D. D. & L. Ltd. Form/C.2118/13.

Army Form C. 2118.

WAR DIARY
or
INTELLIGENCE SUMMARY.
(Erase heading not required.)

Place	Date	Hour	Summary of Events and Information	Remarks and references to Appendices
TERDEGHEM	July 2nd 1918		1 Coy T.M. Battery came in to section for the defence of the 3rd line with 4 Guns of the BLUE LINE with 8 guns. Detached section of the 30th D.A. in action for the defence of the 2nd position. Received S.O.S. line for the Defence of the BLUE LINE & was in direct communication with the Group of 30 DA. they were to support. By position the defence of the 2nd position was taken by 30th D.A. were recruited by Pumps & artillery cucumbers covered	

H.C.B. Fitzwilliam

5.8.18

WAR DIARY
or
INTELLIGENCE SUMMARY.
(Erase heading not required.)

Army Form C. 2118.

36th Bde Arty
14th Corps 2nd Army

1st August 1918

Place	Date	Hour	Summary of Events and Information	Remarks and references to Appendices
Terdeghem	1/8/18		During the greater part of the month the Krisooune Artillery supplemented by the 76 H.D.H Bde continued to cover the same sector as during the preceding month. The Batteries remained in positions which could cover the entire blue line. The main positions were kept as silent as possible and harassing fire was maintained at the rate of 200 x 18pr. 150rd. 4.5 Shor from forward section positions. Hostile Artillery actively showed an increase on the previous month. Two deliberate counter battery shoots were carried out by the enemy, but away were shot up at one time or another. The O.P.s on the Mts des Cats without there were also harassed. Brig Gen. H.J. Brock CMG DSO Rt proceeded on a fortnights leave	

Army Form C. 2118.

WAR DIARY
or
INTELLIGENCE SUMMARY.
(Erase heading not required.)

Instructions regarding War Diaries and Intelligence Summaries are contained in F. S. Regs., Part II. and the Staff Manual respectively. Title pages will be prepared in manuscript.

Place	Date	Hour	Summary of Events and Information	Remarks and references to Appendices
			In the Enemy his absence the Divisional Artillery was Commanded by Lt Col H C Simpson DSO RFA.	hoops
			During the last week of the month it was noticeable that hostile Batteries were shewing an unusual amount of activity	Belgium
			Several Guns forward were covering a withdrawal of the Heavy Artillery	France
			Aug 30	The enemy withdrew from Ballant's Battery advanced position	Sheets 7/1 28
			moved to Jans Capel	Sheet 3
			31	Batteries again advanced to position S.10 v S.16
				In spite of the rapid made movement of Guns & Supply of Ammunition were difficult but had difficulties were overcome

WAR DIARY
or
INTELLIGENCE SUMMARY.
(Erase heading not required.)

Army Form C. 2118.

Place	Date	Hour	Summary of Events and Information	Remarks and references to Appendices
	Aug. 1		Minor Operations are carried out during the month of August by the Infantry of the 36th Division and were supported by the Stokes Mts. The 36th Div.l Artillery also assisted the flank Divisions in minor operations carried out by them.	
			Projector operation by Special Coy. R.E. against Mouse Farm (X17d35.75)	
	1/2	10.30pm	The Brothers July fired a barrage round the farm & present the escape of any of the enemy and 2 hours after the discharge of the Projectors the Artillery supported an Infantry raiding party.	
		2.15 AM	Gas Concentration fired on Billets of Support Battalion S14c 78 44 S14a 05 46	
	4/5.	7.30pm 3.30 A.m 3.37 A.m	Gas Concentration fired on Mouse Square in Ballast S15c 55 00	
	10th 11th	10.30pm 2.5 AM	Gas Concentration fired on Road Junction S14d 35 52	

Army Form C. 2118.

Instructions regarding War Diaries and Intelligence Summaries are contained in F.S. Regs., Part II. and the Staff Manual respectively. Title pages will be prepared in manuscript.

WAR DIARY
or
INTELLIGENCE SUMMARY.
(Erase heading not required.)

Place	Date	Hour	Summary of Events and Information	Remarks and references to Appendices
	Aug 12/17	10.15 pm	Gas concentration fired on Craters of Crater S31 A 65 & X 15 C 7075	
	1/8	9.30	Aeroplane photographs showed the effect of the bombardment. His tracks across the strewn were both seal dry	
	3 Aug		Hurricane bombardment of enemy line carried out. No previous registration allowed – too foggy were Infantry reported no flatos had compelled, but Rate of fire intense for 15 minutes.	
	14		Raid on Trench Lines. Objectives gained — prisoners taken. Counter attack repulsed by artillery	
	15		34th Division attacked enemy positions on the Stranghe Ridge.	
	21		34th Bull Arty assisted in the Creeping barrage	
	7/8/21		The 34th Division attacked positions round Louis Road, firm hold obtained. Counter attacks by the enemy repulsed by Arty & M.G. fire	

WAR DIARY
or
INTELLIGENCE SUMMARY.

(Erase heading not required.)

Army Form C. 2118.

Place	Date	Hour	Summary of Events and Information	Remarks and references to Appendices
	Aug 22	3 A.M.	Hurricane Bombardment on enemy line	
	26.	7 A.M.	26th Division attacked & captured enemy trenches toward La Bonne Vie	
			SSC: Creeping Barrage was fired and Smoke Screen put on Raucourt Hill and Bellive Asylum.	
			All objectives gained. Slight enemy retaliation.	
	27.		Lt Col McSimpson, 250 RFA assumed duties of CRA	
			Brig Gen A.J. Rock CMG DSO RA commanding the Division	
			During the night enemy heavily bombarded Pres Capel	
			10th Bn. Our casualties being slight	
	28.		The Divisional Right boundary changed to	
			the new front held by our Bde of Infantry with 2 Batts	
			in the line. The Artillery worked with a man group &	
			one Sub-Group.	

Army Form C. 2118.

WAR DIARY
or
INTELLIGENCE SUMMARY.
(Erase heading not required.)

Instructions regarding War Diaries and Intelligence Summaries are contained in F. S. Regs., Part II. and the Staff Manual respectively. Title pages will be prepared in manuscript.

Place	Date	Hour	Summary of Events and Information	Remarks and references to Appendices
Erquingham	29/Aug	7.30	The 31st Division have been relieved by the 38th Division on this sector but enemy counter attacks withdrawal owing to heavy casualties which were cancelled and the 31st Division advance was	
	30		Orders for the Division Right Coastal army holding any Battalions advances trying to hurry to positions in the St Jean Capel Area	
	31		Barrage fired on Ravelsberg Hill which was captured by the Infantry. Batteries moved forward to position. "A" SO 5.16 "B" SO 5.16	

31/8/18

W.E.R.
Lt Colonel R.H.A
Cmdg 36th (Aust) Divisional Artillery

Army Form C. 2118.

H.Q.
H. Div. Only

968 36

WAR DIARY
or
INTELLIGENCE SUMMARY.
(Erase heading not required.)

Instructions regarding War Diaries and Intelligence Summaries are contained in F. S. Regs., Part II. and the Staff Manual respectively. Title pages will be prepared in manuscript.

Place	Date	Hour	Summary of Events and Information	Remarks and references to Appendices
1st Bn Cdn Inf Bde	Sept 1st		Potter Group in action in S.22; Simpson Group in J.15. Fire was maintained on targets such as machine gun emplacements, trenches &c &c. Enemy artillery was fairly quiet throughout the period, slight attention being paid to the roads.	
2nd Bn Cdn Inf Bde	2nd		Early in the morning the Potter Group moved up to positions in T.7.d. They were all in action by 9 am. 10th Bde wheeled in 109 Bde + went to escape from Sylve by 5pm. After a preliminary bombardment the 2/11 R.S. line west of King Sylve was captured. In the evening 3 Batteries of the Simpson Group moved up to positions behind Arbre Sylve. Headquarters showed slight increase in activity. Divisional Headquarters (?) moved to ST INS CAPPEL will be the reserve.	
	3rd		The advance was continued to a line roughly H.29 d 70 05 T.11 central & V.13 d. Remainder of the Simpson Group moved up to positions near the other batteries. A land mine	

A5834 Wt. W4973/M687. 730,000 8/16 D. D. & L. Ltd. Forms/C.2118/13.

WAR DIARY or INTELLIGENCE SUMMARY.

Army Form C. 2118.

(Erase heading not required.)

Instructions regarding War Diaries and Intelligence Summaries are contained in F. S. Regs., Part II. and the Staff Manual respectively. Title pages will be prepared in manuscript.

Place	Date	Hour	Summary of Events and Information	Remarks and references to Appendices
Sjaw Capell	3rd		exploited on to C/152 position causing 5 casualties, all wounded	
	4th		Early in the morning 29th division on our right in conjunction with our Bde they attacked & gained a footing on Hill 63. Our infantry advanced unsw to the old front line but the enemy was forced to gun ground a little. During the night the Rifles group moved to positions in T3. Y Simpson Group to positions in front of Nieuw Eykse. Hostile artillery showed increased activity especially H.V. guns.	
	5th		There was no change in the situation. During the right the enemy shelled the area around Nieuw Eykse with gas. Our casualties to 173 Bde suffered most having total casualties of all batteries 1 killed 5 wounded 38 gassed including 5 officers.	
	6th		At 4 pm the 107th Bde in conjunction with the 30th division on the left attacked hostile trenches on what of became rdge. Field & heavy artillery fired a barrage for this. All objectives were reached without much opposition except from Baylio Fm.	

Army Form C. 2118.

WAR DIARY
or
INTELLIGENCE SUMMARY.
(Erase heading not required.)

Place	Date	Hour	Summary of Events and Information	Remarks and references to Appendices
Afqine Cappl	7th		A quiet day. At midnight 18pr, 4.5 howitzers & heavies fired concentrations of fire & HE on to enemy company & battalion & brigade headquarters that had been obtained from a captured enemy map dated 4th. Symptoms of gas poisoning were noticed among D/153 horses.	
	8th		At 2.15 am an aeroplane dropped bombs near Sot aerin area. Unfortunately 2–3 bombs fell in the lines of the 2 section DAC Canadiens near. 5 killed & wounded. 50 horses killed. 25 wounded	

Army Form C. 2118.

WAR DIARY
or
INTELLIGENCE SUMMARY.
(Erase heading not required.)

Instructions regarding War Diaries and Intelligence Summaries are contained in F. S. Regs., Part II. and the Staff Manual respectively. Title pages will be prepared in manuscript.

Place	Date	Hour	Summary of Events and Information	Remarks and references to Appendices
St Jans Cappel	9/9/16 to 17/9/16		According to instructions from X Corps the 36th Divisional Artillery carried out a harassing fire programme daily, harassing fire programme	
	18/9/16		The 36th DA supported a minor operation by the 31st Division (on our right) who advanced their line slightly at U 26 & C 2 (Sheet 28)	
	20/9/16		On the night 18th/19th 153 Bde RFA was withdrawn to their wagon lines ", " " 19th/20th " 173 " " " " " "	
	21/9/16 to 27/9/16		On the night 21st/22nd the 163 Bde RFA and No 1 section DAC marched to the HAANDEKOT area and on arrival came under command of the 9th DA (II Corps.) The 173 Bde RFA marched on the night to the BUSSEBOOM area (Sheet 28 G 16) and came under command of the CRA 35th DA, No 2 section of DAC accompanying them	

A 5834 Wt W4973/M687 750,000 8/16 D. D. & L. Ltd. Form C.2118/13.

Army Form C. 2118.

WAR DIARY
or
INTELLIGENCE SUMMARY.
(Erase heading not required.)

Instructions regarding War Diaries and Intelligence
Summaries are contained in F. S. Regs., Part II.
and the Staff Manual respectively. Title pages
will be prepared in manuscript.

Place	Date	Hour	Summary of Events and Information	Remarks and references to Appendices
StaurCapp.	20/9/15		On the night of 20/21 the medium Trench Mortar Batteries moved to ZWYNLAND Brewery (L.12.c.1.4 SW of POPERINGHE and came under the command of the II Corps	36 D.A. Order No 73 of 19/9/15
	19/9/15			
ESDALE	24/9/15		The 36 Divisional Artillery Headquarters closed at ST JANS CAPEL up to 10 am on September 20th and reopened at the same date from at ESDALE camp (K.6.b.7.7)	36 D.A. Order No.73 of 19/9/15
	2/9/15		The 36 D A H Q was out of the line	
	25/9/15			
	1/10/15			

A 5834 Wt.W4973/M687 750,000 8/16 D. D. & L. Ltd. Forms/C.2118/13.

WAR DIARY
or
INTELLIGENCE SUMMARY.
Army Form C. 2118.

Place	Date	Hour	Summary of Events and Information	Remarks and references to Appendices
	27/9/18		The 36th Divisional Artillery HQ closed up ESDALE Camp on 27/9/18 and opened at the CONVENT VOGELTJE at 4 pm	
	28/9/18		DAHQ assumed Command of 173 Bde and 153 Bdes RFA and closed at the Convent VOGELTJE and opened at the Ramparts YPRES at 4 pm. 173 Bde RFA was placed under the command of the GOC 109th Inf Bde for operations. 56th RGA came under command of the CRA 36th DA for operations.	Commanding 36th Divisional Artillery Lt Col R.V.S.F
	29/9/18		The roads running EAST and NORTH EAST from YPRES are in a very bad state, great difficulty experienced in moving guns and ammunition forward. The Bdes (173 & 153) moved Eastward slowly and came into action in 30 wk.	
	30/9/18		The 153 Bde RFA came into action in Steel 25 K15 p-m then HQ at K15.d.6.3. The 173 Bde RFA in K21.c & K27.a	

Army Form C. 2118.

WAR DIARY
or
INTELLIGENCE SUMMARY.
(Erase heading not required.)

Instructions regarding War Diaries and Intelligence Summaries are contained in F. S. Regs., Part II. and the Staff Manual respectively. Title pages will be prepared in manuscript.

Place	Date	Hour	Summary of Events and Information	Remarks and references to Appendices
Ferme at K7d 3.1 (Sheet 28)	5/10/18		On the night of the 5th/6th 6" Stoke mortars were put into action that EAST of VIJFWEGEN in K24B (sheet 28) for the purpose of cutting the enemy wire on the NORTH EAST slope of Hill 41	
	6/10/18			
	7/10/18		From 1800 The Artillery available to cover the Divisional Front consisted of (1) Simpson group { 153 Bde RFA { 173 Bde RFA (2) 113 Army Bde RFA (3) 3 Batteries of Artillery - 4th French Cavalry Division. The latter were superimposed for defensive purposes on selected points.	367A. order No 76
JUNCTION CAMP C27c 8·7	8/10/18		Advanced Divisional Headquarters withdrew to JUNCTION CAMP C 27 c 8·7 (Sheet 28)	

WAR DIARY
or
INTELLIGENCE SUMMARY

Army Form C. 2118.

Place	Date	Hour	Summary of Events and Information	Remarks and references to Appendices
Junction Camp	9/10/18 to 11/10/18		The Divisional Artillery maintained their harassing fire programme and on the 11th inst co-operated with the 108th Bde trg to capture GOLDFLAKE FARM. The attack was successful. Two Batteries of the 113th Army Bde RFA (B & D Batteries) came under the command of the CRA 36 Divl Arty. Advanced BAHQ transferred to K7c	
K7C	12/10/18 13/10/18		Situation remained unchanged. Harassing fire was maintained and the Batteries of the 173 and 153 Bdes RFA and B & D Batteries of the 113 Army Bde RFA moved forward to Battle Positions in K16, 17 a 23	
"	14/10/18		At 05.00 on the 14th inst the Enemy put down a counter-preparation on the forward areas. At 05.35 the Divisional Artillery opened on their barrage line and our infantry advanced to the attack. The barrage fire ceased at 07.51. Very little information as to progress was received except at 06.40 the DAC were ordered to move forward to K15 & The two 18 pdr Batteries detailed for close support of the infantry moved into action A/173 ii L22b (SILVER FARM) C/153 " L15 d 4.2	

Army Form C. 2118.

WAR DIARY
or
INTELLIGENCE SUMMARY.
(Erase heading not required.)

Place	Date	Hour	Summary of Events and Information	Remarks and references to Appendices
	14/10/18		The remainder Batteries were ordered to move up to the vicinity of HILL1. At 1300 a wireless message timed 12.15 reported that our infantry were in GZINDENHOLE and the batteries in the vicinity of HILL1 were ordered to move up to the area L.15.a.16 at 13.15. At 14.50 a message timed 14.10 was received reporting infantry just west of GULLEGHEM. At 15.15 the Batteries not in close support were ordered to move up to L.17 and if the situation permitted to reconnoitre in G.9 (Sheet 28). At 15.10 the 86th Heavy Bde R.G.A. were ordered to reconnoitre positions from which an advance on COURTRAI could be covered. A message timed 16.30 was received at 5.5 p.m. reporting that our infantry were held up just west of GULLEGHEM by machine gun fire.	

Army Form C. 2118.

WAR DIARY
or
INTELLIGENCE SUMMARY.
(Erase heading not required.)

Place	Date	Hour	Summary of Events and Information	Remarks and references to Appendices
K.7.c	14/10/18		Our line was reported at the same time to run through G.14.c. G.20.b.d. (Sheet 29) and then South West to L.30 central (Sheet 28)	
ASHMORE FARM	15/10/18		Advanced Divisional Artillery Headquarters opened at ASHMORE FARM Sheet 28 L.15.c 9.0 at 0800 on the 15th inst. The 113 Army Field Artillery Brigade came under the command of the C.R.A. 36 D.A. few operations on the 15th and were ordered to reconnoitre and occupy positions in L.17 & further EAST if the situation permitted.	
	16/10/18		At 0525 news was received that the infantry had penetrated into the Western outskirts of COURTRAI and were established on the NW western banks of the canal in H.25 & 26 (Sheet 29). The Bridges across the canal had been demolished and our infantry were forced to halt. The 36 Divisional Artillery was withdrawn from the line to area just North of LEDEGHEM. The Command passed to	

Army Form C. 2118.

WAR DIARY
or
INTELLIGENCE SUMMARY.
(Erase heading not required.)

Place	Date	Hour	Summary of Events and Information	Remarks and references to Appendices
Ashmore Farm L15c9.0	16/10/18		CRA 41st Divisional Artillery at 1800 on 16th inst. 36 DAHQ moved to the FARM at F26B 35.50 (Sheet 28)	
Farm at F26B 35.50 (Sheet 28)	17/10/18		The Divisional Artillery were out of the line	
LEDEGHEM (A18d2.3) Sheet 29	18/10/18		The 36 Division took over the sector previously held by the 118th Regiment 3rd (Belgian) Division of Infantry. The Divisional Boundaries were as laid down in 36 Divisional Artillery Order No 82 of 17th inst. The 173 Bde RFA moved into action in support of the 109 Infantry Bde occupying positions in the approximate area B10.B16 (Sheet 3) The Belgian Artillery withdrew from action after the 173 Bde RFA reported their Batteries in action. The 153 Bde RFA was held in reserve in their wagon lines West of LEDEGHEM and were ordered to move thereafter under and to hold themselves in readiness to occupy positions to reconnoitre positions for occupy their at B23.19 B21.32	

WAR DIARY or INTELLIGENCE SUMMARY

Army Form C. 2118.

Place	Date	Hour	Summary of Events and Information	Remarks and references to Appendices
ERQUELINNES	8/11/18		Advanced Headquarters of the Divisional Artillery opened at A18.d.2.3 (Sheet 47) at 19.00 on October 18th 1918.	
A18.d.2.3 Sheet 47			The Command of the Artillery forces operating with the CRA 36 Div Arty as at 1630	
	11/6/18		The 36 Divisional Infantry forced a crossing of the Lys on O19 and based under cover of a creeping barrage. The Advance commenced at 19.05 on 19th. The infantry battled successfully May-June at Somaing, North East through Cast central Sh.D.11. At 0500 an infantry attacked on a NORTHERLY direction and established themselves on the line Read Junction C31 & 447, 16-6122 & B-7 where they remained pain its general advance = ordered for 05.00 an 20th October.	
			The advance recommenced under a creeping barrage at 0630 and push forward in effective the line 117 x S12 along stream to 1.11 & 9.0 Hence to road (inclusive) at 15 d 7.5 thence 1 x 6 thence to SPITAAL N DRIES including Byevron were reported pene...	

WAR DIARY
or
INTELLIGENCE SUMMARY.
(Erase heading not required.)

Army Form C. 2118.

Place	Date	Hour	Summary of Events and Information	Remarks and references to Appendices
INDFLEDE	20/10/18		In the evening our line were reported to run approximately as follows: sheet 5-29 L. Heart of SPITAAL 5.1.5 central thence S.W. to 1.10 central.	
"	21/10/18		The 36 Division was ordered to advance at 07.30 on the morning of the 21st. Their objective were on high ground in 36 Divisional area. Littres spur No 88 of reels and there was no barrage for a 18/lbs batteries were allotted to be in close support of the infantry brigades. The 173 Bdy Artillery were to be in Divisional Artillery Reserve after 07.30. The two mettles of Newton Mortars were attached for the support of the 108th Bde. New men being slow in coming back must the pace could not be definitely determined.	

WAR DIARY or INTELLIGENCE SUMMARY

Army Form C. 2118.

Place	Date	Hour	Summary of Events and Information	Remarks and references to Appendices
LEDEGHEM	22/10/18		On the night of the Divisional Front our infantry were reported to have reached J.19.a.	
	23/10/18		Two batteries of the 173 Bde RFA were ordered forward to be under the command of the OC 153 Bde RFA. The came under the orders of the OC 153 on the 23/10/18.	
House at J3a.55.90	24/10/18		Divisional Artillery Headquarters moved to House at J.3.a.55.90. Hostile shelling showed an increase of activity on forward and battery areas and there was a general stiffening of enemy resistance.	
	25/10/18		The 36th Division with the 9th on their right and the 184th French Division attached under a barrage at 0900 on the 25th inst. The objective was as given in 36th Divisional Artillery Order No 486. The Field Artillery available to support the advance consisted of the following groups:	

IVENS GROUP { 153 Bde RFA
             15th Bde RHA

SIMPSON'S GROUP { 173 Bde RFA
                  113 AFA Bde RFA

WAR DIARY
or
INTELLIGENCE SUMMARY.
(Erase heading not required.)

Army Form C. 2118.

Place	Date	Hour	Summary of Events and Information	Remarks and references to Appendices
House at Sassega	25/10/18		The attack started satisfactorily for later on much milk succeeded machine gun fire. The first objective was not reached gamed by nightfall.	
	26/10/18		The line was adjusted as follows J34 are central to J28a central to J22b 3.3 to Railway at J16 4.0 thence North along Railway to D26 central. On the night of the 26/27 the 153 Bde RFA was relieved by the 160 Bde RFA. On completion of the relief the 153 Bde RFA concentrated at their rear wagon lines. On the morning of the 27th the 153 Bde RFA and DAC marched to the LAUWE area. On the evening of the 27th the 173 Bde RFA was relieved by the 152 Bde RFA and concentrated at their wagon lines on completion of the relief.	
	28/10/18		Divisional Artillery Headquarters closed at their present location at 1100 and opened at BELLEGHEM at 1350	

Army Form C. 2118.

WAR DIARY
or
INTELLIGENCE SUMMARY.
(Erase heading not required.)

Instructions regarding War Diaries and Intelligence Summaries are contained in F. S. Regs., Part II. and the Staff Manual respectively. Title pages will be prepared in manuscript.

Place	Date	Hour	Summary of Events and Information	Remarks and references to Appendices
BELLEGHEM	28/10/18		The 173 Bde R.F.A. marched to area 29/N 25, 31 on the morning of the 26th. Locations were as follows. Refer Sheet 29	
			Headquarters 36 Divisional Artillery N 33 B 50.85	
			153 Bde R.F.A. } M 21 a 80.35	
			Batteries and vicinity	
			173 Bde R.F.A. M 36 β 30.30	
			A/173 T 1 a 30.60	
			B/173 N 31 a 30.60	
			C/173 N 25 c 30.70	
			D/173 N 31 a 10.70	
			T.M's M 21 a 70.30; D.A.C. Headquarters M 21 a 70.30	
			N°1 section M 15 d 30.90. N°2 section M 21 c 70.80	
	28/10/18		The Divisional Artillery were	
	31/10/18			

J. F. R. ——— Lt Col
Commanding 36 D.A.

Army Form C. 2118.

WAR DIARY
or
INTELLIGENCE SUMMARY.
(Erase heading not required.)

Place	Date	Hour	Summary of Events and Information	Remarks and references to Appendices
BELLEGHEM	1/11/18 to 4/11/18		The 36th Divisional Artillery was at rest at BELLEGHEM RAHQ moved to MOUSCRON on the 4th inst.	
	8/11/18		Bdes were in action in the neighbourhood of AVELGHEM. 173rd Bde fired on the canal bend at 1745 hours on 8th inst. Hostilities ceased at 1100 hours on November 11th 1918	
	11/11/18		Brigades withdrew to TOURCOING area	
	12/11/18 to 30/11/18		A programme of Education, recreation and military training was inaugurated and proceeded with.	

C.W. Menzies
Brig. Genl.
CRA 36th Div.

WAR DIARY
or
INTELLIGENCE SUMMARY.

Army Form C. 2118.

HQ RA 36 Vol 39

Place	Date	Hour	Summary of Events and Information	Remarks and references to Appendices
MOUSCRON	1.12.18 to 31.12.18		The 36th Divisional Artillery was at MOUSCRON. A programme of Education and recreation was carried out.	
	31.12.18		Demobilisation commenced.	

A.J.L. Drewker
Brig Gl. R.A.
C.R.A. 36 Division

Army Form C. 2118.

WAR DIARY
or
INTELLIGENCE SUMMARY.

(Erase heading not required.)

AQ RA 36D
Vol 40

Place	Date	Hour	Summary of Events and Information	Remarks and references to Appendices
MOUSCRON	1.1.19 to 31.1.19		The 36th Divisional Artillery was at MOUSCRON. A programme of Education and Recreation was carried out, and demobilisation was continued.	
	30.1.19 to 31.1.19		H.R.H. The Prince of Wales visited the 36th Divisional Artillery	

C.12. Walker Brig Genl R.A.
C.R.A. 36th Division

WAR DIARY
or
INTELLIGENCE SUMMARY.

Army Form C. 2118.

Place	Date	Hour	Summary of Events and Information	Remarks and references to Appendices
MOUSCRON	1.2.19 to 28.2.19		The 36th Divisional Artillery was at MOUSCRON. A programme of Education and vocation in reconstruction was carried out; lectures were held, and debates on topical subjects were given. Demobilisation was continued.	

H.E. Pipe
C.R.A. 36th Division

www.ingramcontent.com/pod-product-compliance
Lightning Source LLC
Chambersburg PA
CBHW080842010526
44114CB00017B/2355